CAPTURING KAHANAMOKU

Duke Kahanamoku with his surfboard, date unknown.

CAPTURING KAHANAMOKU

HOW A SURFING LEGEND AND A SCIENTIFIC OBSESSION REDEFINED RACE AND CULTURE

MICHAEL ROSSI

HarperOne
An Imprint of HarperCollinsPublishers

Without limiting the exclusive rights of any author, contributor or the publisher of this publication, any unauthorized use of this publication to train generative artificial intelligence (AI) technologies is expressly prohibited. HarperCollins also exercise their rights under Article 4(3) of the Digital Single Market Directive 2019/790 and expressly reserve this publication from the text and data mining exception.

CAPTURING KAHANAMOKU. Copyright © 2025 by Michael Rossi. All rights reserved. Printed in the United States of America. No part of this book may be used or reproduced in any manner whatsoever without written permission except in the case of brief quotations embodied in critical articles and reviews. For information, address HarperCollins Publishers, 195 Broadway, New York, NY 10007. In Europe, HarperCollins Publishers, Macken House, 39/40 Mayor Street Upper, Dublin 1, D01 C9W8, Ireland.

HarperCollins books may be purchased for educational, business, or sales promotional use. For information, please email the Special Markets Department at SPsales@harpercollins.com.

harpercollins.com

FIRST EDITION

Designed by Kyle O'Brien

Title page art © Kelly Headrick / Adobe Stock; Photo on page ii © Alpha Historica / Alamy Stock Photo; Photo on page 16 © American Museum of Natural History; Photo on page 90 © Alpha Historica / Alamy Stock Photo; Photo on page 96 © Kauai Historical Society; Photo on page 120 © Bettmann / Getty Images; Photo on page 156 © ullstein bild / Getty Images; Photo on page 182 © John Hay Library at Brown University; Photo on page 201 © Bernice Pauhi Bishop Museum; Photo on page 202 © Library of Congress; Photo on page 238 © Granger; Photo on page 271 © Getty Research Institute; Photo on page 274 © Library of Congress; Photo on page 290 © Alpha Historica / Alamy Stock Photo

Library of Congress Cataloging-in-Publication Data has been applied for.

ISBN 978-0-06-327997-1

25 26 27 28 29 LBC 5 4 3 2 1

For my parents, Linda and Joe and Paul and Loretta, who taught me to love words and waves

CONTENTS

1 The Cast of David Kahanamoku   1

2 The Gospel of the Body   17

3 The "Model Youth"   97

4 A Passion for Measuring Naked Men   157

5 Barbarians and Demigods   203

6 "Quite a Different Man"   239

7 The Discovery of Nothing   275

8 This Was Your Life!   291

Acknowledgments   303

Notes   307

Select Bibliography   341

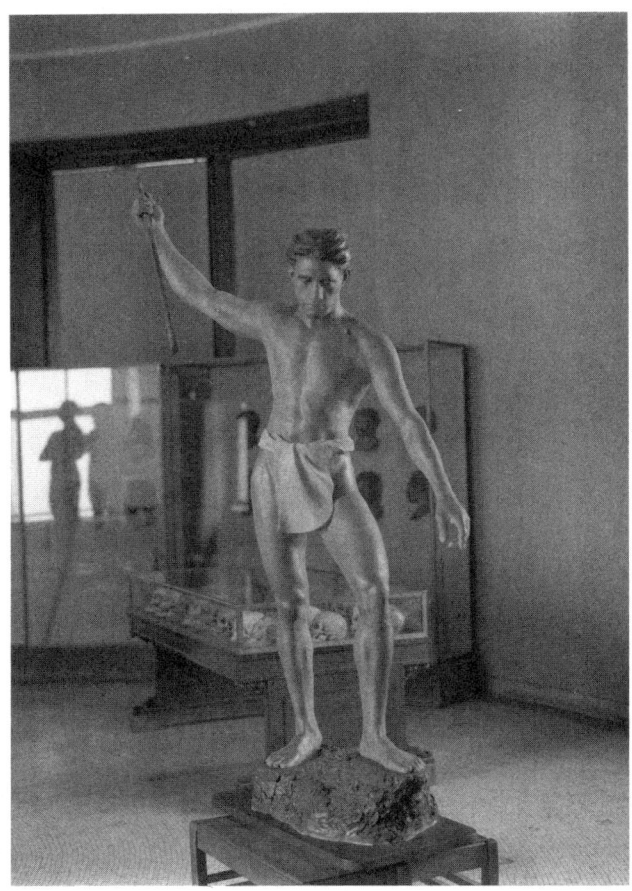

The finished cast of David Kahanamoku, on display at the American Museum of Natural History.

1

THE CAST OF DAVID KAHANAMOKU

David Kahanamoku was beautiful. Startlingly so. Scientifically so. Six feet tall, broad chested and slim, he had a champion athlete's build and a glittering smile. His eyes were dark and dovish and enveloping, and when he swam—which was pretty much all the time—he slipped through the sea like a porpoise, water eddying in arabesques behind him. Known around Honolulu as a "beach boy," he was "modeled like a bronze god," as one of his admirers put it, and had a "charismatic personality" to match. But it was on a surfboard that he utterly dazzled. Posed on the face of a roaring, foaming "bluebird"—1920s surfer speak for a huge wave—he looked like an immortal of the sea: chest thrust forward, arms cocked at his sides, toes clinging onto twelve feet of solid redwood as he rocketed through the water.

In the summer of 1921, at twenty-seven years old, he was one of the best surfers and swimmers in all of Hawai'i, which meant that he was one of the best surfers and swimmers in the world.

But on July 20 he found himself immobilized, covered from foot to neck in plaster. It was a hot afternoon in the basement of the Bishop Museum of Natural History in Honolulu. Upstairs, in the cavernous main hall, curious museumgoers browsed glass cases filled with feathered cloaks and helmets of the ancient chiefs of Hawaiʻi. Displays of shell fishhooks, octopus traps, musical instruments, and weapons from around Polynesia—Hawaiʻi, Aotearoa, Tahiti, Samoa, Te Henua Enana—intrigued visitors with their exquisite workmanship. Giant surfboards, fifteen feet long and once the property of Hawaiian kings, hung from the walls. Outside, car horns honked. The tram ground by and chattering people hurried on and off. The city was busier than ever before, bouncing back with vigor from the recent world war and subsequent worldwide flu pandemic.

Inside the room, David was alone.

The men who had entombed him were eugenicists—race scientists from the American Museum of Natural History (AMNH) in New York City, five thousand miles away. They had come to Hawaiʻi to take measurements, photographs, and plaster casts of the people of Hawaiʻi, to trace the origins of Polynesian people, and to study the effects of "race mixing" on the American population.

The term "eugenics"—coined by the British statistician Francis Galton in the late nineteenth century—derived from the Greek words "eu" (good) and "genos" (birth). Seeking to improve humanity's genetic lot, eugenicists believed that intermarriage and reproduction among people of good racial "stock" should be encouraged, while people of "poor stock" ought to be discouraged—even prohibited—from reproducing.

The ultimate goal of the eugenicists in Hawaiʻi was to

"capture" a cast of David's older brother, Duke. Duke was a world-famous swimmer, an Olympic gold medalist, and the best-known surfer on the planet. He, too, had a "perfect" physique, perhaps even fuller and more powerful than David's. It was his perfect form that had convinced the eugenicists—perpetually interested in athletic skill and manliness—that Duke was the ideal example of what a Polynesian person, and perhaps even a human male in general, should look like. To complete their collection of the people of Hawai'i, therefore, the eugenicists needed a cast of Duke.

Unfortunately, Duke had given them the slip as they moved around the Hawaiian Islands, so the scientists busied themselves making facial casts of other people as they searched for their main target. Eventually, Duke had agreed to come and get cast, but on the morning of his appointment, David had shown up instead and had been covered with plaster in Duke's place.

Now, David was stuck.

The eugenicists had grown hungry from their work and left for lunch.

The plaster squeezed his chest, making it difficult to breathe. The heat inside the mold rose steadily, sending rivulets of sweat down his forehead. He tried not to panic. He was overheating, felt like he was suffocating. His breath came in short bursts. The casting session had turned from an odd errand into a "fight for survival," as he later recalled. He struggled to maintain his composure and shifted his broad chest as much as he could in the plaster to get some breathing space. He might have wondered, not for the first time, about the validity of eugenic science. He doubtless thought of Duke, who could have been encased instead of him.

One thing was for certain, he vowed, as the plaster bore down, patient as a python: if he got out of this, neither he nor his brother would ever again have dealings with "museum artists."

• • •

A century later, I stood in a quiet tower in an out-of-the-way corner of the American Museum of Natural History in New York City, looking at rows of plaster heads. As I gazed down at them, they stared back—silent and unblinking and dusty and white. The room was bright and sunny. The building's heating system thrummed quietly in the background. My sneakers squeaked on the tile floor when I moved, and a chill crept down my back. I fought a superstitious urge to look over my shoulder at an unseen presence, hovering somewhere, just behind my head. A quiet morning in the anthropology archives seemed an improbable setting for a haunting. But the phantoms there ran amok.

I'd come to this tucked-away part of the museum—far from the crowds of dinosaur seekers and schoolchildren on field trips—to look for the cast of David Kahanamoku. I'd first come across mention of him on a slip of paper in the museum's archives while I was researching another project. It was just a name, quickly jotted down on a form from 1926, stuck in a folder, and deposited in a box deep in the interior of the museum, but it had ignited my curiosity. It was somewhat unusual for anthropologists of this period to write down the names of their subjects—and it was still more unusual for those subjects to be famous surfers. As a historian of science, I was trying to understand the ways in which science, culture, and ideas of physical perfection and athletic beauty wound around one another, both in the past and in the present.

Now, in the archives, I sifted through the remnants of that research program: some photographs, a ledger on lined paper, and, of course, the white plaster faces. Some had smudges of dirt on them or chips of plaster missing due to their passage through the better part of a century. Some still had fibers embedded in them from the casting process. Most portrayed a bust in full—from the neck up, hair, shoulders.

It was tempting to see these casts as works of art. They were exquisite and weirdly beautiful. Each expressive face appeared to capture the moment of its creation. One man seemed distressed, his brows furrowed, barely holding his composure against the weight of the plaster on his face. A woman smirked ever so slightly, as if amused at the weirdness of being covered with plaster by an anthropologist. The cool, hard plaster appeared as warm and yielding as flesh. The expressions of the casts changed when the light shifted. They seemed almost animated, sizing me up.

But if the casts were, in some ways, timeless works of artistry, they were also—and unavoidably—medical technologies: early twentieth-century tools for studying human population genetics. They had been used for generating and preserving data about human variation, and ultimately, for controlling the demographic destiny of twentieth-century America.

In an era before gene sequencing, when the very concept of a "gene" was new and little-known, the purpose of the casts was to demonstrate with total scientific accuracy the physical features that differentiated one "type" of person—one "race"—from another. Such physical features, a great many scientists believed, could be tracked from generation to generation using tools like casts, photographs, and measurements. Indeed, the physical characteristics that marked "types" of people could even serve as an index of underlying mental characteristics: one "type" might be better suited to democracy, another more prone to crime. One might have greater physical prowess, or musical ability, or facility with money (to name just a few possibilities). By understanding how different "types" of people passed on heritable traits, many of the most progressive American scientists and policy makers of the early twentieth century felt that it would be possible to shape human society for the better.

I did not find casts of David or Duke Kahanamoku among the plaster heads that day in the archive. Nor did I see their names recorded in the well-preserved, neatly collected, and obsessively filled-out piles of note cards recording the physical statistics of Hawaiian people. The two most prominent of the subjects of the anthropological study were not on any ledger. Their casts were not in the collection. There were no photographs or measurements of them among the hundreds of records that I eventually looked at. They had disappeared like waves on the beach—or ghosts in the archive.

• • •

The shades of Hawaiian subjects were not the only specters haunting the museum. The creator of these casts, too, was something of a phantom. Louis R. Sullivan was only twenty-eight in 1920, when he was charged with the task of conducting the anthropological survey of Hawaiʻi, and with the particular duty of measuring, photographing, and casting Duke Kahanamoku.

It is something of a truism that anthropologists tend to be the real subjects of their anthropological studies. Anthropologist Bronislaw Malinowski, for instance, left explicit—in every sense of the word—diaries about his participation in the societies of the Trobriand Islands. These records allow us to see how his own appetites and attitudes informed his invention of "participant observation"—the anthropological technique of immersing oneself in one's subjects' lives. Margaret Mead famously struggled against the constraints of early twentieth-century American society and in the 1920s found a form of personal liberation in revealing the ways in which people in the South Pacific defied the norms of middle-class America. And Franz Boas folded his own past fascinations with physics, geography, exploration, and political liberalism into the foundations of American anthropology. On a more basic level, the archives of the American Museum of Natural History are replete with photographs and memoirs of anthropologists—exploring, measuring, interviewing, disembarking, returning, practicing their craft.

But Sullivan left little such record of himself. When he embarked for Hawai'i, he was still a graduate student and hadn't yet acquired the thoroughgoing self-regard that is so often incumbent on successful academic research. His letters betray a shy, inexperienced introvert—eager to please, bent on doing a good job. No time for egoism or self-promotion.

He was also quite young when he died. Although it was tuberculosis that killed him at thirty-three years old, he had suffered respiratory ailments for years—a victim of long-term complications from the 1918 influenza pandemic. His anthropological career spanned less than a decade, and thus left little room for detailed self-reflection.

But even without a written autobiography, his story still lingers in his work.

Sullivan was a specialist in anthropometry—the measurement of human beings. The sheer quantity of photographs, measurements, and casts that he took in Hawai'i speaks to his obsessive work ethic, and the quality of his measurements suggests an uncompromising eye for detail. Most of all, what comes through in the remains of his research is an unwavering belief in the idea that humans can all be classed into "races" and "types" and that—through the administration of eugenic science—it might be possible to use this knowledge of "races" and "types" to genetically promote better, stronger, and smarter humans.

It's strange to find someone so completely defined by their work, especially when that work is to define others. Or maybe not so strange at all. One thing that anthropology teaches us is that the people around us frame us; shape us. Sullivan appears in the archival record as a ghost defined by ghosts.

• • •

This same ambiguity did not trouble Sullivan's boss and the president of the American Museum, Henry Fairfield Osborn. Where Sullivan was diffident, Osborn was outspoken, even bombastic. An imperious man, Osborn left no doubt about his intentions. He wanted to transform the American Museum into a worldwide powerhouse of paleontology, biology, anthropology—and, crucially, eugenics.

Under his direction, the museum mounted its first exhibits of dinosaur bones in 1905. This marked an exciting turn for the museum, which had, in its original days, been characterized by row after row of dusty glass cases filled with jumbles of fossils. Now, visitors could imagine the great creatures as if they were really alive—lumbering, swimming, flying their way through hundreds of millions of years of deep time. Osborn then sought to revolutionize the American Museum's taxidermy displays, poaching the legendary hunter and taxidermist, Carl Akeley, from the rival Field Museum in Chicago. Akeley was famous for his dynamic taxidermy displays that made viewers feel as if they were immersed in the scene before them. He filled the halls of the AMNH with dioramas of gorillas beating their chests, ostriches defending their eggs from warthogs, lions pacing the savanna, monkeys screeching from trees: little wildernesses frozen in time and confined in glass.

Osborn also expanded the museum's collections of anthropological and archaeological displays, sending collecting expeditions to Central America, Africa, Asia, and the Northwest Coast of North America to gather the arts and crafts of Native peoples for display in the museum. Cataloged within glass cases or hung on mannequins, these displays did for humans what taxidermy did for animals—provide a view of unadorned, "savage," human nature so that the residents of sprawling New York could understand the notional antecedents of their own civilization. As Osborn put it, "realizing the rapidity with which not only animals, but races of mankind with their beliefs and customs, are being swept out of existence by what we are pleased to call the march of civilization, special effort has been made of late years to gather objects and information while they are yet to be had."

Starting in the early 1910s, Osborn turned his focus from

"man" and "nature" to eugenics. A strange hybrid of medicine, racism, scientific rationality, and an occult faith in the dark magic of history, eugenics was—as Osborn put it—the science of "improving health and morals, first, by diminishing or preventing the multiplication of the unhealthy and immoral elements of our population, and secondly by encouraging the multiplication of the intelligent, healthy and moral elements of our population." Eugenics, in other words, was the science of selectively breeding human beings—ideally through choice; if need be, through force.

Eugenicists believed that all of humanity's problems—poverty, war, inefficiency, dishonesty, disease—were accidents of human evolution. The traits that caused some humans to be virtuous and others to be wicked; the traits that caused some humans to be brilliant and others to be inept; the traits that caused some humans to be cooperative and others recalcitrant, they believed, had taken hold over eons of higgledy-piggledy human reproduction. In contrast, eugenics was "the self-direction of human evolution." This meant selectively encouraging some people to reproduce while discouraging or even forbidding others, all according to strict, seemingly scientific principles.

In the 1920s, the concept of the "gene" was poorly articulated. It seemed clear that certain traits were passed along from parents to offspring, and leading biologists hypothesized that these traits were carried by "hereditary factors." Biologists called these hereditary factors "genes" and thought they were carried in "germ plasm"—that is, heritable material—contained in sperm and egg cells. This "germ plasm" was the source of the "genetic stock" of a particular species or race. But when pressed, beyond the somewhat vague suggestion that genes might ultimately be an as-yet-unknown chemical that acted through an unknown mechanism, biologists were at a loss to describe what, precisely, genes were—other than to suggest in circular fashion that genes were hereditary factors, and hereditary factors were those factors that could be inherited.

Nevertheless, eugenicists felt sure that, with enough research, they could distinguish the different "factors" that led some people to succeed in society and others to fail. Moreover, they felt certain that these factors were characteristic of different "races"—and so it was vital to study the racial makeup of different populations, using techniques such as measurement, photography, and plaster casting.

Not everyone was convinced. Social reformers pointed to political and economic conditions—colonialism, capitalism, the legacy of slavery in America, wealth inequality, and uneven access to social resources like public health and education—as among the main drivers of "failure" among some people and "success" among others. Religious groups—the Catholic Church in particular—tended to see the salvation of humankind as a matter of ministering to souls, rather than modifying genes. And historians and anthropologists like W. E. B. Du Bois and Franz Boas insisted that there was little evidence to suggest that "racial" differences were as determinate as eugenicists believed.

Nevertheless, it was easy for eugenicists and their allies to dismiss such objections as sentimentality in the face of objective facts. After all, eugenics had the appeal of a "science" that confirmed the biases of powerful people in government and industry. Eugenicists and their clients were convinced that there were distinct and immutable "races" of humans, and that it was beyond dispute that different "races" had different capacities for social achievement in the modern world. They thought that these alleged facts should be obvious to anyone who observed American society. The only question, in the eyes of eugenicists, was how to curtail the reproduction of the great masses of deficient people in the population and increase the production of efficient, intelligent, modern people.

Along with many of the powerful trustees of the American Museum of Natural History—former US president Teddy Roosevelt, lawyer and environmentalist Madison Grant, and naturalist John Muir, among others—Osborn wanted to make the museum a clearinghouse for eugenic research, using its tremendous resources to promote eugenics from the lowest school grades to the highest levels of American government. A prodigious opportunity presented itself in 1921, in the form of the Second International Eugenics Congress. Osborn was thrilled to host the congress—the first in nine years—at the AMNH. In 1912, the eugenicists of the world had convened in London for the first ever International Eugenics Congress, gathering roughly seven hundred fifty people from across Europe and North America. World War I delayed the Second International Eugenics Congress, originally scheduled to take place in 1915, but counterintuitively strengthened international interest in eugenics because so much of the allegedly best genetic "stock" of the world's leading nations had been destroyed on the battlefields of Europe. What could be more necessary than a comprehensive program to replenish the best of civilization, and limit the spread of bad genes?

Holding the overdue Second International Eugenics Congress at the AMNH would cement the reputation of the museum as a center for eugenics research, and Osborn as one of the world's leading eugenicists. This was the reason that Osborn had dispatched Sullivan to Hawai'i—to gain material for an exhibit that would be the centerpiece of the Eugenics Congress. And this was the reason that David Kahanamoku found himself interred in plaster, in place of his brother, on a hot July afternoon in 1921.

• • •

Gazing into the plaster eyes of people from a century before, I realized that this long hidden history was still very much alive.

The people that the masks represented had lived a century before, but the times in which they lived bore telling similarities to my own. In the early 1920s, they, too, were reeling from the aftershocks of a global disease outbreak—the 1918 influenza pandemic—and wondering with some hope and much doubt about the state of medical science. They were part of a booming economy that brought tremendous wealth and power to some people and left others out in the cold—or, in their cases, on the warm beaches at Waikiki, hustling to make a living by ingenuity and physical strength. They would've viewed rumblings of war from around the world with trepidation, but not too much concern—America was so far away from trouble spots, even in its island outpost in the Pacific. They would have reveled in new media technologies—like movies and radio—and wondered what these new media meant for the shape of their society. They read the words of politicians who spoke of the "good" and "bad" blood of immigrants—and they discussed with great curiosity the work of scientists like Sullivan, who—using new technologies, and new discoveries like "genes"—

promised easy solutions to complicated political problems through (pseudo) science.

Today, we are living through a period of political and scientific revolution that uncannily mirrors the world of a century ago. On the one hand, cutting-edge genetic technologies like CRISPR, well-known companies like 23andMe, and public initiatives like the Million Veteran Program (to name a few) promise an understanding of human biology and development as well as active intervention in matters of health, disease, even social and economic justice. At the same time, we are publicly grappling with questions of identity, gender, sexual desire, physical and mental ability, and representation in everyday life. Politicians still speak of the "blood" of immigrants as "good" and "bad." We debate what it means to be an American and what defines American "greatness." Some of those debates shade over into discussions about what it means simply to be human, to be understood as valuable, as worthy of respect, worthy of good-faith dialogue, worthy of truth.

These quandaries, moreover, transcend time and space, surpassing both the here and now and the past of a century ago. At their core are tangled human values: matters of truth and goodness, of rightness and beauty. They encompass questions like: *Who are we (as a people, as individuals)? How do we know who we are? What constitutes authentic understanding, and what are the best—most proper, most morally rich—means for understanding ourselves and others? What place does "science" have as a lens for understanding self and other, and what are the limits of science? Who should we trust to help us answer these questions? And what about "culture"—a word that carries so much weight, but that's so amorphous? Where do "culture," identity, and biology cross paths, and where do they diverge?*

The temptation when faced with questions such as these is to look to science as a neutral and infallible arbiter of right and wrong. But history teaches us that science—particularly when social science meets biological science—is always bound up with matters of subjective perception. As the philosopher Michel Foucault put it, "in the war between history and nature, history always has the upper hand."

In the twenty-first century, we tend to think of history as running in more or less straight lines. Society moves forward. It "progresses." This progress might occur faster than some people would like, or slower than others would prefer. Even those moments when things seem to go wrong can be described pejoratively as history moving "backward" or "advancing too fast": a court decision with which one disagrees takes us back to the 1950s, for instance; or we have "progressed" too far and need to go back to a mystical time when all was well. Forward and backward: we imagine history as a freight train.

When I left the archive that day, I still didn't know what had happened to David, or to Duke, or to the casts that had been made of them—or not made. The archivists I'd spoken with said that the casts didn't exist anymore—if they ever did, in the case of Duke. Duke was a legend only for swimming and surfing—not for transforming anthropology.

I took one last look. The eyes of the casts were open. Their silent faces stared at me, vital and expressive. I gazed back—into their eyes, through their eyes—into a past that was still very much alive.

Henry Fairfield Osborn.

2

THE GOSPEL OF THE BODY

In April 1920, Henry Fairfield Osborn, then sixty-three years old, gave an impromptu lecture at the Fairmont Hotel in San Francisco on the impending extinction of the Hawaiian "race." He had just arrived in California on the steamer *Lurline*, fresh from a monthlong stay in Hawai'i. His time in the Islands had convinced him that the Indigenous people of Hawai'i were succumbing at alarming rates to the influenza pandemic that had claimed some fifty million lives worldwide since 1918.

These "stateliest of people," Osborn told the assembled crowd, "are being carried off by the influenza scourge that makes an easy victim out of the susceptible native." He emphasized that by his count, there were only "10 per cent left of the original Hawaiian race"—about 25,000 people. Their numbers were dwindling, Osborn said, because "they possess little resistance against disease propagated by the whites," but also because their "purity" was being further diminished through intermarriage "with other races." As a result, Osborn concluded, "this highly developed race is extremely hard to preserve." He urged his audience to prepare for the inevitable extinction of Indigenous Hawaiians.

Osborn was a leading American paleontologist who specialized in the study of extinct mammals, a trained physiologist with an early career in genetics and mind sciences, and the president of the American Museum of Natural History in New York—a powerful position through which he had established himself as a global scientific leader as well as a kind of evangelist for the ways in which science could help to save modern humans from themselves.

From Osborn's perspective, it was not just Indigenous Hawaiians who were in trouble. Modern civilization itself was teetering on a sort of precipice. As a paleontologist, Osborn understood the world in evolutionary terms. The fittest members of any class of living thing survived to reproduce; the less fit members perished, making room for further, more robust creatures. This was what gave rise to the diversity of life as well as what Osborn believed were fundamental hierarchies within the natural world. At the same time, as the fossil record made clear, those species that found themselves on top one day were gone the next. The greatest of dinosaurs had succumbed to the smallest of mammals. The greatest of mammals—woolly mammoths, ground sloths, saber-toothed tigers—had, in their turn, vanished in the face of puny but intelligent humans.

Now, in Osborn's view, humans were the highest forms of life—and of those humans, the "white race" was supreme. "White" civilization, for Osborn, was therefore synonymous with "civilization" itself.

But there was a problem. For even as the so-called white race had, in the eyes of men like Osborn, made great strides against disease; even as it had built sprawling cities; even as it had connected the globe with markets for the distribution of sophisticated goods; even as it had, according to Osborn, "civilized" the supposedly backward people of the world so that they, too, could appreciate the benefits of white civilization—indeed, even as it had invented *science* through which superstition was vanquished and the light of reason shined forth—that very science also told civilized man (for civilization was, indeed, the purview of *man*) that he was in danger of decline.

Examine his muscles. Peer into his eyes. Did civilized man have the physical strength and mental fortitude to wrest survival from the fangs of cruel beasts? Did civilized man dream of mastering fire and raising cities from the mud to save his race from darkness? Did the blood of civilized man boil with the desire to do bare-fisted battle with Nature itself, to conquer the elements and establish his superiority on the earth? No. Civilized man spent his days preoccupied with numbers on a stock ticker or accounts in a book; he fretted over the cut of his suit; he worried about what wine he was going to have at dinner. Civilized man was losing his vigor. He was growing decadent, weak—even unmanly and effete. Through its very achievements, civilization was ridding the world of nature, and that loss of nature would, itself, be the downfall of civilization. It was nature, after all, that had supposedly given white men the power to transcend nature by endowing them with superior genes. And yet, it was nature—in the form of genes—that men like Osborn regarded as the greatest risk to white men and white civilization.

This was Osborn's vision not of human history, but of *natural* history—a field that, in his eyes, fused nature and time into a powerful, elemental force. Natural history, for men like Osborn, was a quasi-mystical view of history in which nature (in the form of biological evolution) provided the powerful, motive force that gave meaning to life and to time itself. Without nature there could be no change; all of life would be eternal and undifferentiated. Natural history, for men like Osborn, was therefore the architecture for nature's power—it described the advancement of natural forces (like evolution) in regular, cosmic rhythms.

Human history, in contrast to *natural* history, was a perpetual attempt by human beings to break free of natural forces, to wrest agency from the grip of biology. All humans, to some extent, battled nature—by using language and tools, by building shelters, by fashioning clothing. The only humans who had fully achieved *human* history, however ("white" humans, in Osborn's estimation), were those who could seize nature through science and create "civilization" in its place, to save humankind from the storms, predation, and disease; to fully develop human agency. This could be seen in the apparent dominance of white humankind across the globe.

Some people (social reformers, humanitarians, sentimentalists) might think that it was social factors—education, income inequality, work opportunity, racial and ethnic strife, for instance—that limited the ability of a particular population to thrive, or even to "advance." But when Osborn lectured about the plight of the Hawaiian people, he saw not the injustices of colonialism, not the ravages of imperialism, not the inequalities of modern capitalism, but a battle between human history and natural history that Hawaiians were clearly, inevitably, losing.

The problem for men like Osborn was that this very struggle between human and nature necessarily distanced the most "advanced" humans (like him) from nature—and therefore moved them away from the source of biological power, and, indeed, history itself. It was predictable, thought Osborn, that a docile, static society such as that of ancient Hawai'i should be completely enveloped by an energetic, dynamic civilization such as that of the United States. This was, in his eyes, the natural order of things. But those humans who had superseded the limits of nature came by this birthright at the cost of taking their fate into their own hands, and—potentially—subverting nature itself. In this way, by no longer confronting nature as they used to, by living modern lives, "civilized" humankind was exposing itself to great jeopardy.

In this sense, the lecture that Osborn gave to curious onlookers at the Fairmont Hotel in San Francisco on April 7, 1920, was less about Hawaiians and influenza than it was a personal horror story about the way that nature could lay a formerly "stately" civilization low. Hawaiians had once been great; now they were in decline because they could not handle the modern world. Might the same not happen to white people? There were leviathans lurking in the waves of deep time, biding their time, waiting to drag even the most advanced people into the depths of extinction. Science—genetics—was Osborn's key to avoiding civilization-wide collapse.

But what Osborn did not reveal—at least, not at that moment—was that during his trip to Hawai'i, he had glimpsed an advantage in the war between history and nature. Better yet, he had found a lifeboat.

That lifeboat was embodied by Duke Kahanamoku.

• • •

The ancient people of Hawai'i were not the first or only humans to ride waves. People in Africa, Peru, and China all appear to have had traditions of wave riding. As Peruvian surf champion Felipe Pomar argued in 1988, fishermen of the pre-Incan Chimú civilization (circa 850–1470) on the coast of modern-day Peru likely used small canoes to ride waves after fishing. These canoes—today called *caballitos de totora* (reed horses)—are made of long strands of thick grass bundled together to form a small boat with a flat back and a sharp, upturned point at the front, like a giant *pigache* slipper. The result is a cheap, strong, and maneuverable craft, but one that is generally short-lived—the reeds tend to become waterlogged and decay quickly. Although their fleeting nature means that no archaeological evidence of *caballitos* has been found, ceramic pots that appear to show people riding the canoes have been dated to 1100 BCE. This led Pomar to the conclusion that Chimú people could have been riding waves for fun—indeed, possibly before the Polynesian diaspora reached the islands of Hawai'i.

The earliest European accounts of surf-riding in Africa, meanwhile, date to the seventeenth century. Believing themselves to be witnessing swim lessons, observers along the Gulf of Guinea in 1640 and 1679 recounted seeing children "strapped" to boards, riding the surf toward the beach. As historian Kevin Dawson points out, this is an improbable way to teach swimming, especially as coastal African people tended to be adept swimmers from a very young age. Rather, the children were almost certainly riding waves in the prone position, holding carved boards in front of them to speed their passage through the waves and lengthen their rides. This was evidently a common practice along the west African coast from what's now called Senegal to Cameroon, and maybe as far north as Libya. Surf-riders in Africa used boards and canoes, and subsequent observers remarked on the skill and daring of the surfers. These cases underlined the robustness of African surfers as well as—to later readers—suggested the invigorating effects of exercising in the surf.

Finally, evidence suggests that daring young men in Song China (circa 960–1279) may have ridden the tidal bore of the Zhe (now Qiantang) River. Unlike ocean waves driven by wind, tidal bores are long, periodic waves caused by rising ocean tides rushing up a river with precisely the right contours at precisely the right speed. The Qiantang River's tidal bore is a yearly occurrence and is the largest in the world. The single wave can be up to thirty feet high and travels upstream at roughly twenty-five miles per hour. In the twenty-first century, it often breaches the river's bank, sweeping away street signs, mopeds, and spectators alike. Scrolls from the thirteenth century depict young, tattooed men swimming in the bore, holding banners aloft—a practice that contemporary historians have speculated might be like surfing. The practice appears to have been relatively short-lived, however.

While surfing in various forms did occur elsewhere in the world, nowhere else was surf-riding so intricately entwined with the religious, cultural, and economic life of a civilization as it was across Polynesia.

Early Polynesian voyagers took surfing—along with crop plants, tools, technologies, stories of gods and heroes, pigs, dogs, and chickens—across the archipelagos of the Pacific: from Fiji, Tonga, and Samoa, south to Aotearoa (New Zealand); then east to Rapa Nui (Easter Island); and north to Hawai'i via the Marquesas and Tahiti in two successive waves.

Each cluster of Polynesian civilizations had a different relationship to surfing. In Samoa and Tonga, surf-riding on bellyboards was a common children's activity. In Aotearoa, people of all ages body-boarded on long, thin boards. On deforested Rapa Nui, people made surf platforms from reeds, not unlike in Peru. And in Tahiti—most culturally similar to Hawai'i—people of all sexes and ages and social strata surfed on a variety of boards in standing as well as kneeling and prone postures.

The first settlement of Hawai'i might have occurred as early as 400 CE, the second as late as 1200 CE, and it was here that surf-riding reached its apotheosis as a form of spiritual, political, physical, and aesthetic expression.

Anthropologist Marshall Sahlins has described ancient Hawai'i as a stone-age "affluent society"—that is, a society in which "all the people's material wants are easily satisfied" and where distinctions between designated work and leisure times are blurry. Among the kingdoms of Hawai'i, people grew taro, breadfruit, and sweet potato; raised livestock like chickens, dogs, and pigs; farmed prawns, mullet, and milkfish among other species in human-made ponds called *loko i'a*; fished in the sea; and gathered food and building materials from the shoreline, lava fields, mountain jungles, and fertile valleys. These abundant resources provided ample sustenance for a Hawaiian population up to 1,000,000 people. Using sophisticated stone tools, they created elaborate architectural structures, fine woodwork and stonework, and a range of arts and textiles.

This is not to say that life in ancient Hawaiian society was utopian or easy. There was constant warfare among kingdoms on the islands. Natural disasters from high seas to volcanic eruptions could destroy villages, taro fields, and fishponds, bringing death and famine to the population. *Aliʻi* (royalty) and headmen who acted as land stewards could be overzealous in demanding tribute from their people. And the system of "kapu"—a common-law tradition of crime and punishment—meant that commoners could be put to death for seemingly small offenses such as stepping on the shadow of an *aliʻi*.

But, as Sahlins points out, the comfortable abundance of economic life for people of Hawaiʻi left ample time for a diversity of activities that were at once technologically innovative, spiritually significant, and aesthetically pleasing.

Ancient Hawaiian people enthusiastically practiced sports like *moku-moku* (an especially bloody style of boxing), *hakoko* (wrestling), *ulu-maika* (a kind of bowling), spear dodging (what it sounds like), foot racing, and cliff jumping, to name a few activities. But it was surfing that people loved the most.

Surfing was aphorized as the "favorite activity of chiefs" but nearly everybody surfed: commoners and royalty, women and men, children and the elderly. As the nineteenth-century Hawaiian chronicler David Malo remarked, "it was not uncommon for a whole community, including both sexes and all ages, to sport and frolic in the ocean the livelong day."

Communal surf sessions could be riotous affairs. Inhabitants of the biggest and most populous island, Hawaiʻi, carved specialized *heiau* (temples) into rock faces adjacent to surf beaches. These temples featured specially made freshwater pools for rinsing off after a session in the waves and tiered seating so that people could watch surfing contests and cheer their favorite athletes. At the Makahiki—a monthslong festival to honor the return of the god Lono—people shouted encouragements and insults from the beach as riders competed to catch the best wave, to surf the longest, and to surf the most stylishly. Gambling on the outcomes of surf runs was as integral to surfing as boards and water. People wagered cloth, animals, canoes, and sometimes their own lives on surfing.

These sessions were more than just religious celebrations or entertainment—surfing was also a show of physical and political strength. A high-ranking official in the nineteenth century recalled that "physical fitness had always been deemed a part of Hawaiian chieftainship. Feats of physical skill were greatly admired and an absolute necessity . . . we all took part in water sports—surfing, canoe racing, swimming."

Strength—physical and mental—was an attribute of leadership best demonstrated on a wave. In one tale, ʻUmi, a young man who was secretly the son of the king of Hawaiʻi, criticized a famous local surfer named Paiʻea. Enraged, Paiʻea challenged him to a *heihei*, or surf contest, betting four canoes against ʻUmi's bones that he would emerge victorious. During the contest, Paiʻea bumped ʻUmi, attempting to drive him into a reef where he would crash. ʻUmi injured his shoulder on the coral but still managed to win the contest. Years later, ʻUmi fought his way to the top throne of Hawaiʻi, taking the place of his father. He hadn't forgotten the way Paiʻea attempted to sabotage him during the surf contest, however, and one of his first acts as king was to have Pai'ea seized and baked in an oven.

But as much as it was a stage for demonstrating political strength, as much as it was a source of community bonding and entertainment, surfing was also, perhaps above all, about beauty and eroticism. As Hawaiian chronicler Samuel Kamakau put it in the middle of the nineteenth century, surfing not only "showed which man or which woman was skilled . . . but which man or woman was the best looking."

Surfing and seduction were woven into the very fabric of Hawaiian history. In one story, Kiha-a-pi'ilani—an attractive young prince made excellent from his constant swimming in the sea—went surfing with Kōleamoku, the daughter of a powerful *ali'i*. For the better part of the week, they surfed the waves of Kapueokahi, on Maui. Then, taken with his skill and physical beauty, Kōleamoku seduced him. In another story, Lā'ieikawai, a powerful priestess, wished to marry Kekalukaluokewa, a prince of Kaua'i. Her grandmother cast a spell so that she could surf with the prince in a dense mist. As her grandmother told her, "when the mist clears, then all shall see you riding on the wave with Kekalukaluokewa; that is the time to give a kiss to the Kaua'i youth" and then "to return with your husband to your house, become one flesh according to your wish."

It is worth noting that neither of these legendary love affairs went smoothly. Kōleamoku's father opposed her relationship with Kiha-a-pi'ilani, and the two men became bitter enemies. For Lā'ieikawai, an even stranger twist awaited, when a different suitor, Halaaniani, "a young man of Puna noted for his debaucheries" (but an excellent surfer), also took a liking to the priestess. He had his own grandmother cast a spell over Lā'ieikawai, so that Lāʻieikawai thought that the debauched young man was her beloved prince. She surfed as planned with the man she thought was her husband-to-be—once, twice, thrice in the mist—then kissed him, and took him to bed. It was only in the morning that she realized her mistake, when she woke up with the wrong man. Her mother cursed her, and she was exiled from her community.

• • •

Scared of water, uncomfortable with sensuality, leery of leisure, it is little wonder that early nineteenth-century Europeans found surfing terrifying. Everything that made it beautiful also made it profoundly threatening. Like icebergs that could bash mighty ships to splinters or ancient ruins that made modern cities suddenly seem flimsy, the improbable sight of men and women courting death as they communed with the awesome strength of the ocean was a sublime, devastating experience for Western viewers.

The British explorer James Cook and the crews of his two ships, the *Resolution* and the *Discovery*, were the first Europeans to record Hawaiian surfing in 1778. A seasoned navigator, Cook was on his third voyage through the Pacific when he happened upon the western islands of Hawaiʻi.

The people Cook's crew encountered were friendly, keen businesspeople, and extremely skilled in the water. Cook and his men had witnessed wave riding before in Tahiti, where they saw people careening through the surf on canoes, but what they found in Hawaiʻi was completely different. The people of Hawaiʻi, wrote Charles Clerke, captain of the *Discovery*, had a "convenience for conveying themselves upon the Water, which we never met with before." Unsure how to translate *papa heʻe nalu* ("wave sliding boards"), the British took to calling them "sharkboards." Maneuvering these sharkboards through the water, Hawaiian people of all sexes and ages were astoundingly fast, literally paddling circles around the dinghies that the *Resolution* and *Discovery* dispatched to parlay with the Hawaiians who came in enthusiastic crowds to greet the British ships.

More startling still, the Hawaiian people rode these boards through the roughest of waves while standing up—an act that seems to have filled the men of Cook's party with equal parts dread and fascination. One ship's mate, David Samwell, wrote in his diary that "these People find one of their Chief amusements in that which to us presented nothing but Horror & Destruction." For British seamen—many of whom couldn't swim in calm water, let alone choppy—the ocean was an enemy, a watery grave waiting to happen. Samwell wrote that he and his fellows witnessed "with astonishment young boys & Girls about 9 or ten years of age playing amid such tempestuous waves that the hardiest of our seamen would have trembled to face." To encounter such waves, wrote another sailor, would be "no other than certain death" to any European.

The Hawaiian people were "so perfectly Masters of themselves in the Water," according to Clerke, "that it appears their perfect element." Some of Cook's men evidently did try surfing—*Discovery*'s midshipman reported that "the most expert of our people at swimming" couldn't stay on a board for "half a minuit [*sic*] without rolling off." But for the most part, Cook's men were content to gawk at the sight of men, women, and children perfectly at ease skimming the border between water and air.

Cook was killed on the Big Island of Hawaiʻi almost exactly

a year later. While there's little historical debate as to *what* happened, *why* it happened is contentious. Some historians think that Cook's first visit coincided with the Makahiki, the festival of the god Lono. As such, Cook appeared to be an instantiation or effigy of Lono: something like a living statue of the god. According to the legend that underwrote the Makahiki, Lono would sail three times around the islands, then return to be killed. When Cook left and then returned, he seemed to be fulfilling this part of the Lono story, and the Hawaiians killed him as the natural conclusion to the ceremony. This account, however, is complicated by the fact that on his second visit, Cook was received much less warmly than before. A Hawaiian man took some iron from Cook's ship and Cook's men murdered several Hawaiians in retaliation. Cook then took a local ruler captive, and ultimately, negotiations for his release erupted into bloodshed. Either way—whether as an instantiation of a mythic cycle or as a violent interloper—Cook met his end in Hawai'i.

• • •

From the vantage point of Cook and his clients in the Royal Society—or to any of the thousands of foreigners who swarmed to Hawai'i over the course of the next century—it would have made very little sense for a distinguished man of science like Osborn to go looking for the future of civilized humankind in Hawai'i. As no less an authority than Herman Melville put it in 1851—having spent time in Hawai'i, Tahiti, and Nuku Hiva—the islands of Polynesia were "insulated, immemorial, unalterable countries, which even in these modern days still preserve much of the ghostly aboriginalness of earth's primal generations, when the memory of the first man was a distinct recollection." Hawaiian society, to this way of thinking, was static, unchanging, and timeless. It was populated by humans, true—but they were not like civilized people. They submitted to the passage of biological time, of natural cycles, of the rhythms of the ocean and the cosmos, rather than productive, progressive human will. Though human in form, they were possessed mainly of *natural* history, rather than the fullness of civilized, human history.

Osborn shared this view, more or less. "Savagery" might be noble—it might have its own sort of reason, its own mysterious logic, its own potential to tap into the power of nature itself. But as soon as the unsuspecting "savage" was brought into contact with white civilization, that spell broke, and the man in the state of nature crumbled into submission. This was what made Hawai'i so interesting to Osborn. For the people of Hawai'i had not evidently crumbled into submission, though he was sure they were in decline. They had weathered better than most their contacts with white men, and in fact while they had diminished, there were still those—like Duke and David—who were magnificent. To Osborn's way of thinking, the Kahanamoku brothers were akin to fossils, like living versions of the petrified bones that he assembled in his museum so that schoolchildren could better understand prehistoric horses and sloths and hippopotamuses. Hawai'i in this sense was part laboratory, and part time machine—a way to see how humans in a state of nature adjusted to modern civilization.

This said, as he steamed into Honolulu in April 1920, Osborn would not have seen a primal island, but a small, bustling, twentieth-century metropolis. Boats from all eras of Hawaiian history skittered across the harbor: outrigger canoes, whaleboats, sampans, junks, and ketches. Stevedores shouted to each other as they unloaded freight from chugging cargo ships that came from as far away as China, Japan, Australia, and Alaska. The Hawaiian Pineapple Factory along the nearby Oʻahu railway was the largest fruit canning operation in the world, and the clang of trains passing through the harbor on the Oʻahu Railroad nearly drowned out the baying of ship horns and the jangle of the uniformed brass bands that the Matson Steamship Company placed on their docks to greet their passengers. Telephone and electrical lines crosshatched the city streets, smoke from ships and factories smudged the sky, and the acrid smell of coal, the sweet smell of canned fruit, the stench of fish, and the heady scent of flower leis filled the air.

Disembarking from the vessel, Osborn would have stepped into the controlled mayhem of high industrial capitalism. There were 6,384 cars on Oʻahu in 1920, and at times it seemed like they were all in downtown Honolulu at once—crowding the harbor quays, honking through the King Street marketplace, jockeying for position with horse carriages, and disappointing visitors from the mainland sold on visions of an untouched island paradise.

More shocking still was the racial diversity of the city. Laborers from the Azores and Portugal tore up the streets and put down new tram lines while Chinese shopkeepers sold goods supplied by white American importers. Portuguese, Italians, Puerto Ricans, Black Americans, and Native Hawaiians worked as longshoremen, hoisting sacks of sugar packed by Japanese warehousemen who received the shipments from Filipino plantation workers. Beat cops, often Indigenous Hawaiians, turned a blind eye—and an outstretched hand—to the city's booming sex work and drug trades.

This is not to say that the city was a paradise of industrial harmony and racial rapport. When striking or staging labor negotiations, workers often organized along racial and ethnic lines. Skilled unions tended to be exclusively white, and anti-Asian sentiment flared when Japanese and Chinese workers began leaving the inland sugar plantations and taking skilled work in Honolulu. These sentiments were exacerbated by constant worries—fanned by newspapers and discussed at community meetings—over the intentions of the Japanese empire, a short three thousand miles away. Was Japan girding for war with the West? Would Hawai'i be on the top of its list as a place to strike? Employers, meanwhile, often used these divisions to their advantage, hiring and firing ethnic groups en bloc, and paying different wages to different groups.

In other words, in the early twentieth century, Honolulu was a bustling American city. It was cosmopolitan, corrupt, modern, urbane, fast-paced, fast-growing, and future oriented. It took a particular sort of myopia—a jaundiced understanding of humankind and human history—not to see that. Convinced that all history was, in essence, a matter of biology, Osborn had that sort of vision. It was impossible for men like him to see human actions and human history as distinct from expressions of biological race and "race memory."

But what Osborn didn't see—what he couldn't see, looking at history as a version of biology—were the accretions of everyday human choices and interactions and chance encounters that had, over the course of more than a century, created the Hawai'i that he encountered in April 1920. Before following Osborn in his eugenic quest, it's important to take a more gimlet-eyed appraisal of the history of Hawai'i.

From the perspective of the people he most wished to study—people like David, and Duke, and their neighbors who had to navigate the complexities of a colonial outpost of the world's newest, least experienced imperial power—even a cursory sketch of the history of Hawai'i's interactions with its continental neighbors would reveal a Hawaiian society with more improvisational churn and vitality than Osborn could have imagined.

Shortly after the *Discovery* and the *Resolution* returned to England bearing tales of Cook's death, a steady trickle of foreign vessels began arriving off the Hawaiian Islands. Their objectives were various: they came to trade, to resupply and repair their ships, to proselytize, to map and catalog the natural history of the islands, and (often) to quietly weigh the idea of taking Hawai'i as an overseas colony. At first they came mainly from Britain, France, and Russia; later in the century they came from Japan and Germany.

Of all the foreigners to stop at the Islands, however, it was the Americans who had the most lasting influence.

The United States first entered Hawaiian politics in a roundabout fashion, when two American sailors were taken captive in 1790 during an internecine war between Kamehameha I—a fearsome warrior and visionary politician—and the rest of the chiefs of Hawai'i's major islands. At the time, the Hawaiian archipelago was divided into four kingdoms, each connected to its neighbors by culture, but not government. Just before the *ali'i* of the Big Island had died, he named his son, Kīwala'ō, his direct successor and appointed the powerful position of Guardian of Ku to his nephew, Kamehameha. Huge, unsmiling, and serious, Kamehameha was unsatisfied with being second in command—he aspired to rule. Indeed, he wanted to rule not just the island of Hawai'i, but the whole archipelago. After a brief, tense period of peace, Kamehameha insulted Kīwalaʻō by failing to include him in an important ritual, Kīwalaʻō's men encroached on Kamehameha's lands, and the two went to war.

In the midst of this conflict, two American vessels—the *Eleanora* and the *Fair American*—dropped anchor off the southern shore of the Big Island. In the course of a routine negotiation over trade goods, the captain of the *Eleanora* got into an argument with one of Kamehameha's lieutenants on the Big Island and had the man flogged. Compounding this offense, the captain of the *Eleanora* then sailed to Maui, where he massacred the residents of a village in another trade negotiation gone wrong. In response, Kamehameha's lieutenant captured the *Fair American* on its return to the Big Island, taking two sailors prisoner. Kamehameha's lieutenant then brought the sailors to the ambitious conqueror. Kamehameha gave the two men a choice: advise him on the best use of the guns on the *Fair American*, or die. The two sailors chose the former and went on to have distinguished careers as Kamehameha's military attachés throughout his wars to unify Hawaiʻi.

By 1810, Kamehameha had subdued his enemies and consolidated control over the Hawaiian Islands. He established his capital at Honolulu and began expanding the economy of his kingdom. One of his first acts was to grant a monopoly over lucrative sandalwood exports to a group of American merchants in return for a quarter of their profits. This added to Kamehameha's coffers and gave Americans a preferential toehold in Hawaiʻi. In 1819, the first New England whaleships stopped to refit in Maui, and shortly thereafter the Islands became a hub in the Yankee sperm whaling fishery, further tethering the United States to the future of the island. Boardinghouses, brothels, bars, banks, and blacksmiths sprouted up around port cities like Lahaina and Honolulu to accommodate them. In 1835, the Hawaiian crown granted an American firm, Ladd & Co., a lease for 980 acres of farmland in Kauaʻi to grow and refine sugar—the first and most profitable agricultural export in the kingdom. To keep an eye on the growing business interests of its citizens, in 1821 the US government opened a consulate in Honolulu—the first such foreign office in the kingdom—and a steady parade of American warships paid ports of call in the harbor.

All of these interactions set the stage for the Honolulu in which Duke and Osborn would meet—but of the many Americans who established a presence in nineteenth-century Hawaiʻi, it was Calvinist missionaries who left the biggest footprint. The first cohort of missionaries arrived on the western shore of the Big Island in 1820, intent on spreading Christian civilization to the "savage" people of the islands. To do this, they made alliances with *aliʻi*, from the top of the kingdom to the local chiefs. Leveraging these connections, the missionaries set up schools and a printing press, built churches, houses, and seminaries, transliterated the Hawaiian language into the English alphabet, and promoted European-style dress. They also convinced *aliʻi* to institute prohibitions against those aspects of Hawaiian life that seemed to the missionaries most un-Christian. It was this sort of influence that convinced the governor of Oʻahu to make sex trade a crime in Honolulu—a decision that made missionaries unpopular with the less pious American and British merchants and sailors with whom they shared white, expatriate life. With these early successes, twelve additional companies of Calvinist missionaries arrived in Hawaiʻi over the course of the next forty years.

Successive Hawaiian rulers responded in different ways to this growing American presence. Some, such as Kamehameha II—or more accurately, his aunt, Kaʻahumanu, who was the de facto ruler of the kingdom during his dissolute years of rule (1819–24)—embraced the values of the missionaries, scouring the kingdom of traditional Hawaiian rules and customs and replacing them with laws that reflected Protestant teachings. Others, such as King David Kalākaua (r. 1874–91), chafed against American dominance in Hawaiian social and political life and tried to restore traditional sports, arts, dance, and Indigenous governance. Mostly, though, Hawaiian rulers were pragmatists, content to employ American influence and trade to further their own political and economic aims while attempting to keep the most avaricious ambitions of their notional allies at bay.

Exemplary in this regard was Kamehameha III (r. 1825–54). Early in his rule, his adviser, the Hawaiian historian and intellectual David Malo, told him that "if a big wave comes in, large fishes will come from the dark ocean which you never saw before, and when they see the small fishes they will eat them up.... The ships of the whitemen have come, and smart people have arrived from the Great Countries.... They know our people are few in number and living in a small country; they will eat us up. Such has always been the case with large countries: the small ones have been gobbled up."

In order that Hawaiʻi not be gobbled up, Kamehameha set about making his kingdom legible as a modern nation-state to potential European and American predators. In very short order, he transformed the kingdom from an absolute monarchy with a political economy based on communal land use into a constitutional monarchy with a liberal political economy based on the private ownership of land and freedom of contract.

His reforms included a "Declaration of Rights" that put commoners on equal legal footing with *ali'i*; a new constitution that abrogated the absolute power of the monarch in favor of a tricameral legislature in which the monarch shared executive power; and a reform called the Great Māhele, in which, for the first time, the Hawaiian government distributed land to commoners for outright ownership. This last became particularly significant when in 1850, Kamehameha extended land-ownership laws for the first time to non-Hawaiians. Americans—mainly missionaries and their children—began purchasing large swaths of property at bargain prices from people who didn't fully understand the implications of giving up prime real estate.

All told, Kamehameha III's reforms meant that, by the middle of the nineteenth century, Hawai'i was recognizably a sovereign, industrializing nation-state, on the model of England, France, and the United States. It had a modern, liberal government; property rights backed up by a well-run judicial system; a market economy; and a cosmopolitan population. It also had a well-oiled machine for international diplomacy. In 1843, Britain formally recognized Hawai'i as an independent nation, followed by France, the United States, and Belgium.

In theory, diplomatic recognition meant that Hawai'i was less of a target for hungry European nations—though this didn't stop a few rogue naval captains from trying their luck. In 1843 a British captain, attempting to arbitrate a British citizen's land dispute, sailed into Honolulu Harbor and forced Kamehameha III to cede control of the islands on threat of bombardment. He was eventually reprimanded by government officials in London for making war on a sovereign state and ordered to return control of Hawai'i to its proper rulers. Six years later, a

French captain likewise invaded Honolulu for a short period of time as a reprisal for what he saw as anti-French policies (these included proscriptions on Catholicism, taxes on French wines, and diplomatic documents written exclusively in English). He, too, was scolded by his government and ordered to return the Hawaiian government to power.

The incidents suggested two things at once. On the one hand, Kamehameha III's efforts had succeeded. European governments recognized Hawai'i as a nation with the same sovereign rights as any other, and honored these rights accordingly. On the other hand, for all of the kingdom's legible modernity, it still remained vulnerable to foreign military strength—or, for that matter, to any scoundrel with a warship and a bad idea.

More to the point, as historian Noenoe Silva argues, the reforms passed by Kamehameha III might well have made Hawai'i *more* of a target for takeover, albeit of an economic and diplomatic sort, rather than a strictly military invasion.

Ultimately, if indirectly, these modernization efforts proved to be the undoing of the Hawaiian Kingdom. Following the example of Ladd & Co., missionary families who purchased land after the Great Māhele largely turned their vast holdings into sugar plantations (and later, pineapple plantations). Although Kamehameha III died in 1854 and thus didn't live to see the greatest extent of it, sugar production rapidly took over the Hawaiian economy. After the American Civil War cut off Union access to Louisiana sugar, Hawai'i's sugar exports flooded California's ports in a glittering, white tsunami.

The fortunes made in sugar gave its main producers—a cluster of companies known as "the Big Five"—nearly oligarchic control over Hawaiian commercial, legal, and cultural life. They took a hand not just in the production of sugar itself, but also in the shape of infrastructure, politics, and demography. The Big Five financed banks, built railroads, dug canals, and razed villages to make room for more cane fields. They colluded to keep sugar prices high and production costs low and lobbied for political favors from the Hawaiian government and tariff-free markets from the United States. Finally, and most enduringly, when Native Hawaiians resisted working in the poor conditions of the sugar plantations, the oligarchy made deals to import hundreds of thousands of laborers from China, Japan, Portugal, and the Philippines to work the cane fields. Sugar producers brought workers from around the world to Hawai'i and promoted judges and local officials who would keep immigration open and labor cheap.

The heavy hand of the Big Five was a persistent sore spot for Hawaiian monarchs—one that came to a head during the rule of David Kalākaua (r. 1874–91). Nicknamed "the Merrie Monarch" for his love of dance, sports, and drinking, Kalākaua was also a serious nationalist with a burning antipathy for American influence in Hawaiian affairs. Under the motto of *Hawai'i no ka poe Hawai'i*—"Hawai'i for the Hawaiians"—he made a point of populating his cabinet posts with more Native Hawaiian ministers than his predecessors, funding and promoting Hawaiian language newspapers, and reviving "the Ancient Sciences of Hawai'i"—medicine, poetry, genealogy, and surfing among them—through a society called Hale Nalu.

The Big Five viewed Kalākaua's nationalism as a direct assault on the foundations of their economic and political existence. In 1883, a group of foreign businessmen—largely Americans, but some British—formed a secret society, the Hawaiian League, equipped with its own armed militia, the Honolulu Rifle Company.

In July 1887, the League, backed up by its riflemen, showed up at 'Iolani Palace and surprised Kalākaua with the demand for a new constitution—one they had taken the liberty of composing. The so-called Bayonet Constitution stripped the monarchy of its power, reserving the right to appoint cabinet positions to elite landowners. Literacy and wealth tests effectively excluded most Native Hawaiians from voting, and Asian people of any wealth or literacy were denied suffrage. The result was a government run almost exclusively by American businessmen.

This was the beginning of the end of the Hawaiian monarchy and the independent Kingdom of Hawai'i.

King Kalākaua died in 1891 and was succeeded by his sister, Queen Lili'uokalani. For a brief period, it looked as though she might restore the Hawaiian monarchy to its previous position of power, but once again, a group of American businessmen—this time backed by the American consul John L. Stevens—intervened. When, in 1893, Lili'uokalani called for a referendum on a new, pro-monarchy constitution, Stevens summoned a contingent of US marines from the warship *Boston*. They occupied the royal palace and placed Queen Lili'uokalani under house arrest. In 1894, the usurpers declared a new state, the Republic of Hawai'i, with the business leader Sanford Dole as president.

The new Hawaiian Republic never had more than a shaky legal and political relationship with the United States. The administration of President Grover Cleveland was mortified to discover that an American official had freelanced a coup d'état against a sovereign foreign nation and considered forcing Dole to restore Liliʻuokalani as monarch. But the United States was also potentially interested in annexing Hawaiʻi, which would be made easier by the pro-American, pro-business, pro-annexation Dole administration. For four years, successive administrations argued the matter in a desultory fashion.

Ultimately, the matter was decided in 1898, when the United States went to war with Spain, ostensibly to liberate the oppressed Spanish colonies. After a brief conflict, the United States found itself in possession of Spain's holdings in Cuba, Puerto Rico, Guam, Samoa, and the Philippines. In the Pacific, the Philippines became an American territory over the objection of those Filipino revolutionaries who had assumed that they would be able to form their own government after throwing off the yoke of Spain. Their objections to US rule led to four years of open war between the United States and the nascent Philippine Republic, plus another twenty years of sporadic guerrilla war, with the United States exerting its own form of tyranny over the people it had saved from tyranny—an irony that it would fail repeatedly to reflect on over the next hundred years.

The needs of defending a new Pacific empire drove home the importance of Hawaiʻi as a strategic outpost. Within a month of US warships sinking the Spanish Navy in Manila Harbor, in April 1898, Congress voted to annex Hawaiʻi. Two years later, in 1900, Congress passed the Hawaiian Organic Act, officially declaring Hawaiʻi a territory of the United States.

The incorporation of Hawaiʻi as a US territory was controversial, not least of all because of its multiracial composition. Territories are allowed nonvoting representation in the House of Representatives, which meant that the people of Hawaiʻi would, necessarily, become members of Congress, over the objection of those who wanted the lower house to be a whites-only affair. Worse still, territories could become states. Could anyone imagine, asked one congressman, the "shame when a Chinese Senator from Hawaii, with his pigtail hanging down his back, with his pagan joss in his hand, shall rise from his curule chair and in pigeon [sic] English proceed to chop logic with George Frisbie Hoar or Henry Cabot Lodge?" The very idea was greeted with laughter from his peers. A nonwhite person speaking on equal terms with the great orators of the American Senate? Outrageous!

Nor was this question limited to Congress. In 1901, the Supreme Court heard the case of *Downes v. Bidwell*, one of a group of so-called insular cases attempting to iron out territorial law. The legal matter at the heart of *Downes* technically concerned whether US territories that were formerly nations or colonies of other nations should be considered fully part of the United States for the purpose of tariff law. Justice John Marshall Harlan, however, took a broader view of the issues at stake. The question of territories was not simply about borders or tariffs, he said. The question was "whether a particular race will or will not assimilate with our people, and whether they can or cannot with safety to our institutions be brought within the operation of the Constitution." The answer, often as not, was "no," though it was up to science—or, rather, pseudo-science—to decide.

• • •

For Osborn and his eugenicist peers in the 1920s, the question of whether a people could or could not "assimilate" into American society was in many ways a matter of public health as much as one of cultural norms or beliefs. This was because, for eugenicists, culture *was* a matter of biology, and therefore a matter of physiology, and physical health. The "race" of a people—their genes, as expressed in their physical forms—shaped the kinds of societies and beliefs and customs that they would adopt. This was especially the case where nonwhite people were concerned, though many of the attributes that Osborn and his peers celebrated about American civilization—industriousness, ingenuity, rationality—could supposedly be traced to the healthful influence of "Nordic" or "Caucasian" "stock."

This was why Hawaiʻi—and Hawaiian athletes like surfers and swimmers in particular—so readily captured the imaginations of American eugenicists. Before contact with Europeans, the Hawaiian people were thought to have been among the most magnificent people on the earth. "Anthropologists agree," wrote Osborn's contemporary, Vaughan MacCaughey, "that the ancient Hawaiian was one of the finest physical types in the Pacific, and compared very favorably with the best types from any other part of the world. They were tall and well developed, with splendidly shaped torsos, and fine muscular limbs of excellent proportions." Now, however, the Hawaiian "race" was in decline. As MacCaughey put it, "a variety of influences, racial and sociologic, have led to the decimation of what was at one time one of the finest peoples in the Pacific Ocean."

How, wondered Osborn and his peers, in this moment of early twentieth-century decline, did men like Duke and David persist? How to account for their physical perfection? And what did their perfection say about the possibility of using eugenics to harness biology for the advancement of "civilization"?

Osborn's focus on Duke—as a famous Hawaiian swimmer,

practitioner of the ancient art of surfing, and paragon of masculine healthiness—represented a change in American attitudes toward health, fitness, and nature. From a Euro-American fear of both the ocean and Indigenous customs (and Indigenous people), over the course of the nineteenth century, elite Europeans and Americans pivoted to a fascination with the possibilities of healthfulness—and even moral redemption—to be found in Indigenous traditions and relationships with nature. In a perverse way, the very attitudes that formed the bedrock of eugenics also made people like Osborn interested in surfing.

• • •

For the people of ancient Hawai'i, surfing was central to healthy living because it involved interaction with the ocean. From this interaction, people acquired *mana*—a term referring at once to "spiritual life force," "spiritual power," "status," and "belonging." *Mana*, as historian Noenoe Silva explains, is not a power that simply inheres in objects or people. Rather, *mana* is actively created by interactions between beings with the power to feel, to think, to speak, and to act. These willful beings might be human, but they can also be nonhuman. The ocean was a central nonhuman actor in ancient Hawaiian life, recognized as kin to people and as alive as any bird or fish or human.

Surfing was one way of accessing or building *mana*. Daring acts on the ocean like surfing, explains waterman Tom Pohaku Stone, were both proof of strength and a way of interacting with the power of the ocean, the power of the natural world. Because of this, surfing was a central source of spiritual and political power.

Indeed, many Europeans recognized this equation between daring in the ocean and physical health. In 1806, the Swiss philosopher Isaak Iselin declared surfing "a fine exercise, in which the natives show their skill as swimmers to great advantage." As late as 1851, Henry T. Cheever, a whaler, visited Maui and wrote that surfing was an "easy and unequalled means of retaining health, or of restoring it when enfeebled." He felt it was "unwise, not to say criminal, in such a climate, to neglect so natural a way of preserving health."

Nevertheless, between Cook's first encounter with Hawaiians in 1795 and the arrival of Calvinist missionaries in 1820, the healthfulness of the Hawaiian population had declined steeply. Epidemic syphilis and gonorrhea exploded through Hawaiian society, leaving death and infertility in their wake. Those mariners who followed Cook—whalers, merchants, and military detachments—added a battery of other European diseases to the raging epidemic of sexually transmitted illnesses. The most feared of these—measles, smallpox, mumps, cholera, influenza, tuberculosis, and later leprosy—scorched Hawaiian populations in regular waves. At the time of contact with Cook in 1778, the total population of Indigenous Hawaiians may have been as high as 1,000,000 people. By 1820, the population was 200,000. By the end of the nineteenth century, an official census counted just under 30,000 people of Hawaiian ancestry living on the islands.

To explain these catastrophic epidemics, European observers of the nineteenth century looked to the principal medical theories of their time. In the absence of any theory of pathogenic microbes as causes of illness, nineteenth-century medical explanations for suffering tended to come in three related varieties.

First, most medical and laypeople tended to think of climate as a central source of sickness. It was obvious to nineteenth-century observers that extremes of temperature and humidity could wreak havoc on the bodies of those who were unprepared. This explained, for example, why people got colds and flus more frequently in cold weather. But it also explained why Europeans who journeyed to tropical climates—English elites who went to Jamaica to oversee sugar plantations, for instance—appeared to be more susceptible to diseases like yellow fever than Native or enslaved peoples. European bodies were simply not used to the heat, according to the best medical theories of the time, and could only achieve states of comparable health if they were "seasoned" by carefully adjusting to hot climates.

At the same time, "bad airs"—known medically as "miasmas"—were believed to cause sickness. Miasmas were generally putrid, emanating from dirt, effluvia, and decaying matter. In other words, miasmas were caused by "filth." To learned medical minds this explained, in no small part, why those who lived in poverty tended to suffer more disease (and more varieties of disease) than the wealthy. Since the poor tended to live in environments that their social betters considered "filthy," they would therefore tend to be more afflicted by miasmatic airs and would be more prone to sickness. Conveniently, miasmatic theory was compatible with notions of climate-based sickness. After all, it was apparent that organic matter decayed more quickly in hot climates, which emitted foul-smelling, disease-causing miasmas.

Finally, the moral constitution of an individual was seen as the ultimate arbiter of disease and health. Diseases like syphilis clearly tended to follow sexual promiscuity. Absent a theory of contagion, the best explanation was that a sort of moral turpitude or dissolution caused maladies of this sort. In a similar way, overconsumption of alcohol and tobacco could be sources of "dissipation," which would weaken the body and open the door to diseases caused by climate or miasma. For that matter, moral character also explained the higher prevalence of disease among the impoverished members of society, since the lack of industry that was assumed to make poor people poor in the first place could also be interpreted as a precursor to sickness. The poor lived in filth (so the theory went) because they lacked the moral uprightness to bring themselves into more healthy circumstances—thus did medical theory, social theory, and moral theory form a tight and self-reinforcing feedback loop.

In the case of Native Hawaiians, it seemed manifestly clear to European observers that it was this last factor—a lack of good moral character—that drove the ill health of Native peoples. After all, the climate of Hawai'i was salubrious for white people as well as Hawaiian people, and there were no known miasmas on the islands. This left only moral character as the cause of disease.

Which particular moral characters? Medically minded missionaries tended to focus principally on the characters of sexual permissiveness and "indolence." Both seemed unchecked in Hawaiian society, both were deemed to be detrimental to health, and both came to the fore in the practice of surfing.

As much as surfing in ancient Hawai'i was a display of political power, physical strength, and beauty, surfing was also—perhaps inevitably—about sex. In Hawaiian tradition, surfing was both a way of admiring a potential lover and a stylized mode of courtship. When people "surfed to flirt," as one nineteenth-century Hawaiian writer put it, they would put on their finest surf wear: a red *malo* loincloth for men, and a red sarong for women. Then "all [would] go surfing together, the men mixing with the women. When they surfed, they would catch the same wave. . . . The end result was a love affair." Common expressions codified the connection between surfing and sex. "Hāwāwā ka heʻe nalu haki ka papa" translates to "when the surfer is unskilled, the board is broken"—that is, an inexperienced man will not satisfy his lover. More optimistically, the woman who says "O ka papa heʻe nalu kēia, pahʻe i ka nalu haʻi o Makaīwa" means that she is so excellent at lovemaking that her body is like a surfboard that will transport her lover as though over the rolling waves of the famed surf break, Makaīwa.

This strong association between surfing and sexuality scandalized missionaries. As Sarah Lyman, a missionary teacher on Oʻahu's North Shore, remarked in 1834, surfing was the "source of much iniquity, inasmuch as it leads to intercourse with the sexes without discrimination." An editorial in the missionary newspaper *Ka Hae Hawaii* agreed, drawing a parallel between surfing, hula, and other "shameful" and "impure activities . . . related to sex."

This sort of unrestrained sexual liberalism was bad, but to American eyes, "indolence" was even worse.

By "indolence," Calvinist missionaries meant a perceived resistance on the part of Indigenous Hawaiians to sustained, capital-producing labor. From the perspective of American missionaries, traditional Hawaiian society was radically underproductive. The agricultural potential of the land was rich, but people worked only as much as they had to in order to live comfortably and make satisfactory tributes to their *aliʻi*. This is not to say that ancient Hawaiian people shunned labor. Life in the ancient affluent society was hard work. The production of canoes, the making of fishponds, and the clearing and planting of taro fields—among many other activities—were all arduous affairs, sometimes requiring the coordinated effort of thousands of people.

Nevertheless, the idea of overproducing in order to accumulate wealth—what Europeans would come to call "capital"—was anathema in ancient Hawaiian society. Indeed, a principle way that chiefs cemented their power was by periodically giving away their material goods in displays of largesse.

To missionaries and those they converted, this casual attitude toward productive labor and private property suggested an epidemic of indolence among Native Hawaiians—and indolence was not simply a moral failing, or an economic barrier, but a source of disease. This was a clear refrain among missionaries in the first part of the nineteenth century. As missionary John Smith Emerson remarked, "these people are indolent and much of the improvidence and sickness and death are often the result of this [indolence]." Reverend B. W. Parker likewise reported that "both the moral and physical health of the natives is most seriously affected (injured) by their indolence, indifference, and improvidence."

To missionaries and those they converted, nothing seemed more indolent than the obvious preference of people of Hawaiʻi for surfing over undertaking sustained, economically productive labor. In an 1842 letter to Mataio Kekuanaoa, the governor of Oʻahu, a concerned Hawaiian father stated baldly, "surfing is wrong." It was wrong because it was "dirty"; it was wrong because it made people idle; it was wrong because it distracted children from school. The letter writer implored the governor to combat the "evil" of surfing by banning it entirely from the island. Another writer, a converted Christian going by the name of Owlahie, laid out a similar case in clear, condemnatory prose in an editorial titled "No Ka Molowa," or "Laziness." "It is clear that [the people] are lazy," the author wrote. "The men would spend their time surfing and the women and children would spend all their time jumping and diving into the ocean." As one observer put it, when the surf was up, farmers would leave their fields, hurry home to grab their board, and then go surfing: "All thought of work is put off, and all they think about is the sport. The wife may go hungry, the children, the whole family, but the head of the house does not care . . . all day there is nothing but surfing."

For these mid-nineteenth-century observers, far from being a source of power and health, surfing seemed to many like a wellspring of disease. An editorial in the *Pacific Commercial Advertiser* proclaimed that the decline of indigenous populations could be linked directly to traditional recreations, since they promoted "indolence and vice among a race which *heaven knows is running itself out fast enough*, even when held in check with all the restraints which civilization, morality, and industry can hold out." In other words, the Hawaiian peoples' health might be improved en masse if only they would work more, and work in the mode of American civilization, morality, and industry.

Perhaps the best expression of this sentiment came from Kaili'aumoku, a Native Hawaiian who had converted to Christianity, in a news report about a boy who had died while surfing.

The report strongly implied that it was the immoral character of surfing itself that was fatal, and called for a full accounting of the ills of surfing. "We have seen the immoral side of surfing. It is the reason people become indolent and the root of lasciviousness. What are we to think of this senseless death? Is it not possible to quit surfing?"

The author summed up his argument with the aphorism: "Go and sin no more"—by which he might as well have said, "go and surf no more."

• • •

To remedy the "unhealthy" practices that were supposedly driving the Hawaiian people to oblivion, missionaries and their allies in government lobbied Hawaiian leaders to pass sweeping restrictions. As US naval captain Charles Wilkes wrote in 1840, "Such was the proneness of all [Native Hawaiians] to indulge in lascivious thoughts and actions, that it was deemed by [missionaries] necessary to put a stop to the whole, in order to root out the licentiousness that pervaded the land."

Some of the reforms implemented by missionaries and their allies targeted behaviors directly. In 1829, for instance, Kamehameha III passed an edict against adultery and premarital sex titled "No Ka Moe Kolohe," or, "Concerning Mischievous Sleeping." This directive made it a crime to engage in any sexual union not sanctioned by Christian marriage. In 1830, the Hawaiian government also banned the practice of hula—a traditional, sometimes sensual, storytelling dance—in public places.

Other measures undermined Hawaiian customs indirectly

by targeting its next generation. The missionaries briskly established schools for the education of elite people of Hawai'i modeled on the "Indian Industrial Schools" of the mainland United States. These schools had the stated goal of maximizing the "physical growth, mental growth, and character" of leading Hawaiian youth. The programs taught in these schools included English, Christianity, music, and the arts. In boys' schools in particular, military training and sports like baseball also figured heavily. Very little attention was given to Indigenous sports or lifeways, nor were sports like surfing encouraged.

It is not the case, as is often claimed, that American missionaries to Hawai'i banned surfing outright. Indeed, in 1847, the leader of the first wave of missionaries, Hiram Bingham, remarked somewhat sniffily that "the decline and discontinuance of the use of the surfboard, as civilization advances, may be accounted for by the increase in modesty, industry and religion, without supposing, as some have affected to believe, that missionaries caused oppressive enactments against it." In other words, missionaries did not *outlaw* surfing. It was simply the advance of *civilization* that had naturally led people to give up surfing, mostly for their own good. This, of course, ignored the very active hand that American missionaries had in shaping the contours of "modesty, industry, and religion" to say nothing of "civilization" in Hawai'i, tout court.

The missionaries found that even subtle measures could suppress surfing. As Bingham noted with some satisfaction, the Native "adoption of our costume"—that is, Hawaiians wearing European clothing—"greatly diminishes their practice of swimming and sporting in the surf, for it is less convenient to wear it in the water than the native girdle, and less decorous and safe to lay it entirely off on every occasion they find for a plunge or swim or surf-board race." Bingham went on to point out that the very habit of making European-style clothes, or working for wages in order to buy such clothes, left less time for activities like surfing. This was, for Bingham and his fellow missionaries, an unalloyed good.

Thus without ever explicitly banning surfing, the influence of American "civilization" led to a noticeable diminution in the practice. In 1836 the US naval surgeon W. S. W. Ruschenberger posed the matter as a loaded question. "Can the missionaries be fairly charged with suppressing these games?" he wrote. "I believe they deny having done so. But they write and publicly express against the laws of God, and by a succession of reasoning, which may be readily traced, impress upon the minds of the chiefs and others, the idea that all who practice them, secure to themselves the displeasure of offended heaven." As far as Ruschenberger was concerned, missionaries were clearly to blame for the decline of surfing.

These edicts made it seem as though surfing was a "nearly forgotten sport" by the end of the nineteenth century, as one wealthy missionary descendant wrote. Nevertheless, surfing never really died out—Hawaiians just stopped surfing in places frequented by Europeans and Americans. Outside of these power centers, surfing was still an active pastime, carried on by enthusiastic participants and passed from parents to children. Waikiki, for instance, was far enough away from Honolulu proper that it remained an active surf spot into the twentieth century.

Moreover, some rulers—such as King David Kalākaua, who

reigned from 1874 to 1891—began promoting surfing as an act of political independence, along with lifting the ban on hula and supporting independent Hawaiian language newspapers. Indeed, it was three of Kalākaua's nephews—Jonah Kūhiō Kalanianaʻole, David Kawananakoa, and Edward Keliʻiahonui—who are credited with first bringing surfing to California. In July 1885, on a trip to Santa Cruz, they caused a stir when they crafted three boards out of redwood and took to the waves.

Between the beginning of Kalākaua's rule in 1875 and Osborn's visit in 1920, surfing experienced a transformation in the eyes of American scientists and reformers, from an insalubrious activity that contributed to iniquity and indolence, to a healthful activity that might well be civilization's salvation.

In 1891, the American folklorist H. C. Bolton, passing through the small island of Niʻihau, snapped the first known photographs of people surfing. There he found surfing avidly and very publicly practiced among the hundred or so Native Hawaiians on the island. At his request, "six stalwart men . . . assembled on the beach of a small cove, bearing with them their precious surf-boards." They posed for Bolton's camera, then donned *malos* and headed into the sea. The photographs Bolton took of their surfing exhibition show a few blurry figures kneeling, lying prone, and standing on their boards as they slide down some gently sloping waves toward a rocky shore. The waves were not very big that day, Bolton reported, and the surfers "soon tired of the dull sport," though Bolton found the activity exciting. He even tried it himself, and although he could "boast of little success" in the waves, he did enthuse that it would not be difficult to obtain a working skill in surfing if one was well-versed in ocean swimming.

More intriguingly, while Bolton made a few perfunctory comments on the general decline of surfing in Hawai'i (it was "once so universally popular," he wrote, "and now but little seen"), he was more interested in contrasting the healthful activity of the surfers to the very *unhealthful* qualities of civilization itself. "The pleasure-loving Hawaiian aborigines," he wrote, "formerly practiced a variety of athletic sports and games peculiar in part to their isolated community." However, he went on, "under the *enervating influences of civilization*, the people now neglect the dashing sports of their ancestors, and have adopted in their stead modern games, such as cards, dice, etc. with which they satisfy their love of gambling with less physical exertion." In contrast to more populated islands like O'ahu, Ni'ihau in the 1890s was largely under the singular control of an abstemious Scotsman who, Bolton felt, protected the Indigenous people of the island from the "evils of civilization." The specific evil in this case was alcohol, but more generally, the Scotsman encouraged the practice of traditional sports like surfing as a hedge against the corruption of modern life.

By the end of the nineteenth century, it was clear that the "civilizing" effects of plantation labor, wearing European-style clothing, and speaking English had not improved the general health and prosperity of Indigenous Hawaiian people.

In 1880, King Kalākaua's administration released a report titled *Sanitary Instructions for Hawaiians in the English and Hawaiian Languages*. This report, authored by Kalākaua's adviser, Walter Murray Gibson, came to a damning conclusion. "The Hawaiian child has not done well," Gibson wrote, "at least physically, under the alien tutelage"—meaning, in the main, governance by Americans. While it was true that Americans had brought modernity and markets, their proscriptions against activities like surfing had emasculated and enervated Hawaiian society, Gibson thought. Other than traditional Hawaiian sports, Gibson lamented, "What is there for the cause of Hawaiian manliness? . . . Where is the hero? He is gone; but you will find in his place, the tricky lawyer, the lying kahuna, the hypocritical preacher, and the civilized loafer." This verdict, Gibson explained, was not meant to insult the Hawaiian people. Rather, it was rendered out of necessity. He urged the Hawaiian people to get back to their roots. "It is not necessary, or expected," he wrote, addressing his Hawaiian readers directly, "that you should train to be warriors of the olden time. But let the youth of the nation keep up the bold surf riding . . . and other athletic sports; and thereby an increased vigor of health will be promoted . . . and win at least a world's praise for Hawaiian manliness."

This was striking testimony from a Hawaiian government official placed in charge of public health. In both Gibson's and Bolton's accounts, surfing no longer appears as a cause of disease. Instead, it is civilization itself that promotes ill health, and even unmanliness, and surfing that is the cure.

What happened to redeem surfing as a healthful activity in the eyes of science-minded officials? Many things, but scientifically speaking, three major developments in medicine and science in the middle of the nineteenth century radically restructured the ways that doctors, scientists, and everyday people thought about health and disease.

First, there was the development of the "germ theory" of disease. In the 1860s, scientists like Louis Pasteur in France and

Robert Koch in Germany posited the novel idea that sicknesses in humans and animals were not caused by climatological, environmental, or moral failings, but were the results of infections by microscopic organisms. Since the 1500s, observers peering through well-crafted lenses had known that the tiniest drop of water—or semen, or blood, or milk, or beer, or wine—might be home to thousands of wriggling "animalcules." However, only the very uneducated and very superstitious actually thought that these organisms reproduced and caused disease in other creatures. Indeed, the prevailing scholarly wisdom held that microorganisms "spontaneously generated" (emerged without any parent organism) from the chemical conditions created by decay or fermentation. Pasteur and Koch, however, proved that these organisms were species of living things, just like macroscopic creatures. Some of these microorganisms caused bread to rise; others converted grape juice into wine. Still others caused disease.

Second, a new sort of scientist emerged in Europe following the French Revolution: the physiologist. The physiologist did not merely investigate living things, but "life itself." This meant not simply understanding organisms as machines designed to metabolize and reproduce, as philosophers like René Descartes had proposed. Rather, it meant thinking about "life forms"—a word that, as anthropologists Sophia Roosth and Stefan Helmreich point out—emerged in Germany in the 1820s and 1830s to describe not just a "living thing" but the ways in which the shape of an organism might be "determined by inner life forces and grounded in life itself." "Life" could be studied in terms of electrochemical congeries of cells, but it was more than just the sum of these parts. Life was an abstract, unifying force that gave living things meaning. As German scientist and political reformer Rudolf Virchow put it in 1848, the body—especially the human body—was best understood as a "republic of cells." This was a radical notion, because it implied that the body was akin to an industrial nation, each portion doing its part to contribute to the well-being of the whole organism. When all these systems functioned together, each responding to the others and to the outside world, the organism was in balance: a state known as homeostasis. This balance could be interrupted by disease caused by germs, which might be envisioned as invaders. It might also be overturned by rogue forces within the body itself—a hidden fifth column of stressors, anxieties, cellular malfunctions—which acted as saboteurs, disrupting the harmonious state of the body. Crucially, both the cells that made the body function and germs that "invaded" the body had to play by the same electrochemical rules. All living things, in this sense, were connected by similar, shared, biological processes.

Third, Charles Darwin's theory of evolution—published in 1859 in *On the Origin of Species*—drew these elements together into a powerful way of rethinking not only health and disease, but the relationship of humans to the natural world, to history, and to other humans. Darwin's theory held that the diversity of all life on Earth was simply a matter of variations on a basic theme (life), brought on by changes in environment. This basic theme involved the same electrochemical processes of interest to the physiologists, and had—at some point in the distant past—begun with microorganisms. From a singular, perhaps accidental, form of microscopic life came all other forms of life. Some of those subsequent forms of life had characteristics that gave them an edge that allowed them to thrive in their particular environment. These life forms propagated, changing over time to become even stronger, and eventually became species. Others failed to adapt, and died off. Sometimes, changes in the environment, or adaptations in other species, caused established forms of life to die and others to take their place.

One of the important implications of this was that all life forms were connected, through deep time, by the common thread of simply being alive. Darwin's theory—and the elaborations of his theory by his various successors—wove human history, natural history, physiology, germ theory, and theories of human society into a singular fabric, with powerful implications for understanding ideas of morality, goodness, health, and governance.

These theories were neither easily nor immediately adopted into everyday practices. When they were, however, they brought on a wholesale reconsideration of what sickness and health meant. It was no longer possible to blame health and disease on indolence, immorality, climate, or bad airs. Instead, it became the job of the state—or of people in positions of authority—to make at least rudimentary interventions to ensure the health of its people. "Public health," in the modern sense of the term, was born.

This period, starting in the late nineteenth century, in which governments and businesses were seen as newly accountable for the health of their citizens and workers, gave rise to a group of vocal social reformers in the United States. Journalist Upton Sinclair railed against the squalor and danger of the meatpacking industry. Novelist Sinclair Lewis wrote about the obstacles placed in the path of good public health by capitalism. Others pointed toward the dangers wrought on the bodies and nerves of urban dwellers by streetcar accidents, loud noises, and the spiritually enervating aspects of office work. Even underregulated medications could do more harm than good, necessitating the passage of the Pure Food and Drug Act in 1906, a predecessor to the contemporary FDA.

It became increasingly clear that the emerging ways of living associated with the modern, industrial world brought new forms of ill health. It was true that capitalism increased production, and efficiency, and wealth, at least for a select few. But at what cost? The experience of civilization in places as disparate as the beaches of Hawai'i and the slums of the great European and American cities began to tarnish somewhat the idea that civilization was an unalloyed good, a panacea that would bring all people into light and prosperity.

But only somewhat. For what civilization—industry combined with modern science—had broken, civilization could also fix, through the new, scientific tools at its disposal.

• • •

Born in 1857, Henry Fairfield Osborn—"Fairfie" to his family—grew up in the highest stratum of Gilded-Age Manhattan society. He was the second of four children, born to William Henry Osborn, a railroad tycoon, and Virginia Osborn, the daughter of a railroad tycoon. His uncle, J. P. Morgan, was a financial tycoon.

During colder months, the Osborn family inhabited a looming, Victorian Gothic mansion on Park Avenue in Manhattan, its dark, orange brick facade punctuated by white stone boldly framing the windows and a high mansard roof. It had been designed by Richard Morris Hunt, the most famous architect in America, who would go on to design Cornelius Vanderbilt's Biltmore estate, the Metropolitan Museum of Art, and the pedestal of the Statue of Liberty. In warm weather, the family migrated upstate to their sprawling estate, Wing-and-Wing, in Garrison, an enclave overlooking the Hudson River near West Point.

As a young American plutocrat, Osborn enjoyed a life of profound material ease and deep, spiritual exertion.

At Wing-and-Wing he learned to swim and fish, and he and his brother, William, planted an experimental peanut garden in the yard. One of his playmates in the country was Theodore "Teddy" Roosevelt, whose family had a neighboring estate. The future president of the United States and advocate of vigorous living was then a sickly and timid child. Fairfie, too, was shy—a delicate, almost foppish boy—though he was physically strong. In Manhattan he went to the elite Columbia Grammar School and the Lyons Collegiate Academy before entering Princeton, where he was a middling student. His classmates called him "Polly" due to his fine features and princely manner.

From his father, Osborn learned to conceal his shyness and insecurity behind a stony, businesslike exterior.

From his mother, he learned that the key to both earthly prosperity and spiritual salvation was struggle. A devout Calvinist, Virginia Osborn insisted that to live a life of privilege devoid of effort would make a person no better than a "poor, weak, delicate" plant. Realizing the full purpose of life meant exerting oneself—exceeding one's mere birthright and thereby developing into a more elevated sort of human being. For one already born into the material and social advantages of the

Osborn family, this sort of exertion would mean not simply achieving greater wealth but striving to better the condition of humanity.

Osborn had initially contemplated entering business like his father, and perhaps politics or philanthropy thereafter. In 1876, however, during his junior year at Princeton, he fell under the twin spells of Arnold Guyot and James McCosh. Guyot was a geology professor and naturalist who taught that the earth and everything on it changed gradually, according to the plan of a divine intelligence. Guyot was sufficiently devout that students called his program "Christocentric," but he was also dedicated to science and insisted that students should look to nature rather than the Bible to contemplate God's plan. McCosh was a noted moral philosopher and Princeton's president. He had caused a stir by championing Darwinian evolution at a time when the theory was under fire in American schools for its apparent disavowal of God. Against this criticism, McCosh asked: Was it not possible that a divine hand guided the evolution of species—even Man? McCosh thought the answer was "yes" and saw the ascendancy of white humanity as a sign of the divine hand behind evolution.

This sense of the deep history and divine purpose behind the study of living things gripped Osborn. In 1878, he and a friend, William Berryman Scott, spearheaded an expedition to Wyoming, Colorado, and Utah, where they and three other recent Princeton graduates dressed as cowboys and collected fossils. He published his first scientific paper, "On the Lower Jaw of Loxolophodon" (an extinct, hippo-like mammal), based on their finds. Osborn's newfound passion for the primordial world led him to study anatomy and physiology at Bellevue

Hospital in New York before decamping to England to work on embryology and comparative anatomy.

In England, Osborn flirted with girls, hobnobbed with Oscar Wilde, and studied with scientific luminaries like Thomas Henry Huxley, who was known as "Darwin's Bulldog" for his tenacious support of evolutionary theory. At one point, an aged Darwin visited one of Huxley's lectures, and Osborn could only stare, starstruck, at the elderly scientific luminary who had transformed the life sciences.

But of all the distinguished thinkers Osborn met in England, none exercised a greater, or more lasting, influence than Francis Galton. A cousin of Darwin, Galton was a respected statistician, writer on heredity, and the founder of eugenics. His mammoth tome, *Inquiries into Human Faculty and Its Development* (1883), introduced the term "eugenics" to general readers as "the science of improving stock." He later clarified that by "stock" he meant "the inborn qualities of a race," and thus eugenics was "the science which deals with all influences that improve the inborn qualities of a race; also with those that develop them to the utmost advantage." *Inquiries into Human Faculty and Its Development* took readers through the basics of eugenics—what "heritable qualities" were, the statistical techniques for studying them, the fine balance between mental and physical energies that inhered in all humans.

Galton was obsessed with the idea that statistical methods could be coupled with natural sciences to explain human social characteristics in a scientifically rigorous way. His scientific papers—such as "The Weights of British Noblemen During the Last Three Generations," "On Head Growth in Students at the University of Cambridge," and "The Measure of Fidget"—

show his preoccupation with applying exact measurement to human qualities. He also undertook side projects such as a "beauty map" of the United Kingdom and a study of the most scientific way to cut a cake so that it remains fresh. (London had the most beautiful women, according to Galton—and to scientifically cut a cake, it was best to first make two long, parallel cuts down the middle of the cake and take the initial pieces from this portion. That way, you can push the two remaining halves together to preserve their freshness. For subsequent slices, rotate the cake by ninety degrees, and repeat as needed.)

But the bigger question that he sought to answer was: How do traits accrue to children? Which parts are heritable and which are not?

It had been clear for centuries to even the most casual observer that children tend to take after their parents in both physical traits and psychological demeanor. It was equally clear, however, that children are not exact copies of their parents and often vary in unpredictable ways. This led to two related conundrums for European philosophers of the seventeenth and eighteenth centuries. First, what accounted for the similarity between parents and children? Indeed, what caused humans to give birth to humans, and not, say, horses? Second, if humans generally gave birth to similar-looking humans, what accounted for variations—children who looked more like their grandparents than their parents, red-headed children, to say nothing of those more extreme variations known at the time as "wonders" or "monsters"?

To answer these questions, early modern doctors turned to ideas of "impressions" and "vital spirits" that they distilled from the writings of Aristotle. As the physician Pierre-Sylvain Régis put it in 1654, "I am of the opinion that . . . the image of the thing seen is communicated by the power of the animal spirits present in the brain, through the mediation of the arterial blood, further on to the uterus, and at last through the umbilical vein to the fetus itself. And this happens in a manner in no way dissimilar to that whereby images of visible things are depicted upon the retina of the eye. The tender fetus, moreover, on account of its softness easily takes upon itself the image strongly impressed upon it from the imagination of the mother."

In other words, when two people were so enamored of each other that they were moved to reproduce, they spent a great deal of time looking at one another, admiring one another, gazing into each other's eyes. The strongly felt images that the future mother experienced when obsessively mooning over her child's father would be carried from her eyes to her womb by "animal spirits"—a sort of fluid contained within blood that allowed all animals to sense things. (Plants and lower animals like oysters or sea anemones had "vital spirits"—which was why they were alive—but they did not have "animal spirits," and thus were not able to see, smell, hear, etc.) These images of the father-to-be would "impress" themselves on the fetus developing in the mother's womb—imprinting aspects of the father's features (and perhaps personality) on the developing child.

Various other factors— maternal diet, temperature, and emotional state among them—might also shape the development of the child. Indeed, strong emotional states like obsessions or terrors might deliver equally strong impressions to the womb. In a scandalous case from the 1720s, a London woman—Mary

Toft—claimed to have given birth to baby rabbits after she was startled by a rabbit when she was pregnant. A number of the most prominent physicians of the day examined her and declared her claims to be legitimate, especially as she continued to expel rabbit parts and the occasional whole rabbit. It was only later—after her husband was caught buying baby rabbits from a local butcher—that she was exposed as a fraud. The larger point, of course, is not that Mary Toft was a fraud (if an imaginative one) but that the leading scientific minds of the classical age found the doctrine of impressions plausible enough to explain the most remarkable of circumstances.

By the 1800s, accompanied by the development of fields such as histology (the study of tissues) and physiology (the study of the chemical processes of the body), physicians and scientists began rethinking the ways that living things inherited traits. Clearly, the doctrine of "animal spirits" did not quite hold water, since nobody could identify what an "animal spirit" was. At the same time, it wasn't clear what, precisely, should replace them, or really how heritability worked.

In 1809, French naturalist Jean-Baptiste Lamarck proposed that organisms passed traits acquired in the course of their lives to their offspring. The classic example was that of an early ancestor of a giraffe stretching its neck to feed on leaves in tall trees, and then passing the trait of a slightly stretched neck on to its offspring, who would then stretch their necks, and so on until a modern giraffe emerged. In 1859, Charles Darwin disputed this account with his own theory of evolution by "natural selection": organisms with traits that were suited to the particular environment in which they lived would survive—or be "selected"—to pass those traits on to their offspring.

Those that were less well-suited would perish, and their traits would be lost. Both theories attempted to explain how traits were inherited and how they changed, albeit over a long period of time and at the level of the species as well as the individual. And both theories lacked an explanatory mechanism, which allowed them to compete with one another for more than half a century.

In 1865, an obscure Moravian monk name Gregor Mendel proposed that heritable traits came in discrete bundles that combined according to definite rules. Working with pea plants, he saw that certain traits would appear in predictable patterns in hybrid plants. For example, crossing a pea plant from a strain that always had purple flowers with a pea plant from a strain that always had white flowers would always yield offspring with purple flowers. However, when Mendel crossed the offspring of this hybridization with another plant with white flowers, three fourths of the resulting hybrids would have purple flowers, but a minority—one-fourth—would have white flowers. This suggested to Mendel that traits—which he called "factors"—followed regular, deterministic patterns. Although Mendel himself did not express it this way, such traits could be mapped in a square grid—a so-called Punnett square.

Mendel's paper was largely unknown for almost forty years. In the intervening years, another scientist, August Weismann, theorized that an element he called "germ plasm" was the ingredient that carried "heritability factors." This germ plasm, Weismann said, was found in cells, but he didn't say precisely in which part of the cell. By 1900, Mendel's paper had been rediscovered, providing important conceptual if not material evidence of how germ plasm might work. In 1905, Nettie Stevens and E. B. Wilson, working at Columbia University, proposed that peculiar structures in the nucleus of every cell—chromosomes—are the basis of sex. In 1909, Danish scientist William Johannsen coined the term "gene" to describe the fundamental, biochemical unit of heritability. And in 1911 Stevens and Wilson's teacher, Thomas Hunt Morgan, proposed that chromosomes carried genes.

Although scientists still couldn't explain the mechanism by which genes worked—a development known as the "modern synthesis," which would take place in the 1930s—these discoveries and theories put the new science of eugenics on firmer ground and fueled Galton's enthusiasm.

While Galton was writing *Inquiries into Human Faculty*, he and Osborn collaborated on a survey of memory and mental imagery titled "Visualizing and Other Allied Faculties." The survey dealt with "the degree in which different persons possess the power of seeing images in their mind's eye, and of reviving past sensations"—in other words, the power of imagination. This did not immediately bear on questions of heredity, but would, as Galton wrote, "throw light upon more than one psychological problem"—not least of all, how different "types" understood mental constructs such as numbers, images, colors, and so forth. Studies of mental visualization were central to the project of eugenics because, as Galton wrote, "energy is the most important quality" in "human improvement," and visualization was one way to discern how much energy people used on cognitive activities versus physical activities. Osborn distributed the survey to Princeton and Vassar undergraduates and discovered that, in general, women were better at visualization than men. In the text, Galton thanked Osborn warmly for his collaboration.

Upon his return to America, Osborn's rise to prominence

was brisk. Bolstered by his prestigious European contacts and armed with his father's patronage, he became the first professor of paleontology at Princeton in 1881 (his father endowed the chair). In 1891, Osborn moved simultaneously to the Zoology Department at Columbia University where he became the university's first professor of biology, and to the American Museum, where he became the museum's first curator of vertebrate paleontology. It was from this post that he pioneered the mounting of dinosaur skeletons—bringing dead bones back to life—and commissioned the painter Charles Knight to make extravagant murals of extinct animals.

By any measure, these efforts were a success. A large photograph of Osborn's first fossil mount—a brontosaurus—graced the front page of the *New York Tribune* when the exhibit opened in 1905. The accompanying article praised the already "magnificent" museum for entering into a "new phase of usefulness" and lauded Osborn and his exhibition team for their "rare combination of mechanical skill, anatomical knowledge and special familiarity with Ancient form [*sic*] of life." Osborn himself thought his efforts were "epoch making."

In 1894, in the midst of Osborn's ascent to the heights of American biology, his father died. The railroad executive had, since the 1870s, suffered from ailments related to what one doctor called a "highly strung nervous organization." In the medical parlance of the era, this meant that his nerve cells were prone to overexcitement because he worked too hard. State-of-the-art nineteenth-century science regarded the nervous system as a vibrating electrical system. When it vibrated harmoniously, the result was a productive, happy human. When it vibrated unharmoniously, pathology occurred.

Modern life was an unending source of pathological vibrations. From the flickering of electrical lights to the shriek of locomotives and clanging of trolley cars, the senses of modern humans were under attack. (Osborn's home in Manhattan was mere blocks from the building that would become Grand Central Station, which was then a noisy and chaotic open-air train depot.) Then there was the pace of the modern workday, which kept a busy executive tied to ticker tapes, telegrams, and telegraphs day in and day out. As the neurologist George Miller Beard wrote in his book *American Nervousness*, "Many of the appliances and accompaniments of civilization . . . are the causes of noises that are unrhythmical unmelodious and therefore annoying if not injurious. Manufactures, locomotion, travel, housekeeping even, are noise-producing factors, and when all these elements are concentrated, as in great cities, they maintain . . . an unintermittent vibration in the air that . . . may be unbearable and harmful." The trappings of civilization conspired, it seemed, to fray the nervous system. Moreover, it was the captains of industry—the very white men at the forefront of civilization—who were believed to be the people most overwrought by the constant demands of civilization. It was a condition sometimes known as neurasthenia, meaning "nervous exhaustion," or, more colloquially, "Americanitis."

Americanitis depleted the high-powered executive of his body's vital energies, without which he could not sustain himself. The theory was, in essence, that the human body had only a finite amount of mental and physical energy. This "vital" energy varied in absolute quantity from person to person, but it could only be used for a discrete amount of activity at any one time. White men were especially prone to nervous disorders because—

the theory went—they used so much of their vital energies in the activities that made civilization function: planning, invention, calculation, and engineering. In contrast, the "uncivilized" people of the world had much more vital energy to spare for their physical health because they didn't use their energies on such anxiety-making cognitive tasks, instead leading lives of purely sensual pleasure. Without such physical pursuits, white men's nerves tended to be jangled, their health precarious.

The death of Osborn's father did not so much shatter Osborn as it compressed him—squeezing his thinking into a diamond-like conviction, as one of his colleagues later put it, in "'creative evolution' in a somewhat mystical sense" and a "strong disbelief in 'chance' as a factor in personal history." "Creative evolution" in this instance meant the idea—articulated by the French philosopher Henri Bergson—that evolution was not a matter of randomness, as Darwin had supposed. Rather, evolution was a result of a mysterious "élan vital," or vital force, that shaped life itself, from the smallest microbe to the largest whale. Élan vital was related to consciousness, and, indeed, could be interpreted as a variety of will or will power. Although Bergson himself did not personally promote a sense of hierarchy among creatures, some of his acolytes nonetheless concluded that humans possessed the greatest élan vital of all creatures—they simply had not yet discovered an efficient way to direct it.

Osborn's thinking combined natural history and human history into a potent explanation for change in species and in individuals. Vital force was responsive to history—not only the "life force" of the individual at any one time, but the life force of history at a given moment. In a lecture given at the Marine Biological Laboratory in Woods Hole, Massachusetts,

Osborn told assembled luminaries that "if the environment be changed to an ancient one, then ontogenic variations tend to regression or reversion . . . or practically to repetition of an ancient type." In other words, all beings had within them the power to access previous bodily states from previous centuries, even prior millennia.

The implication of this for paleontology was that transformations in species were already extant in their genetic material, rather than brought on through random chance. Through repetition of particular behaviors, creatures would unlock this potential for change. By implication, these changes might be good for creatures—that is, they might allow a species to adapt to new circumstances. But they also might be maladaptive, leading to a species' eventual degradation. Humans, Osborn felt, were an excellent example of this. The descendants of modern Caucasians had originated in the arid steppes of Eurasia, Osborn believed, where harsh, strenuous living had forced them to behave in ways that allowed them to reach an ideal racial type. Fanning out into Africa, with lush, plentiful jungles (so Osborn thought), human behaviors had changed—they degraded—and along with these behaviors, so too did body types change. Different human populations had different "race memories" and different sorts of élan vital.

The implication of this idea for the lives of Osborn's contemporaries in America, however, was much more immediate. Modern life would endow individuals with a "modern" constitution—one that was, perhaps, more highly strung than the constitution of humans in "ancient" environments. Osborn's father was a perfect example. He was a powerful man, a titan of industry, but also a workaholic neurasthenic—and therefore prone to breakdowns and even premature death. If, however, the individual was able to engage in "strenuous" activities more commensurate with an "ancient" environment, the individual could acquire such "ancient" characteristics as fortitude and resilience. Osborn had "the increasing conviction that our intellectual, moral, and spiritual reactions are extremely ancient and that they have been built up not in hundreds but in thousands—perhaps hundreds of thousands—of years." Indeed, Osborn believed in what he called a "racial soul"—a sort of vibratory living memory in which the characteristics of a "race" were held by the individual.

This idea was not only a fixation for Osborn. Versions of the notion of a racial soul conditioned by past actions was accepted by a vast swath of (white) Americans as a crucial ingredient of American character.

These views were neatly summarized by the historian Frederick Jackson Turner in his epoch-making paper, "The Significance of the Frontier in American History." First debuted as part of the "Historical Congress" portion of the 1893 World's Columbian Exposition in Chicago, the "frontier thesis," as Turner's theory came to be known, held that American greatness had been forged not through the institutions set down by the "founding fathers," but in the very physical bodies of Europeans as they moved west across the North American continent. "American development has exhibited not merely advance along a single line," Turner told a small, hot, and tired audience on July 12. Rather, American greatness could be imagined as a "return to primitive conditions on a continually advancing frontier line."

For Turner, this "return to primitive conditions" had shaped the vital force of the American people. Those Europeans who spread out across North America had needed to be clever, resourceful, and physically strong in order to conquer nature, to bend the savage wildness of the land to their wills and make it productive. Moreover, as they annihilated or relocated Indigenous peoples, Euro-Americans had assimilated the best of the supposedly "primitive" characteristics of these people. As Turner said, "this perennial rebirth, this fluidity of American life, this expansion westward with its new opportunities, its continuous touch with the simplicity of primitive society, furnish the forces dominating American character." Euro-Americans had assembled the best part of "the primitive" and "the civilized" into their very bodily makeup.

Although initially greeted with indifference, Turner's thesis quickly found admirers. One newspaper editor called it "the most informative and illuminating contribution to American history that I have read in several years." Theodore Roosevelt—then US Civil Service Commissioner and author of numerous books about hunting and exploration in the American West—thought that Turner's talk was full of some "first class ideas" and praised him for giving a structure to "a good deal of thought that has been floating around rather loosely." With growing numbers of allies, Turner's thesis was republished countless times between its initial debut and the turn of the century—in popular magazines, in anthologies of essays for schoolteachers, in newspaper digests.

Turner's thesis offered both a warning about American decline and a possible solution. It implied that the rugged, willful spirit that had made America great was under attack from within. Modern life was enervating and emasculating the frontiersmen, diluting their "race memory." People of a formerly ascendent "stock" such as Anglo-Saxons risked what Theodore Roosevelt, an avowed white supremacist in ideology if not in name, called "race suicide"—demographic capitulation to the triune evils of enervation, immigration, and race mixing. But the frontier thesis also implied a cure.

In 1899, Roosevelt—by then governor of New York and a hero of the Spanish American War—penned an essay called "The Strenuous Life." In it, he argued that American expansion was the key to maintaining the "frontier spirit" that had made America so great in the first place. Americans had to maintain their "strenuous" conquest of the "uncivilized" peoples of the world in order to benefit those people and the American body politic through the expenditure of their energies on heroic exploits.

The British writer Rudyard Kipling had made the case in verse the very same year when he penned "The White Man's Burden"—a poem exhorting the United States to annex the Philippines and other Spanish holdings it had taken in the Spanish American War. "Take up the White Man's burden," he wrote, "The savage wars of peace—Fill full the mouth of Famine / And bid the sickness cease." In other words, American expansion might necessitate waging "savage wars" against those who resisted colonization, but ultimately American victory would bring peace in the form of public health, better nutrition, and other notional benefits of American civilization. Kipling sent a copy to Roosevelt, who thought it was terrible poetry, but a generally good idea.

For men like Roosevelt, shouldering the "White Man's Burden"—as he suggested in texts such as "The Strenuous Life"—was, in its own way, therapeutic. Not only would Americans help spread health and prosperity across the supposedly benighted corners of the globe, they would, themselves, benefit from the salubrious exertion of the effort. Overseas territorial expansion was a test of American spirt and will at the highest level.

To Osborn, this kind of racial-historical logic made sense. What Turner hadn't said explicitly—but what his thesis clearly implied—was that a certain kind of American élan vital had been activated on the North American frontier. This vital spirit might be in jeopardy, but it was possible to salvage and even enlarge it. Just as the Caucasian race had once forged its greatness in the harsh environments of the Asian steppe, now the white, American race would be able to cultivate the best of its "stock" through judicious overseas expansion—managed, of course, under the auspices of eugenics.

Not all of Osborn's colleagues subscribed to this way of thinking. In 1904, Osborn hired thirty-eight-year-old Thomas Hunt Morgan to join the zoology faculty of Columbia. Morgan was one of a new generation of "experimental" biologists. In contrast to the methods employed by paleontologists and comparative anatomists, experimental biologists looked not at organisms' overall body form (or morphology), but at the ways that cells worked.

They examined cell parts, and—although the word "gene" was not coined until 1909—they invented the idea of "germ plasm" within a cell to explain heredity and, by extension, evolution. To Morgan, men such as Osborn and his like-minded peers were not practicing good science. Theirs was simply guesswork based on uncertain theories. Morgan was critical of the mystical aspects of Osborn's thinking and griped that Osborn had "no way to check up on his speculations."

Osborn, for his part, countered that genetics as practiced by Morgan and the new experimentalists did not really explain evolution. It was perhaps true that they were able to isolate the parts of the cell that carried heritable material—and indeed Morgan won a Nobel Prize in 1933 for his 1909 work demonstrating that chromosomes in the cell nucleus contained genetic material. But this by no means showed *why* creatures evolved in particular directions, nor did it account for the apparent purposefulness of evolutionary trends. For Osborn, evolution could be better explained through the concept of energies that flowed through the bodies of living things and shaped their development. These energies, moreover, could be released and channeled through strenuous living. His basis for believing this was his own idiosyncratic understanding of evolution, inflected by his religious upbringing, and cut with a deep admiration for strenuous living and a fear of showing weakness.

By the time Osborn ascended to the presidency of the AMNH in 1908, the concept of "strenuous living" was not simply a byword for personal development—it was a way of thinking about America's place in the world more broadly.

Hawai'i was, in this sense, the ultimate proving ground for American élan vital.

• • •

The writer Jack London penned among the most well-known accounts of strenuous living—and surfing—in Hawai'i. A socialist with a taste for fine living, a white supremacist with a profound ambivalence toward white civilization, a hardheaded rationalist with an occult belief in primal life forces that suffused the universe, London contained many of the contradictions of science and social reform that likewise characterized eugenics.

In the early twentieth century, he was also one of the most famous writers in America. After a peripatetic adolescence spent riding the rails, prospecting for gold in the Yukon, stealing shellfish as an "oyster pirate," traversing the Pacific as a merchant sailor, and performing hard labor in a string of industrial gigs, London rocketed to national literary fame with *The Call of the Wild* (1903). The book tells the story of Buck, a domestic dog stolen from his loving family in California and sold into work pulling sleds in the Yukon. Through his many trials in the untrammeled wilderness of Alaska, Buck grows increasingly more wild, eventually accessing distant race memories of prehistoric canines, and becoming the leader of a wolf pack.

London's other works similarly describe the savagery of nature, the cruel primitivity beating in the heart of civilization, the importance of blood as a repository for ancestral impulses—all delivered in burly, two-fisted, locomotive prose. In his short story "The Son of the Wolf," a white fur trapper in a fight feels "the primal instinct of life, which in turn gave way to the lust of slaughter. Ten thousand years of culture fell from him, and he was a cave-dweller, doing battle for his female." Another man experiences the "race memory" of "steel-shod, mail-clad" Anglo-Saxons: "red-flickering across the dark forests and sullen seas; he saw it blaze, bloody and red."

In 1907, London, age thirty-one and by then a very wealthy man, set out on an ocean voyage from San Francisco to Hawai'i, and then points south, on a custom-built boat called the *Snark*. He was accompanied on this trip by an eclectic crew consisting of London's wife, Charmian; the couple's butler; Charmian's uncle; a Stanford University track star; and a young man who London welcomed aboard due to the sheer charisma of a letter he had written to the famous author.

The point of the voyage, as London said, was to pit himself—"a bit of vitalized matter, one hundred and sixty-five pounds of meat and blood, nerve, sinew, bones, and brain—all of it soft and tender, susceptible to hurt, fallible and frail"— against "the great natural forces—colossal menaces, Titans of destruction, unsentimental monsters that have less concern for me than I have for the grain of sand I crush under my foot." Should he come out on top in this endeavor, he supposed, "the bit of life that is I . . . will imagine it is godlike." This was strenuous living at its most extreme.

And the voyage was, indeed, strenuous, though not because of London's imagined "cyclones and tornadoes, lightning flashes and cloud bursts, tide-rips and tidal waves, undertows and waterspouts, great whirls and sucks and eddies, earthquakes and volcanoes, surfs that thunder on rock-ribbed coasts and seas that leap aboard the largest crafts that float, crushing humans to pulp or licking them off into the sea and to death."

Instead, it was human error that nearly sank the *Snark*.

London had commissioned the boat to be a state-of-the-art cruiser. It was forty-five feet long and twin masted, outfitted with four waterproof chambers to keep her afloat in the most trying of circumstances, a lifeboat just in case, and a seventy-five horsepower gasoline engine to propel her through the water when the winds did not cooperate. The engine also powered a small ice machine to ensure properly chilled cocktails during the voyage. London, a skilled sailor but an inexperienced navigator, felt certain he could learn enough navigation on the water to hit their marks in Polynesia. Questionable as this plan was, the crew soon had other problems.

The building of the *Snark* had been mismanaged by Charmian's uncle, and despite costing three times the estimate, the boat had been constructed with inferior materials and less care than London had specified. It had also, unbeknownst to its crew, borne the brunt of a nautical fender-bender with two lumber scows one night while anchored in San Francisco, and its hull was hydrodynamically compromised: prone to leaking and ever so slightly bean-shaped. The result was that a few days out from California, London and his crew found the *Snark*'s bilges flooding with seawater, its engine destroyed, their food and water supply contaminated, and the boat itself difficult to control. Adding to this, London had trouble determining their location. Every time London took a reading, the boat's apparent position on the map of the Pacific Ocean jumped unpredictably.

At last, after twenty-seven days at sea, they did make it to Hawai'i, but not before newspapers in San Francisco had declared the *Snark* lost with all hands. The crew was by turns amused and appalled by the news of their untimely deaths, but in many ways, the reports vindicated the strenuous life. They had gambled their lives and proved to the sickly shore-dwellers that modern men could still emerge victorious from a contest with nature.

Once ashore, the Londons and their entourage made vigorous vacationing their business—swimming, fishing, riding horses, strolling the bustling city, snapping photos, and meeting with the elites of Hawai'i new and old. In Waikiki, they went to a party at the house of Prince Jonah Kuhio Kalanianole. Charmian found him to be "handsome enough" but was struck by his wife,

Princess Elizabeth, who she judged "every inch a princess in the very tropical essences of her"—although, Charmian thought, there was a "fleeting, shifting glint of the wild in her great black eyes." Beside Princess Elizabeth sat Queen Lili'uokalani, who Charmian judged to be intriguing and refined, if "implacably savage in [her] cold hatred of everything American." Given that she had been overthrown by some of the very Americans that now partied beside her, this was a sentiment that Charmian had to admit could not be held against her.

On a trip up the side of a volcano, the Londons also met forty-nine-year-old Lorrin Thurston, whom they ranked among the "best of Hawai'i's white citizenship." Scion of an old missionary family, Thurston had been a member of the legislature of the Hawaiian Islands under King Kalākaua. By 1887, however, he had turned on the king and was among the leaders of the plot to undercut Kalākaua with the so-called Bayonet Constitution, which stripped the monarchy of its authority. As one of the authors of the Bayonet Constitution, Thurston was in a position of power among the usurpers and had himself appointed to the influential position of Interior Minister in the new government. He served in this post until 1890, then retired only to reemerge in insular politics in 1893, as head of the group that overthrew Queen Lili'uokalani. This gave him the distinction of having toppled not one but two monarchs in less than a decade. By 1907, he was retired from politics, except in that he was the owner of Hawai'i's premier English language newspaper, the *Pacific Commercial Advertiser*, which he used to promote Hawaiian industry to investors and tourists from the mainland.

The Londons' Hawaiian sojourn was on its way to becoming

an amusing but incidental vacation among the conflicted elites of America's newest colony when, as Charmian and Jack sat drinking cocktails one day, they were accosted by a slender man with an enormous walrus mustache and piercing eyes. "You're Jack London, aren't you?" the man demanded. Without waiting for an answer, he barreled on: "My name is Ford." This was Alexander Hume Ford—thirty-nine-year-old journalist, adventurer, failed fiction writer, and energetic booster for all things Hawaiian.

Jack knew of Ford through the man's travel journalism. Ford had gone from South Carolina, to Chicago, to China, to Russia, and back again, filing stringer reports with national papers. In his rambling around the world, Ford had arrived in Honolulu about six months ahead of the *Snark* and had become enthralled with surfing. He decided to stay, spending equal time cultivating his skill on a surfboard and his friendships with Honolulu's political and industrial elites. The orphaned child of rich plantation owners, he was not shy around the wealthy and well-known.

When London confirmed that he was, indeed, Jack London, Ford leaned in. "Now look here, London," he said, and began to talk at lightning speed about his fragmentary fiction plots, the glories of Hawai'i, his plans for promoting Hawai'i to the world, and—most of all—his love of surfing. After two hours and many more cocktails, Charmian was exhausted, but Jack was enthralled.

The next day, Saturday, June 1, 1907, London was lounging on the beach outside of the Moana Hotel in Waikiki, contemplating the limits of strenuous living, when he first experienced surfing.

"What chance," he thought, gazing at a run of large waves breaking far out to sea on an offshore reef, had a human being against these "white headed combers," these "big smokers," these "bull-mouthed monsters"?

"No chance at all," he concluded—and the thought made him feel "microscopically small" and "fragile" and ego-dead, simperingly content to sit and watch the waves from the safety of the beach.

Then, all at once,

> rising like a sea-god from out of the welter of spume and churning white, on the giddy, toppling, overhanging and downfalling, precarious crest appears the dark head of a man. Swiftly he rises through the rushing white. His black shoulders, his chest, his loins, his limbs—all is abruptly projected on one's vision. Where but the moment before was only the wide desolation and invincible roar, is now a man, erect, full-statured, not struggling frantically in that wild movement, not buried and crushed and buffeted by those mighty monsters, but standing above them all, calm and superb, poised on the giddy summit, his feet buried in the churning foam, the salt smoke rising to his knees, and all the rest of him in the free air and flashing sunlight, and he is flying through the air, flying forward, flying fast as the surge on which he stands. He is a Mercury—a brown Mercury. His heels are winged, and in them is the swiftness of the sea. In truth, from out of the sea he has leaped upon the back of the sea, and he is riding the sea that roars and bellows and cannot shake him from its back. But no frantic outreaching and balancing is his. He is impassive, motionless as a statue carved suddenly by some miracle out of the sea's depth from which he rose.

Other American men of letters had addressed surfing. Mark Twain, visiting Hawai'i in 1866 on an assignment for the *Sacramento Union*, tried his hand at surfing. On his first and only attempt, he got badly bumped along the bottom, came up with "a few barrels of water" in him, and concluded that "none but natives ever master the art of surf-bathing thoroughly."

London was aware of Twain's accounts; the *Snark* even seems to have carried a copy of Twain's adventures. But London came to the opposite conclusion as his predecessor. Anything that a nonwhite man could do, London assured himself, he could do better.

London shed his clothes and prepared to "wrestle with the sea." He took a board from a nearby child and joined a group of Native children in the shallows. He attempted to emulate their gleeful rides on the small waves, but he couldn't, much to the children's amusement. At his lowest ebb, a voice called out to him—it was Ford, who had been watching from the beach.

"Get off that board," Ford commanded. "Chuck it away at once. . . . Here, take my board. It's a man's size."

Ford snatched away the small board that London had been using and gave him his own, "man-sized" seventy-five-pound board. Over the next few hours, Ford taught London how to surf. London was hooked. "What a sport for white men it is!" he exclaimed.

The next morning, Ford took London out to the surf break that had so awed him the previous day. It was likely the spot known today as Paradise break, about half a mile straight out to sea from the Moana Hotel. The waves aren't huge in good weather but the chop over the reefs can be challenging. For

London, surfing the break was not a larky new experience. It was an epic confrontation between nature and humanity—a "battle in which mighty blows were struck, on one side, and in which cunning was used on the other side—a struggle between insensate force and intelligence."

Fortunately for London, intelligence intervened in the form of George Freeth, a half-Hawaiian surfer and part-time lifeguard who made his living giving surf demonstrations and lessons to the growing crowds of curious tourists at Waikiki. Freeth, who frequented Paradise break, was surfing there when London and Ford arrived. As London described it, Freeth was magnificent. He zipped effortlessly through the waves, "standing upright on his board, carelessly poised, a young god bronzed with sunburn."

Freeth gave London some pointers, and perhaps a push or two. Ironically, Freeth's central advice to London was, in many ways, the opposite of the doctrine of strenuous living. "When the undertow catches you and drags you seaward along the bottom," Freeth instructed, "don't struggle against it. If you do you are liable to be drowned, for it is stronger than you. Yield yourself to that undertow. Swim with it, not against it, and you will find the pressure removed. And, swimming with it, fooling it so that it does not hold you, swim upward at the same time. It will be no trouble at all to reach the surface." Where London saw himself as doing battle with the sea, Freeth saw surfing as more of a collaboration between unevenly matched but mutually interested parties.

From his subsequent writings, it is apparent that London did not internalize this lesson about waves and life, insofar as he continued to write about the ocean as an implacable opponent to be conquered by superior human will. He did, however, catch a wave. "I saw it coming," he wrote, "turned my back on it and paddled for dear life."

> Faster and faster my board went, till it seemed my arms would drop off. What was happening behind me I could not tell. One cannot look behind and paddle the windmill stroke. I heard the crest of the wave hissing and churning, and then my board was lifted and flung forward. I scarcely knew what happened the first half-minute. Though I kept my eyes open, I could not see anything, for I was buried in the rushing white of the crest. But I did not mind. I was chiefly conscious of ecstatic bliss at having caught the wave. At the end of the half-minute, however, I began to see things, and to breathe. I saw that three feet of the nose of my board was clear out of water and riding on the air. I shifted my weight forward, and made the nose come down. Then I lay, quite at rest in the midst of the wild movement, and watched the shore and the bathers on the beach grow distinct.

Back on land, London wrote about surfing, strenuous living, and racial blood in precisely the evolutionary terms that would drive eugenicists' enthusiasm about Hawai'i. For his short story "The House of Pride," London somewhat unkindly borrowed Ford's name (though not his character), and Freeth's character (though not his name). The story details the relationship between Percival Ford, the passionless, anemic scion of a plutocratic Hawaiian missionary family, and Joe Garland, a charismatic half-Hawaiian laborer. London sketches Ford as a supercilious prig of "meagre blood"—unimaginative, compassionless, quick to judge others though with little capacity for self-reflection. In contrast, Garland is "full-muscled and generously moulded"—a man of physical strength and good humor. He is hard-drinking, popular with women, and brave, while Ford drinks only lemonade, eschews sex, and exhibits cowardly behavior. By no coincidence, Garland, in the story, is also a surfer.

The moral of the story is clear—the people produced by missionary society are "thin blooded" and unlovable, compared with the "warm blooded," athletic, and healthy surfers of Native descent. The twist ending of the story—where Ford discovers to his horror that Garland is his half brother through his missionary father's secret affair with a Native woman—only cements the point: it is not simply the way that Ford *lives* that makes him less of a man than Garland—Garland's manliness is in his very blood.

This "blood" was, in part, what made Hawai'i special to men like London. It was the physical embodiment of the "race memory" that London felt enabled "civilized" man to transcend the feminizing effects of civilization. It was not *necessary* that one possess this blood in order to maximize strenuous healthfulness. But the magnificence of figures like Freeth pointed toward the ways in which activities like surfing could enable white men like London to tap into the primal unconscious of the primitive past. For London, Freeth showed the benefits of strenuous living—the literal and metaphorical benefits of fusing "primitive" and "civilized" blood through surfing.

For all his advocacy of strenuous living, London's lengthy session in the surf—and, later, his continued travels through the South Pacific—did not contribute to his health. After four hours on the ocean with Ford and Freeth, London returned to his Waikiki hotel catastrophically sunburned and had to spend the next several days in bed. After the *Snark* left Hawai'i, London's health worsened as the party continued south to the Marquesas, and then on to Tahiti and Fiji. He had contracted yaws—a type of nonvenereal syphilis that bored holes in the skin around his ankles—and his skin began to slough off in painful, flaky sheets. He was constantly exhausted, at times could barely walk, and he developed an anal fistula. London's biographer, Earle Labor, has suggested that London's extreme reaction to the sun was a manifestation of lupus. London himself felt that he had been "torn to pieces by the ultra-violet rays just as many experimenters with the X-ray have been torn to pieces." Doctors in Australia said that London's declining physical condition must be "nervous" in nature—a diagnosis that must have galled the believer in vigorous living.

The *Snark's* voyage ended in Australia, when London was unable to continue. Eventually he made his way back to San Francisco, where his health continued to worsen. In 1915, toward the end of his life, London—then thirty-nine years old—returned to Hawai'i with Charmian, in part for its healthy climate. He was no longer able to pursue strenuous activity, but the two admired an upcoming generation of surfers, including Duke Kahanamoku, who Charmian wrote was "unsurpassed" among "Hawaiian Youth." London died shortly thereafter.

• • •

Osborn was one of London's many readers, and London's work inspired him. If he disagreed with London's socialism—and could not have identified with London's hardscrabble early life—he nevertheless saw something similar in Hawai'i. True, traditional Hawaiian society was not the equal to white man's civilization in his eyes. It was, nevertheless, an advanced, even spiritual culture, brought low by exposure to modern civilization. Moreover, like London, Osborn was a sort of evangelist. The two men proselytized for the same fundamental things: the purity of nature, the value of the strenuous life, the mystical memories to be found in ancestral blood, the physical benefits of being in nature, and the spiritual benefits of studying nature. The big difference was that whereas London was an atheist, Osborn saw his purpose in an explicitly religious light.

In 1913, Osborn summed up his beliefs about science, spirituality, and the future of humankind in a short essay titled "The New Order of Sainthood." The piece was framed as an encomium to the famous French bacteriologist, Louis Pasteur,

Outside of Honolulu, 1920s.

whose germ theory of disease had "showed us the way of the physical redemption of man." Pasteur, Osborn wrote, was well-known as both a great scientist and a great humanitarian. His theory that microbes were the source of much sickness had engendered a public health revolution: vaccines for previously fatal illnesses, tests to discover sources of contamination in food and water, better public sanitation, and laboratories for the discovery of new pathogens and their cures. But beyond lauding Pasteur and men like him as scientists and humanitarians, continued Osborn, it would be better to think of them as religious figures—modern-day saints who, through science, led humankind toward salvation. This was the "new order of sainthood"—an honor reserved for those who, using science, look for "the causes of a very large part of human suffering" in nature, and in nature find "the means of controlling or averting suffering."

The teachings of men like Pasteur, continued Osborn, could be thought of as the "Gospel of the Body"—a good book describing how to make humankind not just physically healthier or more efficient, but morally healthier as well. "In the study of Nature," Osborn wrote, "man finds intellectual delight; in the laws of Nature man finds his physical well-being; man through nature becomes the redeemer of physical man." The Gospel of the Body showed the way to "the final conquest of Nature, out of which has come man's redemption of man."

Osborn nominated Pasteur as the first inductee to his "new order of sainthood," and he included men like Isaac Newton and Charles Darwin among its ranks. It is not difficult to see, however, that Osborn was writing about himself as well. Rather than microbes, his own chapter of the "Gospel of the Body" would tell the story of how eugenicists like himself harnessed the laws of evolution and heredity to "redeem" humankind from its own most irresponsible impulses. Osborn thought that Hawai'i—with its multiracial population and dwindling but still extant "stock" of "pure" Hawaiian people—was an ideal place to write this chapter.

On February 4, 1920, Osborn finalized his plans for a voyage of "pacific ethnology and anthropology" and prepared to leave New York for Hawai'i. A few weeks later, on March 2, he disembarked the steamer *Matsonia* in Honolulu Harbor, to the welcoming tunes of a brass band and a group of singers. He was left with a "wonderful impression of good government and welfare."

Somewhere in the middle of the Pacific, on February 28, 1920, Osborn had jotted a quick paraphrase of the philosopher John Locke in his journal: "any man who would make the most of his time must spend a large part of it in vacation." Of course, Osborn's idea of vacation involved less rest and relaxation than scientific study.

As he traveled through Hawai'i, Osborn compulsively recorded the race and "type" of the people he met, as far as his discerning eye could tell. John Tamatoa Baker—a former governor of the Big Island—was a "grand old chieftain type." The captain of a ferry to Kaua'i was a "Dublin Irish prot[estant]" type. A school teacher was "Irish . . . blue eyes—brogue—energetic." A driver was a "sturdy scot." The cook at his hotel was a Japanese type (and "excellent"). He noted the various "mixed types" that he found on the island of Hawai'i. The "Hawaiian and Chinese blend," he wrote, "is an excellent one; in the schools, intelligent, upright, persistent." A horse, meanwhile, was a "superb type" with a "highly intelligent head."

He toured the Islands, shaking hands with Hawaiʻi's (mostly white) elites. He borrowed a car from Walter Dillingham, a genial construction magnate known as the "Baron of Hawaiian Industry," visited the plantation of C. Montague Cooke, a descendant of missionaries and a prominent mollusk scientist, and discussed the "early history of the Islands" with William Castle, heir to one of the "Big Five" sugar-producing fortunes.

He also thrilled at what he learned of ancient Hawaiian culture, including surfing.

There were half a dozen different varieties of surfing. *Heʻe nalu* referred to riding ocean waves on a wooden board in either a standing, kneeling, or prone position. *Kaha nalu* meant surf-riding without a board, or bodysurfing. *Pākākā* involved riding waves in an outrigger canoe. *Heʻe puʻe wai* meant surfing on a river or tidal bore. It was even possible to "surf" on wet sand and on rock. *Heʻe one*, or "sand sliding," was a sort of reverse bodysurfing practiced on a steep beach. Watching the waves carefully, the practitioner would pick the right moment, then race toward the water and dive headlong onto the thin layer of water and sand left by a receding wave, skimming on his bare chest down the beach and into the ocean. *Heʻe hōlua* was like surfing on gravel. The athlete stood on a thin, wooden sled called a *papa hōlua* and rode down a steep track carved into the side of a mountain. At times these activities could be combined, as when a *hōlua* rider on a mountainside and a wave-rider on a surfboard raced to a common point on a beach.

Practitioners of *heʻe nalu* made different board shapes and contours for different waves, many of which Osborn saw in the collections of Honolulu's Bishop Museum, the American Museum's Hawaiian counterpart. The most commonly used types of boards were called *alaia*. These boards were tall, flat, and thin, rounded at the front, squared in the back, and tapered slightly along their length, so that when stood on end, the silhouette somewhat resembled a long fish standing on its tail. These boards were typically made of hau or koa woods, ranged from six to nine feet in length, and handled well in many types of surf. Smaller *paipoʻo*—thin and shaped a bit like guitar picks—were used by children, or in very light surf close to shore. *Kikoʻo* were like very large *alaia*—ten to fifteen feet in length and featuring slightly convex bottoms and long, slender, flat decks, they handled well in rough waves, where the length of the board and the curved bottom helped to stabilize and slow what might otherwise be a wild ride.

It was the giant *olos*, though, that represented the ostentatious apex of ancient board making. These boards were made of fifteen to twenty feet of koa or willi-willi woods. Rounded at the ends and convex on both sides, they curved gently from their middles to their edges, and measured up to eight inches thick along their bulging midline. Boards like these might weigh up to two hundred pounds. *Olos* were used exclusively by royalty, and, like the *olos* themselves, surf breaks with the right conditions for *olo* riding tended to be off-limits to commoners. Transgression of these strictures was punishable by death. Osborn came away from this experience with a newfound appreciation of Hawaiian culture, and a sense of loss at what he saw as its decline.

On March 5, 1920, Osborn first crossed paths with Duke Kahanamoku. The circumstances of their meeting are unknown, but the encounter seems to have stoked Osborn's growing interest in the "race question" in Hawaiʻi, and in the physicality of Hawaiian people in particular. Duke was six feet tall and 150 pounds, with enormous hands and feet, dark eyes, and a blinding smile. By that point, he was world famous as a champion swimmer, but on the Islands he was also known as a masterful surfer. Along with some friends, he had founded a surf club called Hui Nalu, an antidote to the stuffier—and racist—Outrigger Canoe Club that had been founded in 1908 by Alexander Hume Ford.

Duke had been a protégé of London's surfing teacher, George Freeth, and, like Freeth, made a living teaching swimming and surfing to the well-heeled tourists who came to Waikiki. Osborn was one of those tourists. Kahanamoku took him into the water and showed him how to ride a board—his own, huge *olo* with "DUKE" inscribed in white letters across the top. By all accounts, Osborn was not much of a surfer. Even in light surf, a wooden board is unwieldy, and Duke's weighed close to 150 pounds. Osborn flopped around in the surf, trying to get the dynamics of the waves. It's not clear whether he managed to stay up for a wave, although he didn't record being laughed at by children like London. The experience, anyway, haunted him as being among the many arts and customs of the Hawaiian people that were endangered by modernity.

Osborn left Hawai'i on March 30, decked in leis and full of ideas for a research expedition to be conducted jointly by the AMNH and the Bishop Museum in Honolulu. The expedition would require a team of anthropologists and craftspeople and would culminate in an exhibit of Hawaiian "types" at the Second International Eugenics Congress in 1921.

Duke Kahanamoku was, in Osborn's opinion, a "model youth." He would be a magnificent centerpiece of the exhibit.

Duke Kahanamoku at a pre-Olympic swim meet in Manhattan Beach, California, July 1920.

3

THE "MODEL YOUTH"

It took a lot to make Duke Kahanamoku angry. In athletics, he accepted victory gracefully and defeat magnanimously. The occasional taunts and trash talking that inevitably accompanied work as an international athlete didn't rattle him, and sports page commentary—positive or negative—seemed to slide off him. "Mahape a ale wala'u," he would say. "Don't talk—keep it in the heart."

Nevertheless, in January 1920, Kahanamoku sued the *Pacific Commercial Advertiser* for libel. Several months earlier, in October 1919, Duke had unexpectedly dropped out of the celebrated Fall Swim Meet in Honolulu, citing exhaustion. He was still recovering from a bout of the 1918 influenza that had swept the world in a lethal pandemic. The disease had nearly killed him. National qualifiers in California for the 1920 Olympics were just around the corner, and Duke wanted to compete—but to do that, he had to build back the muscle he had lost during months of convalescence. He threw himself into a punishing routine of swimming, rowing, surfing, and some beach volleyball and water polo, but the exercise often left him sore. Concerned for his health, Duke canceled his appearance at the swim meet, much to the ire of the organizers.

On October 29, 1919, the *Advertiser* blasted Kahanamoku with a scathing, fifty-point headline: "DUKE P. KAHANAMOKU QUITS COLD." With bilious indignation, the editorial accused Kahanamoku of having "feet of clay," of "sulking," and implied that he was not only a poor sport for dropping out, but an ingrate besides. "Kahanamoku," read the editorial, who "has received local, and even world wide [*sic*] adulation, pages of publicity and many honors, whose picture is featured on the Hawai'i Tourist Bureau booklets and letterheads, had pleaded muscles hardened from rowing that prevents him being at top standard." The editorialist called this a "silly excuse" and went on to label Kahanamoku a "slacker and a loafer" who lacked "backbone." Worse still, the editorial insinuated that Duke brought disgrace on the "Hawaiian race" and for that reason did not deserve to be called a "true Hawaiian."

The byline on the piece was that of Leonard Withington, the *Advertiser*'s sports page editor, but the barrage had all of the hallmarks of Lorrin Thurston—the two-time usurper of the Hawaiian government and the paper's owner.

In portraits of Thurston as a young man, he resembles a goose on the verge of attack—head cocked quizzically atop a slender neck, sideburns well-groomed like ornamental plumage, a glimmer of belligerence flickering in otherwise cold, shining eyes. It's easy to envision him leading a group of armed plantation elites in an overthrow of the Hawaiian throne. Now at age sixty-two and the owner of a newspaper rather than a private militia, he channeled his pugnacity into a habit of pillorying his perceived opponents in print.

Duke was his newest target. Thurston had previously written that Duke was "a credit to his race, to his native islands, and to those who started him upon the road to sobriety, without which his name would not today be blazoned upon the athletic honor roll." In other words, Duke honored Hawaiʻi through his athletic skill, but only because Hawaiʻi—meaning men like Thurston—had lifted him up out of "insobriety." Duke, as a rule, had never been a drinker and had always been highly disciplined, but that hardly mattered. Even if he never touched a drop of alcohol, he couldn't be "sober"—that is, a serious citizen—without the help of people like Thurston. Indolence and lack of discipline were the traits with which missionaries had tarred Native Hawaiians for a century. Now, Duke's failure to show up as the star attraction of an event intended to make Hawaiʻi "the swimming capital of the world" revealed the depths of ingratitude and laziness that lurked in Kahanamoku's heart. In Thurston's world, his associates were either with him or against him—and Duke's refusal to be the star of Thurston's show put Duke on the other side of the line.

• • •

This was not the first time that the Kahanamoku family had dealings with Thurston. In 1893, just after he overthrew Queen Liliʻuokalani, the thirty-five-year-old Thurston had championed Hawaiʻi's entry to the World's Columbian Exposition in Chicago. This was the same fair at which historian Frederick Jackson Turner had pronounced the North American frontier closed and called for the United States to discover new arenas where men might practice the strenuous living that had fueled the nation's greatness. Hawaiʻi, Thurston decided, could be such a place, and he became determined to make the newly formed Hawaiian republic a part of the United States: a vassal state if not an outright territory.

As part of this scheme, he organized a fantastic show to promote the Islands: the "Kilauea Cyclorama." A circular building with a 52-foot-tall, 412-foot-wide painting wrapped around its interior, the cyclorama was intended to give viewers a sense of what it would be like to be inside an erupting volcano. Outside of the cyclorama building, a fearsome plaster statue by Chicago sculptor Ellen Rankin Copp depicted Pele, the volcano goddess, charging on a lava chariot, holding aloft a fiery spear. The grimacing face loomed over the entrance while American flags fluttered from the ramparts of the building. Once inside, visitors crept out onto an "observation platform" that simulated a view from the rim of the crater, down into the "bubbling and thunderous lake of lava." Electric lights, steam vents, and pyrotechnics conjured an eruption. As the guidebook to the exposition put it, "Gazing upward and around, the spectator is encompassed with a hissing, bubbling sea of lava, with tongues of flame and clouds of steam rising from fathomless pits to overhanging crags and masses of rock."

To accompany the pyrotechnic show, Thurston hired a group of Hawaiian singers and dancers to display traditional Hawaiian forms of art. A troupe of hula dancers performed versions of the traditional storytelling form that had only recently been re-legalized after having been banned in the 1830s for its sensuality.

Among the musicians who traveled to Chicago was Duke Kahanamoku's father, whose name was also Duke. The musicians were, as one newspaper reported, "delighted with their trip to America, and especially the sights they saw at the fair."

Some of the cyclorama singers—including Kahanamoku—split off from the exhibition and went to New York for another gig. Kahanamoku returned to Hawaiʻi in July 1894 having made some money and in "the best of health."

The cyclorama was a hit with mainland audiences and, more importantly, popularized Thurston's main point: Hawaiʻi was a land of wonders—beautiful but savage—and it needed the firm hand of American intervention to bring it into the modern world.

Indeed, even as fairgoers flocked to the Exposition grounds, a US envoy, James Blount, was returning to Washington from Hawaiʻi, where he had conducted an investigation ordered by US president Grover Cleveland into the overthrow of the monarchy. His reports stated unequivocally that US involvement in the coup amounted to an act of war on a sovereign nation and recommended that Washington immediately return Hawaiʻi to its status as an independent nation.

Blount's report enraged pro-annexation partisans across the United States and made it into reporting on the cyclorama. The *Rochester Democrat and Chronicle*—a pro-annexation paper—wrote that "The Hawaiian exhibit is one of the most interesting on the grounds" of the Columbian Exposition, though the editors regretted that there was no "wax sculpture" of the American investigator Blount "toadying up to the Royalists and Queen Lili." Other news reports were more circumspect but equally emphatic in calling attention to the putative backwardness of the Hawaiian people. It was true, a concerned citizen wrote to the *Brooklyn Eagle*, that "justice did demand fairer dealing with the ignorant savages than they received." Nevertheless, justice "did not and does not summon us to surrender civilization to their control. Thus does civilization in the Hawaiian islands cry out for help and, as is natural, turns to their powerful neighbors for aid, to a country calling itself the 'home of the free and the land of the brave,' a country governing itself in peace and equity." In other words, Blount may have been right that the United States had dealt very incorrectly with the Hawaiian monarchy—but the higher cause of civilization overrode the earthly laws governing international relations.

Still other news outlets projected the supposed battle between savagery and civilization onto the cyclorama performers themselves. Several papers, for instance, ran sensational stories on the attempt by one of the performers to murder his wife with an axe. Opu, a singer, had been arguing with his wife, Paau, when she threatened to "pray Opu to death." Opu, reported the *San Francisco Chronicle*, was "absolutely clothed with barbarous prejudices"—the victim of dark superstitions. As a result, he believed his wife's threats and reportedly attempted to kill her with an axe before she did him in with spirits. Nothing seems to have come of the incident—if, indeed, it really occurred— and Opu sailed back to Hawaiʻi without having been charged with a crime. He and Kahanamoku Sr. remained friends for years thereafter. But the reporting on the incident—a "champion diver, swimmer, and shark sharp [that is, a shark hunter]" attempting a murder based on dark magic against the backdrop of Pele and an exploding volcano—was precisely the image of crisis in paradise that Thurston wished to project.

From Thurston's perspective, Duke Kahanamoku Sr.—along with the other performers at the cyclorama—had filled a role. They presented to the public the portrait of a charismatic but uncivilized people who needed a civilizing hand. The fact that

Kahanamoku, for instance, was a graduate of the elite Royal School of Hawai'i—a thespian and orator who also had won top honors in the school's military drill—made little difference. In the eyes of the people who flocked to see the cyclorama, he was supposed to be quaint and charming at best and a savage at worst. Thurston needed visitors and readers to believe in this narrative so they would support the cause of annexation.

With annexation accomplished in 1898, and a new tourist industry pumping money into the Islands by the 1920s, Thurston now expected the elder Duke Kahanamoku's son to perform a new role: that of the celebrity athlete and obedient representative of Native talent. But Kahanamoku refused, and Thurston attempted to punish him by disparaging his character. The accusations stung, because they attacked him as both a sportsman and a Hawaiian. Kahanamoku pushed back with uncharacteristic force in the form of the lawsuit.

• • •

Steaming toward O'ahu in the early twentieth century, passengers from the mainland United States were first greeted with the sight of the volcanic mountains of the Ko'olau range, purple-green and shrouded in clouds. Birds dipped and glided around them; rainbows unfolded through shafts of sunlight. Lush forests of koa, ironwood, and pandanus cascaded down their sides.

At the southernmost edge of the range was the jagged mass of Lē'ahi, an extinct volcano with glittering mineral deposits known to European sailors since the nineteenth century as Diamond Head. In the shadow of Lē'ahi's crater, about four miles from Honolulu Harbor, the neighborhood of Waikiki hugged the coast. A marshy stretch of hau trees and white sand beaches interspersed with freshwater streams, it had been a treasured surf spot for ancient Hawaiians. When Honolulu began to emerge as a commercial center, though, it was considered a backwater by most Honoluluans.

A few who could afford automobiles or carriages had beach houses there. Hawai'i's last queen, Lili'uokalani, had a cottage facing a rolling surf break, later called "Queen's" by the boys she sometimes summoned to surf for her. The sugar baron James B. Castle had erected a spectacular, four-story confection of open-air porches and Tiffany stained glass windows about half a mile away along Kalehuawehe, a choppy, expert-only break that came to be known as "Castles." Otherwise, though, the area was countryside—primarily home to subsistence farmers and those who tended taro patches, rice paddies, and duck ponds.

By the early twentieth century, Waikiki was changing. After the Honolulu Rapid Transit Company extended its trolley line in 1907, the area experienced a reawakening as a tourist destination. It was still possible to find people living in traditional grass huts and subsisting off Waikiki's plentiful fish, coconuts, and taro, and surfers had never fully abandoned the area's many breaks, but now a single trolley track unfurled through the swamps. Cheery red and yellow streetcars trundled passengers across the lazy streams to new Waikiki destinations. The Moana Hotel—built in 1901—became the tourist trade's center of gravity: a five-story, Beaux arts layer cake of white wood, Corinthian columns, and open porches. The hotel's pier jutted a hundred feet into the ocean, and colorful umbrellas cropped up along the beaches in front of its broad verandas.

Nearby Kapiʻolani Park soon featured a racetrack for those who wished to gamble, grassy lawns for picnickers, and baseball fields for pickup games. A zoo boasted mongooses, ducks, golden pheasants, and—as one advertisement for the zoo put it—"your ancestors, the monkey family." At the very end of the trolley line, the Honolulu Aquarium at Waikiki showcased the dazzling fish of the Islands' waters. They were remarkable sights, as one tourist from Wisconsin noted enthusiastically, and "practically all *delicious* eating."

Duke Paoa Kahanamoku—the surfer and swimmer who would become Waikiki's most famous son—was born on August 24, 1890, in the Arlington Hotel in Downtown Honolulu. The cheerful, two-story, pink coral residence with breezy porches and wide lawns had once been known as Haleʻākala—the "pink house" or "the house of the sun." It was originally part of the royal estate of Princess Bernice Pauahi Pākī Bishop—the great-granddaughter of Kamehameha I and one of the wealthiest people in Hawaiʻi—and it sat on the well-manicured grounds of ʻIolani Palace, the seat of Hawaiian government. Outside, visitors could stroll the broad lawns lined with palm trees and hibiscus bushes. Inside the hotel, richly paneled koa wood walls seemed to glow from within. Hawaiʻi's last queen, Liliʻuokalani, had lived there as a child, along with Princess Bernice, and the hotel now served a rotating clientele of tourists, government officials, and residents, including the Kahanamoku family. At the time of Duke's birth, his father worked as a clerk and a cab driver for the American Carriage Company, located in a stand across the street from the hotel.

Neither Duke nor his father were, in fact, dukes. Duke's mother, Julia Paʻakonia Lonokahikini Paoa, and Duke's father both descended from *kaukau ali'i*—lower ranked *ali'i* who acted as retainers to higher chiefs. The name "Kahanamoku" had been given to Duke's father's family line by the unifier of Hawai'i, Kamehameha I, to honor their service during Kamehameha's rise to power. Both the Paoa and Kahanamoku clans had acted as retainers to the Kamehameha rulers, including Bernice Bishop. When the elder Duke was born, his mother took the child—named Halapu Kahanamoku—to see Princess Bernice. At the time, Prince Alfred, the Duke of Edinburgh, was visiting Hawai'i from England, so Bernice suggested the name "Duke" as a commemoration of the visit. Alfred—visiting Bernice, one royal to another—was delighted. Evidently, Duke Sr. was too, as he later passed his name on to his own son.

The family relocated from Honolulu to Waikiki in 1893 after American forces from the *Boston* set up their base in the Arlington Hotel during Thurston's successful coup. (There is evidence that hack cab drivers from the American Carriage Company, for which Duke Sr. worked, had smuggled weapons to those opposing the coup, but the elder Duke was not implicated.) The family of Duke's mother owned a plot of land on the westernmost side of Waikiki that had been awarded to them during the Māhele. They lived in a small cottage with wide open porches, called lanais. Its front faced inland, toward rice fields, duck farms, and mullet ponds. Toward the back was the Pacific Ocean and the Waikiki breaks that came to be known as "Kaisers," "Fours," and "Threes." When it rained hard enough, the neighborhood flooded and kids would paddle through their yards and streets on surfboards and in small canoes, scooping up escaped mullet and errant duck eggs.

Most families in Waikiki supplemented their income by

fishing and subsistence farming. In their gardens, people grew a variety of produce. "We used to grow rice and potatoes and taro," recalled one Waikiki resident. Others remembered growing breadfruit, mango, custard apples, lemons, bananas, and water cabbage. Coconuts, dates, and tamarind grew wild. Neighbors organized parties to spear or net fish and shared their catches: hauls of mullet, *uhu* (parrotfish), and *kūmū* (goatfish). *Wana* (sea urchins) were a special treat. Plucked from the coral in October, when they were fattest, they were placed in a canvas bag, shaken vigorously to remove their spines, cracked open, and eaten raw. Pacific lobsters were also abundant and could be trapped in wire cages or nabbed from their crevices in the coral. And *limu* (seaweed)—dank, flavorful, ubiquitous, and delicious—could be picked from the rocks near shore. A merchant named Aima came around once a week selling poi—a paste made from taro roots—for a dollar and a half a bag. The Ah Leong Store delivered canned goods.

By the late 1900s, Duke's father had become a police officer and a minor operative in Honolulu politics. He was initially a bicycle cop, then a patrol wagon driver. He ran for the Democratic seat in Hawai'i's Fourth Congressional District in 1908 on a platform of home rule and better infrastructure, but he lost by a landslide to the Republican candidate. Shortly thereafter, he became a desk clerk, then a sergeant in 1910— an occasion that he commemorated by naming his last son Sargent. Waikiki at the time was sleepy and crime was scarce, other than occasional visits from American military men who would come around to drink, steal ducks, and harass the residents with racial slurs. Otherwise, a neighborhood cop's job mostly amounted to sending kids home when it got dark.

As with many residents of Waikiki at the turn of the twentieth century, the younger Duke had a polyglot upbringing. The family spoke Hawaiian, English, and Pidgin at home. Their neighbors were Japanese, Chinese, Hawaiian, and Portuguese. Many were farmers or shop owners; some of the women in the neighborhood worked in the laundries at the big hotels.

There were other houses on the family lands, all owned by relatives, and Duke grew up surrounded by cousins: thirty-one in total, including the Paoa family. Duke's closest brother, David, was born in 1895. David was followed by a sister, Bernice, in 1897; a brother, William, in 1900; sisters Kapiolani in 1905 and Maria in 1907; and two younger brothers, Sargent and Louis, in 1908 and 1910. There was always someone to play with, and kids were constantly running in and out of the Kahanamoku house.

The neighborhood children were inventive in their entertainment. They would chase the chickens in the Paoas' yard, fish, catch crabs in the sea and streams, scavenge for coconuts, and steal mangos from the trees of their neighbors. Games of pickup football and soccer were popular, and the trolley line inspired still other sports. Kids would collect duck eggs to throw at the cars as they passed or else stand on the rickety trolley bridges over the Waikiki streams as the train approached, then jump off into the water at the last minute.

To make a little extra money, kids would sell newspapers on the trolley and shine shoes in town. Ice cream cones could be had at the local bar in exchange for a few empty beer bottles collected from the neighborhood, or a string of fish.

Even more cash could be had from the blossoming tourist trade. Younger kids—including Duke and David—made money by diving for coins thrown by passengers of steamships arriving in Honolulu Harbor. The kids—mostly male, mostly Hawaiian, Japanese, or Chinese—would wait in the water beside the big ships as they docked. The best divers could identify the type of coin from the way it fell through the water. Silver dollars were the hardest to catch because they zigzagged as they fell. The boys would pop the coins in their mouths to store them and attempt to kick their rivals in the stomachs while underwater to get them to disgorge their mouthfuls of coins. A successful dive session of less than an hour could yield up to six dollars—a princely sum in Honolulu of the 1910s.

Other times, boys would try to entertain tourists with their skill at catching fish. As a younger beach boy, Lemon Holt recalled that when tourists clustered on the quays of Waikiki, he and his friends would dive into the water, peel off their swimsuits, and use the suits to net colorful fish like brightly striped manini. They would then pop out of the water and display their kaleidoscopic catches to tourists. "We'd hold [the fish] up," said Holt, "and if the tourists dropped a nickel, we turned around [without] any tights on and we showed them our 'ōkoles [asses]." On the other hand, if the tourists were grateful enough to drop more money, like a quarter, continued Holt, "we thanked them and did not show them our 'ōkoles." The law of the 'ōkole was unorthodox but principled.

But these amusements paled in comparison to the ones offered by the waves. As Duke's brother recalled, "Number one, we all wanted to learn to swim. Number two, we wanted to learn to surf."

Duke got his first swim lesson in 1894. The elder Duke paddled with his son out into the deep water of Mālama Bay in a canoe. Then he dropped the boy in. In some versions of the story, he tied a rope around his son's waist. In other versions, there was no rope. Either way, the younger Duke recalled, "It was save yourself or drown. So I saved myself." He sank, he sputtered, and then he swam.

The waters of Waikiki at that time were full of children. Hawaiian and Japanese kids did most of the surfing, typically lying on their bellies on improvised boards. They would surf on box tops, scraps of wood, or whatever else was available that would plane on water and give a fast ride. The boards "didn't have any so-called shape," Duke's cousin, Fred Paoa, recalled—the shape was dictated by the materials on hand. Another of Duke's contemporaries agreed: "all we had was one-by-twelve planks, one inch by twelve planks. We got two of them, nailed them together, left the nails protruding under the bottom. Then the front, we had a saw, and we cut the front into a V-shape point. And that was our surfboard."

The "boards" didn't even have to be made of wood. After the Moana Hotel opened, enterprising youngsters would take pillowcases from the hotel, dunk them in water, then inflate them and tie them off like balloons. The water on the pillowcases kept the air inside long enough for the pillowcase to serve as a flotation device that could then be used as a kind of bodyboard. Duke's first "board" was made of a kerosene can pounded flat.

When they weren't plying the waves or egging trolleys, the kids of Waikiki were notionally in school. Along with most of his peers, Duke's formal education started at the Waikiki School, across the street from the newly constructed Moana Hotel, with three rooms: one each for first, second, and third grade. He then moved to the Queen Ka'ahumanu Elementary

School. Duke was not an especially notable or conscientious student, but then, the environment wasn't especially conducive to studying. As a Kaʻahumanu school attendee of that era put it, the habit of the students was "three days of schooling and the rest of the week, surfing."

When he was fourteen, Duke enrolled in the Kamehameha School for Boys—an institution endowed in 1883 by Bernice Bishop. His brother, David, enrolled five years later, and their other brothers followed.

Situated on the northernmost extent of the Bishop Estate at the foot of the Alewa heights, a five-mile tram ride from Waikiki, the school consisted of a cluster of neat, two-story wooden buildings arrayed along a rocky plain. Within the buildings there were classrooms, a printing press, a machine shop, and a library. After 1889, the Bishop Museum opened next to the campus, acting in some instances as a de facto classroom. The students lived in dormitories, wore military-style uniforms, and conducted weekly drills on the school's athletic fields.

The mission of the school was to teach its predominantly Hawaiian student body the skills and discipline necessary for life as proper American citizens. This was all the more needful because the Hawaiian boy, as one teacher explained, was "fonder of ease than of toil"—a prejudiced holdover from Hawaiʻi's missionary days. The school therefore emphasized training in English and science, and "sufficient discussion of the great movements and factors in the history of mankind to cause an appreciation of the struggles and the evolution of the human race, especially during the more recent years of America's and Hawaii's existence." It also required that students learn mechanical skills and trades. Duke recalled that during his time at the Kamehameha School he "started with tailoring, and learned how to make button holes, jackets, and trousers; then went on to machines, blacksmithing, and carpentering."

Beyond learning trades, sports were a central part of the Kamehameha School's curriculum. They were necessary to inculcate students with the values necessary "for a self-controlled life in a democratic society." In other words, sports were valuable because they developed civic fitness and social responsibility, along with physical strength. "The sportsmanship desired in youth," wrote a trustee, "is spoken of as a precept or principle, but it must be experienced and tested out on the field, in the dormitory, at meal time, and during the daily work periods to be sure that it is learned—that is, that it evinces itself in sportsman-like conduct." The sports available at the Kamehameha School in the early twentieth century were mainland American imports—soccer, football, track, baseball, and volleyball—and the Kamehameha students took to these activities with zeal. It was fortunate, one of the school's trustees wrote in 1902, that the "Hawaiian boy is by nature an athlete. Add to this the muscle developed in the shops and in the farm and you have the reason for our success in athletics."

By all accounts, Duke excelled at his activities at Kamehameha School. He was a proficient woodworker, a dexterous machinist, and his ability with textiles stuck with him throughout his life. His athletic experience was similarly broad. He played football, baseball, basketball, softball, and ran track, and he and his classmates were particularly impressive soccer players. As one newspaper report of a game put it, "it certainly was a pretty bit of work to see six Kam men [including Kahanamoku] knock the ball to each other in quick succession with their heads and the play was heartily applauded." Duke's teams would later win the soccer and softball championships in 1909.

In 1908, when Duke was eighteen and finishing up at Kamehameha, Alexander Hume Ford—the surf aficionado, Honolulu impresario, and friend of Jack London—drew on his meticulously cultivated connections among the city's upper crust to establish the Outrigger Canoe Club. The club was in Waikiki, between the Moana and Seaside Hotels, on prime real estate just off the surf break known as "Canoes"—so called for the rolling waves that made it amenable to large craft like outrigger canoes and the largest *olo* surfboards. At the Outrigger Club, well-heeled tourists could kick back with cocktails or rent surfboards and learn to surf.

Predicated on the mission of "preserving surfing on boards and in Hawaiian outrigger canoes," Ford nevertheless banned Native Hawaiians from joining the Outrigger Club, preferring to market surfing as a sport for white people only. Duke knew Ford and was, by all accounts, taken aback by the overt racism of the Outrigger Cub. "The Caucasians began to take to surfing," he later recalled with dry irony, "that was a real switch." His friend, William "Knute" Cottrell, was more emphatic, telling author David Davis that he and Duke "had heard something said by one of the fellows at the Outrigger Canoe Club that disgusted us quite a bit"—that is to say, they'd heard a racist comment about Hawaiian surfers.

Snubbed by the Outrigger, Duke, Cottrell, and their friend Kenneth Winter resolved to start their own surf club. Although they considered naming it the "Very Lazy Surfers," they settled on "Hui Nalu" because, as Duke explained, "'hui' is to get together . . . and 'nalu' is surf." In other words, the club would be home for people united by their love of the sport. The club took up under a hau tree in front of the Moana Hotel. The hotel allowed them to use a room in their bathhouse as their clubhouse. Dues were one dollar per year, and the club welcomed members of all races and classes, and even had a smattering of female members.

Hui Nalu is famous in the annals of surfing as the first Native Hawaiian surf club and is often referred to as beginning the revival of the sport. But it was more than that. It was also a promotional organ for traditional Hawaiian sports and culture, a community-building institution, and—crucially—a labor organization.

Duke dropped out of school shortly after founding Hui Nalu. He took on various odd jobs to get by during this period, but his focus was on swimming, surfing, and developing the club. Little did he know, his efforts to provide an organization through which he and his friends could practice sports and earn a living would lead to one of the most enduring innovations in American cultural history: the beach boy.

• • •

Today, the notion of the "beach boy" conjures images of sun-drenched decadence: a carefree young man, usually with a shaggy mop of sun-bleached, blond hair, carrying a surfboard, untroubled by thoughts of work or money or anything but catching the next wave. He takes life easy, doesn't think too hard, doesn't worry much. For him, each day is much like the one that came before. He's a breezy figure due to his rejection of capitalism and revolution alike. The beach boy offers a promise of counterculture without the danger of change.

A century ago, however, the original beach boys were anything but laid back, anodyne hedonists. They were hustlers and go-getters, sharp businessmen and competitive athletes—men hacking a living out of the fast-paced, fast-changing economy of Honolulu.

When Duke dropped out of school in 1909, the term "beach boy" had yet to enter the lexicon of American slang, but it was understood by people in Hawai'i. "The definition of a beach boy," as one Waikiki resident in the 1920s put it, "was a person, a big man, usually Hawaiian, that earned about probably seventy-five percent of his living from taking people out in canoes, teaching people how to surf and giving them swimming lessons." Usually, although not always, beach boys were young—teenagers or twenty-somethings. They cultivated the air of a bon vivant: they were good looking, liked smart clothes, liked having a good time. Often they were skilled at singing or playing instruments like ukuleles and guitars. Always they hustled. Always they were confident and magisterial on the water.

The genius of the Hui Nalu club was that it allowed beach boys to carve out a way of making money in the semiformal economy of early twentieth-century Hawaiian tourism. Hawaiian vacations before World War II were measured in weeks or even months. Well-heeled tourists from the mainland brought cars, chauffeurs, and servants to Hawai'i with them and rented houses or suites in hotels like the Moana.

The job of the beach boy was to make that vacation feel authentic and special. Beach boys gave one-on-one swim and surf lessons. They played music in hotel ballrooms, in the staterooms of ocean liners, and even in visitors' private rooms. They showed tourists how to fish and cook in traditional Hawaiian ways, and they took them to parties and to neighborhoods in Honolulu where visitors wouldn't dare venture alone. "[We would] walk Chinatown, through the slums and all that," remembered Duke's cousin, Fred Paoa. "I mean, these people are well-to-do people, but [we showed them] something that's unheard of, something different, and that's what they liked very much."

There were other ways of making a living in Honolulu in the early twentieth century. Beach boy "Ah Buck" Yee worked part time as a mechanic. Others sought construction work at the new US naval installation at Pearl Harbor, or at Fort DeRussy in Waikiki. Paoa worked at the docks in Honolulu unloading ships—interisland freighters filled with fertilizer and sugar—and at the Hawaiian Pineapple Company cannery for a little while because, he shrugged, "everybody went there."

But none of the jobs available to a recent high school graduate—let alone a dropout—paid the money a beach boy could make in a few hours of surf and swim lessons. The best jobs in the pineapple cannery and the docks made forty-five cents an hour. The worst barely allowed the employee to scrape by. Paoa recalled that trolley fare from his home in Waikiki to the pineapple factory consumed such a large portion of his twelve cent daily wage that he scavenged pineapple scraps for lunch every day until he quit.

In contrast, a beach boy could pocket two dollars for a surfing lesson, a swim session, or a canoe ride that lasted between ten minutes and an hour. It wasn't unusual to clear ten dollars per day, or hundreds—even thousands—of dollars in a season. "We made money those days," remembered Paoa. Tourists lined up in droves. A writer for *Outing* magazine, for instance, enlisted a band of beach boys to take him spear fishing in 1917, and the experience left him astounded. "Nothing," he gushed, could compare "to the absolute novelty and skill required in the spear fishing of the Waikiki beach boys of Honolulu."

And yet, although the beach boys were renowned for their skill and ranked among the island's busiest entrepreneurs, enduring stereotypes led some visitors to diminish their ventures as the latest expressions of Native indolence and naivete. Novelist Frances Parkinson Keyes described the beach boys as "indulg[ing] in all sorts of pranks and buffoonery, their own childlike enjoyment in these pastimes as great as the amusement they afford others." An earlier travel writer put the matter in darker terms—the beach boy was nothing but a man "who swims all day and plays in a string band at one of the big hotels at night." It was this behavior, the writer suggested, that would lead to the extinction of the "Hawaiian race." Louis Kahanamoku summed up this opinion bluntly, remembering that "everybody say, 'Ey, you a beach boy.' You know, it was kind of like you were the scum of the earth."

Given that being a beach boy was almost the only viable career to a young Hawaiian man, those with the proper skills and connections pursued it. When they reached about thirteen years old, aspiring beach boys would wander down to the Moana Hotel to informally apply for a job with the Hui Nalu crew. "Usually your older brother was a surfer," recalled one. "He would introduce you to the crew and they would size you up.

If they liked you, you were in." First, the new kids would help by moving canoes and surfboards for the older guys, cleaning up the beach, or putting up umbrellas for tourists. This might net fifty cents or a dollar per day. The younger kids might also show tourists how to fish, or how to cook a catch over a fire on the beach.

Then there was teaching swimming. Among the beach boys, David was in high demand as a swim instructor. "The malihinis [tourists] who visit the Island are all anxious to learn how to swim," remarked one article, and David was "in his element in that line [of work]." The tasks of a swim teacher were various. When a student couldn't swim at all—as was often the case—a teacher would have to show them the rudiments of staying afloat. When students could swim, their instructors would try to show them how to perfect their strokes. Many of the swim students were women, and a popular beach song, sung from the perspective of a female student, testified to the sensuality of the experience:

> *Won't you / Come teach me / How to swim / How to swim. / I'd like / To swim with you. / I'd like / To have you hold me / And that's all / You need to do.*

The next verses requested a surfing lesson, then a hula lesson, then a lesson in "wiggling," and then an ultimate, more explicit lesson. That said, it was also the swim instructor's job to protect the honor and safety of his charges—a task that could require forceful action. In one incident, a man on a surfboard collided with one of David's students. David confronted the man and, as David later put it, "tried to impress upon him the need of courtesy in the surf where careless riders are a menace to others."

The man, however, "got 'fresh'" and spoke in a "nasty way," and David slapped him briskly. The man later complained to the Honolulu Harbor authorities, but the woman and her husband both applauded David's conduct and nothing more came of the incident.

Swim lessons were good business, but the best job—the one with the greatest glory, responsibility, and chance for making money—was teaching surfing. Surfing condensed all the beach boys' qualities into one spectacular act of skill, athleticism, and flash. Although many forms of board were used on Waikiki beaches in the early twentieth century, the beach boys' rides of choice tended to be massive *olos*—hand carved on the beach and labeled with the riders' name. As Duke's cousin remarked, all of the surfers in the 1920s used redwood boards. "They were big ones, twelve feet, eleven feet, ten feet," he said. "They weighed about seventy-five to a hundred pounds. . . . And then, when they get waterlogged, oh my God. . . . They're much heavier. We all surfed on those." Duke's favorite was fifteen feet long, with "Duke" lettered in neat serifs on the top. David's was a seventeen-foot redwood board emblazoned with "David." Spectators marveled at the physical power of the person who could hoist such a board under one arm, trot toward the ocean, paddle out, and then cruise gracefully landward, skimming the water in an upright, straight-backed stance that came to be known as "the pose."

The board's style precluded the wave riding tricks common today. For cutbacks, bottom turns, 360s, and other forms of hotdoggery, it is helpful to have a shorter board with skegs (fins) on the bottom, which only became popular after World War II.

In contrast, the 1920s board allowed for long rides at top speeds, often while the surfer performed gymnastic tricks. It wasn't uncommon, for instance, to see Duke or David roll forward into a handstand on the noses of their boards as they rocketed shoreward. After a moment, they'd calmly cartwheel back into standing position as sea spray shot around them. Other times, riders demonstrated their strength by paddling out with a child or a woman on their board, then hoisting them aloft on their shoulders when they caught a wave. Movies and photographs from the era show beaming women in swimsuits on the bare shoulders of impossibly muscular men, zipping through the surf at a rapid clip. David Kahanamoku even trained his black-and-white dog, Spot, to swim out, hop on the board, and surf with him back to shore.

Duke Kahanamoku surfing, 1921.

Like Jack London, visitors to Hawai'i saw beach boys surfing and wanted to emulate them. And, like London, they often found the experience overwhelming. One wrote that a surf lesson fundamentally consisted of "an infinite amount of lugging of a heavy and awkward slab of slippery wood through a mile of thick water, of aching arms and stiff neck induced by trying the feat impossible for an amateur of lying on a board and swimming at the same time, of half-drowning every time a breaker spills the world into a jumble of legs and koa planks, and at last of a thousand mishaps, gurgles and frights till the scornful sea tosses the human wreckage back upon the sandy shore."

The goal of the beach boy was to sublimate the potential for terror into an experience of elation. "We take these people out on the surfboard," remembered Duke's cousin, Fred, "and then push them in on the board. You know, have them stand up. Big deal, you know, hands up. They stand and they fall over, and they like it. Two, three times." Surfing in this way became an exciting activity, but not the life-threatening encounter between human and nature that London had recorded.

Surfing provided more than just the thrill of waves, however. A writer for *Liberty* magazine painted the picture in an article titled "Paradise Gone Mad." "The white woman hires a handsome and muscular brown instructor. She lies prone in her scant bathing suit on the front of the board. The native lies behind, often stripped to the waist, in close proximity, and paddles out a quarter of a mile to the proper breakers. Sometimes they continue on to the outer reef, which is so far from shore that they are entirely lost from view." Readers were left to imagine what came next. In a later interview, Sargent Kahanamoku was less ambiguous on the denouement of these encounters—once the beach boy and his charge were out of sight, he said, they could proceed with a "good Hawaiian fucking."

The *Liberty* writer meant to paint a menacing picture, but others remembered the experience differently. One tourist recalled her surf lessons as exquisitely sensual: "Can you imagine what it was like for me, going to a Catholic school on the mainland, to have a man take me surfing? To sit on top of me, on the back of my legs? The thrill I had. Skin to skin. In the water." Louis Kahanamoku likewise remembered the experience less in terms of "good Hawaiian fucking" and more in terms of the pleasures of close contact. "All the boys liked [teaching surfing]," he said, because it was expected that the beach boy instructor would hoist female surfers onto his shoulders. With "the wahines (women) you go [to] stand up" on your board, he explained, and then you put the girls on your shoulders, and "you put their legs between your arms in the pits, you know." The sudden and strange intimacy of surfing was part of its pleasure.

The erotic appeal of surfing stretched into the night. Once the sun started to descend, the beach boys would often return home, shower, maybe catch an hour of sleep, then head back to the hotels to further entertain their guests. "In the evening, we're different guys, boy," remembered Louis. The beach boy dress code was strict. During the day, beach boys were expected to show up for work neatly dressed, clean shaven, and with short, recently trimmed hair. Dude Miller—a senior beach boy who acted as the de facto business manager of the group—policed their appearance, dishing out slaps and reprimands to those who showed up for work looking sloppy or disheveled, or who let the straps of their bathing suits slump over their shoulders. In the evening, the men returned to work wearing sharp suits and ties and sporting hats with pheasant feathers or flowers. Their flashy and daring outfits—and the color of their skin—set them apart from the staid mainland tourists. "You see a bunch of brown clad boys, Hawaiian boys," recalled Louis, "And we were clean-cut, with a coat and tie. And the girls look at us . . ." he tapered off, chuckling.

An anonymous writer for the *Honolulu Advertiser* filled out the picture. Wandering down to the Moana pier one night, he heard strains of music: "A beach boy was thrumming a guitar. Another beach boy was picking a quarrel with a banjo, and still another thumped a ukulele." A couple was making out at the end of the dock. But this was no ordinary couple, realized the writer, for "he was a beach boy sheik, and she was a visiting tourist!" The scenario—a Hawaiian beach boy with a (presumably) white tourist—was "stranger than fiction," the writer concluded, and could only be chalked up to the night air and the intoxicating effects of the beach boys' music.

Nevertheless, as much as commentators could wring their hands over free love in Waikiki and beach boys and their clients could savor titillating memories, the beach boy lifestyle was—as Louis Kahanamoku remembered—primarily a job. "Women was women," he said, "that's secondary. . . . We go out and think of making money."

Indeed, as historians Peter Westwick and Peter Neushul point out, it's not at all clear that beach boys and their clients commonly extended the erotic promise of surf lessons, swim instruction, and evening music to full-blown liaisons. Although surely such encounters did occur, it would have been a dangerous game, both for the hotels, which had to fastidiously maintain the reputation of Hawai'i as a safe and wholesome place to bring one's family, and for the beach boys themselves, who depended on the hotels for their living.

For that matter, the reputation of individuals was on the

line as well. Duke himself got caught up in a divorce case, wherein a jealous husband accused Duke of seducing his wife. Duke was "very indignant," insisting that his interactions had been "merely those of a swimming instructor to a pupil." Newspapers from Honolulu to Sydney carried items on the story, including the suggestion that Duke could be charged under a federal antipolygamy act. In the flurry of bad publicity, Duke was forced to cancel a trip to Australia. Ultimately, the husband recanted his accusation—he was given to "eccentricities," newspapers noted—and the couple divorced. Duke was off the hook. But the situation underlined the risks of such erotic diversions. Given the potential for a lose-lose situation all around, it's difficult to imagine either side had much tolerance for a revolving door of beach affairs.

Ultimately, Hui Nalu was less a recreational club and more an informal governing body, maintaining order and tradition on the breaks at Waikiki. "Hui Nalu controlled most of the beaches," remembered beach boy Joe Akana, "because we were all the experienced ones."

Conflict was rare, though sometimes rival gangs—or groups of soldiers or sailors—would start trouble. The "Stonewall Gang," for instance, was a group of tough musicians and surfers—equal parts glee club, surf club, and fight club—from up the beach. Occasionally, they would encroach on the beach boys' territory, attempting to "cockroach" (poach) the tourists on the Hui Nalu men's beach. When this happened, the Hui Nalu crew would confront them. We'd say, "You ain't coming down this end," recalled Louis Kahanamoku. Ignore the warning, he laughed, and it was "fight, boy." The Hui Nalu guys, remembered an old-timer, "were pretty rugged buggers."

More often, though, the men of Hui Nalu settled differences through an unspoken but well-understood code. Duke was "the kingpin"—the symbolic head of the group, who often did the diplomatic business of arbitrating disputes between Hui Nalu and other surfers. When other surf crews encroached on Hui Nalu territory, it was Duke who decided which of the more "elite" members of the rival group could work the beaches along with his club. Within the club, the older men would teach the younger ones surf etiquette: don't cross in front of someone surfing a wave; don't steal waves; the person who first starts to ride a wave gets the wave. As Sargent remembered, it seldom took more than one quick slap from Duke's huge hands to drive home the wisdom of good behavior on the beach.

It is ironic that, having established Hui Nalu on the fringes of the developing American empire—and with it an entirely new form of social life—Duke almost immediately set off on a new and entirely different type of endeavor: competitive swimming. Where surfing was improvisational and ad hoc, competitive swimming was rigid and rules-bound. Where surfing was governed by local understanding, competitive swimming was overseen by national and international bodies. Where surfing was a matter of subjective, aesthetic experience, competitive swimming attempted to whittle experience down to objective, quantifiable units. Essentially, by the first decades of the twentieth century, surfing was becoming an art; competitive swimming was becoming a science.

It was part of Duke's genius that he was able not only to straddle these parallel endeavors but to bring them together.

• • •

In 1912, Duke went from being a locally famous beach boy to a world-famous swimmer through a series of swim competitions that culminated in victory at the Olympics. More than a world-famous swimmer, though, Duke became a paragon of "scientific" swimming—a new way of thinking about athleticism that emphasized precise knowledge of physiology and biomechanics. Indeed, through his rise in a new, scientific establishment of swimming, Duke went from being considered simply a very good, if untrained, swimmer to "the most scientific men of swimmers."

It wasn't a foregone conclusion that Duke would be a competitive swimmer. He had always been fast in the water—"he take one stroke while I taking twenty strokes," one of his fellow beach boys recalled—but he had initially considered rowing as his main sport. His other brothers were excellent swimmers, and all aspired to test their talent at the Olympics, the world's grandest stage.

In 1910, however—a year after dropping out of high school—Duke subbed into a swim race between the Healani Beach Club and the Myrtle Yacht and Boat Club. In a relay, he beat George "Dad" Center—the Myrtle's best swimmer. This victory changed Duke's thinking. "That was the first time it dawned on me that I could swim," he said.

His performance against Dad Center also caught the eye of William Rawlins, the assistant district attorney for Hawai'i, a friend of Duke's father, and a leader of the newly formed Hawaiian chapter of the Amateur Athletic Union (AAU). The AAU—founded in 1888 by the duo of James E. Sullivan (no relation to Louis R. Sullivan), a businessman, and William Buckingham Curtis, an athlete-turned-sports-journalist—was a governing body that set rules and standards for amateur contests. The group was also the gateway to international competitions like the Olympics.

Rawlins wanted Duke to compete on the national amateur athletic swim circuit. To do that, however, Duke had to be a member of an AAU-sanctioned club—and so Hui Nalu, the ad hoc beach club Duke had founded, had to be officially registered with the national sporting body. On July 27, 1911, the Hawaiian branch of the AAU accepted Hui Nalu's membership, with Dude Miller as the president and captain and Rawlins as the club's manager. The group adopted a new constitution, which set out its values and goals, and a payment schedule for dues. Most importantly to the style-conscious members of club, the group decided on official Hui Nalu uniforms in sharp black and gold.

After the Hui Nalu was officially incorporated, Rawlins and his associates in the Hawaiian AAU hastily scheduled a "Swim Carnival" to be held in mid-August. The carnival would "put Honolulu on the athletic map"—showing off the island's competitors to the rest of the United States and the world. "It will be interesting to see how the Honolulu swimmers compare with the natatorial experts of the rest of the world," mused a sportswriter for the *Pacific Commercial Advertiser*, previewing the lineup of swimmers. Whatever the result, he had "little doubt that the . . . A.A.U. will get a surprise when the Hawaiian records are forwarded to the mainland."

This prediction was more correct than anyone would've guessed.

• • •

Looking back on the state of the sport in 1918, a writer for the *San Francisco Chronicle* summed up the condition of swimming in the United States. "There has come a recognition of the sport as an art and hundreds of natators have made a study of the science of it," he wrote. Ten years before, only a handful of people in the United States knew how to swim in a strong, fast, efficient manner. Now, the writer explained, "expert coaches have been secured and a scientific study has been made to bring out the best styles for the various distances. Duke started the ball rolling, and we are all willing to take our hats off to him."

At the time of Duke's birth, the term "science" denoted a systematic field of knowledge more than a regimented method for understanding the world. Boxing, for instance, was called the "sweet science" when it was more than just brawling. Poetry was the "gay science" when it was more than just doggerel.

The term for the science of swimming in the early twentieth century—that is, the dedicated study of human movement through the water, and not mere splashing around—was "natation," after the Latin *natare*: to swim. Accomplished swimmers were known as "natatorial experts" and generally went by the honorific "professor"—as with "Professor" Gus Butler, a well-known distance swimmer; "Professor" F. E. Dalton, a championship diver; or "Professor" J. Finney, who held the world record for picking up sunken coins with his mouth while his hands were tied behind him (eighty-seven coins, to be precise).

By the end of the nineteenth century, experts began to imagine swimming as more than just a collection of skills but rather as a codified list of practices with medical and physiological precepts. In 1899, Davis Dalton, a championship long distance swimmer, published *How to Swim*, a "practical treatise on the art of natation." This book promised "the best movements for taking advantages [sic] of the physical laws involved" in moving bodies through the water, as "have been studied by competent men." His treatise outlined the basic physics behind swimming, along with photographs and illustrations. It also gave lifesaving tips and hints on how to perform less crucial feats underwater, such as how to smoke a cigar (surreptitiously turn it around in your mouth before you submerge); how to drink milk (basically, suck it out of a closed bottle and try not to choke); and how to sing (put a pail on your head, submerge head and pail together taking care to preserve the air in the pail. Commence singing—but not for too long).

In his 1904 book, *The Cycle of Life According to Modern Science*, Caleb Saleeby—a British physician, writer, and eugenicist—explained the "science of swimming" to his readers, including the principles of buoyancy, the ways that blood takes up oxygen, and the beneficial effects that swimming supposedly had on the nervous system. Indeed, swimming was the ideal sport, Saleeby thought, since it was less likely than others—such as weight lifting and football—to lead to "absurd lumps of hypertrophied muscle, hideous and useless in all sorts of out of the way places." If practiced scientifically, Saleeby assured his readers, swimming was a sound way of sculpting the human form.

These accounts and others orbited around the general principle that—in order to be a truly useful part of modern society—swimming had to be codified, measurable, and understood in terms of physics, physiology, and psychology. Indeed, in the case of eugenicists like Saleeby, swimming should also be understood in terms of evolutionary biology in order to truly be useful to society.

Duke inadvertently participated in this project by providing a model of what a perfect body should look like. He also defied its basic strictures.

On August 12, 1911, Duke showed up at Honolulu's pier seven in his black, one-piece swimsuit with gold trim and an embroidered gold "HN" (for "Hui Nalu") on the front. He would be swimming against some of his old clubs, the Myrtles and the Healanis. The Outrigger had bowed out of the competition at the last minute, having gotten "cold feet as soon as the entry list of the Hui Nalus was scanned," according to the *Advertiser*. Duke, the paper noted, was one of the "best known natatorial experts in the territory."

The race was to take place in the long steamship berth used for Matson's transpacific liners. A "barnacle encrusted barge" served as a starting block, and a rope at the open end of the pier strung across a line of buoys served as a finish line. Five judges with stopwatches, all officials of Hawaiʻi's branch of the AAU, arranged themselves on either side of it. Crowds lined the sides of the pier—the men in straw hats, women holding umbrellas to keep off the sun. The water was still, the tide gently flowing out. The air was just slightly cooler than usual.

Duke was the favored swimmer in the 50- and 100-yard events, but when the starting gun went off on the 100-yard race, he stunned even his biggest supporters. Diving off the starting block, he tore through the water, quickly outdistancing his closest competitor by more than half the length of the course. When he slipped under the rope that served as a finish line, the judges marked his time at 55.4 seconds—more than four seconds faster than the current American record, held by swimmer Charles Daniels. He repeated this performance in the 50-yard race, where, despite getting a late start off the block, he rapidly outpaced his competitors, finishing with a time of 24.2 seconds—which beat the 50-yard record, also held by Daniels, by 1.6 seconds.

In one sense, it's true that any time set by the swimmers would have constituted an official record insofar as Hawai'i had no records to beat. But in two races and a little under a minute and a half, Duke had not only risen to the top of Hawaiian swimming—he had become the fastest swimmer in the United States.

Race officials immediately knew what was at stake. They emphasized in official reports that all five judges had recorded the same times on their watches. They measured and remeasured the racecourse and hired a surveyor to validate their measurements. Having accumulated what they took to be an airtight set of data and methods, they sent the results through one of the Islands' most respected doctors—one J. T. Gulick—to the AAU in New York.

The reaction of the AAU headquarters was unfavorable. Otto Wahle, the head of the AAU's swimming division—a former champion swimmer himself and the coach to America's current (official) record holder, Daniels—replied to Rawlins with undisguised skepticism. For one thing, Wahle wrote, it was highly improbable that several judges would report such exact times; one would expect more deviation between even the most accurate observers. For another, Rawlins's report hadn't mentioned anything about the precise apparatus used to anchor the floats that defined the racecourse. Perhaps the floats had drifted closer to the starting barge, shortening the distance Duke had covered. Finally, it was simply impossible that Duke's times could have been as good as they were. "The fact that an absolutely unknown swimmer should swim 100 yards faster than the world's champion" (that is to say, Wahle's own protégé, Daniels) "is unheard of," scoffed Wahle.

On one level, the implication was simply that a provincial branch of the AAU had flubbed its first attempt to join the world of organized competitive swimming. At best, the inexperienced territorial residents hadn't understood the proper way to measure and had overlooked their improbable results with naive enthusiasm. At worst, they had deliberately fudged the numbers. Whatever was the case, it was clear to AAU headquarters that they couldn't be trusted with the serious business of modern, scientific athletics.

On another level, however—one not explicitly stated in the message but clear to anyone—Wahle simply doubted that a brown-skinned "native" who'd learned to swim au naturel, in the surf, could beat a white man like Daniels, who had been trained in the "science" of swimming.

Indeed, the scientific supremacy of white athletes was a sort of pet thesis of top members of the AAU, like its president, James E. Sullivan. A science-minded athletics expert, Sullivan had gained notoriety by organizing an "anthropology day" as head of the "Department of Physical Culture" for the 1904 St. Louis Exposition. This contest featured nonwhite people from around the world pitted against one another in the name of racial science. The competition included events like bolo throwing, pole climbing, and a mud fight as well as more standard exercises such as running races and a kind of shot-put competition. The point of the exhibition was to demonstrate that nonwhite athletes were not the equal of white athletes—a goal that the event had accomplished, to Sullivan's mind. This was, of course, patently false—an example of suborning science to prejudice. But Sullivan wasn't about to let science get in the way of his "scientific" views on race and athletics.

For that matter, swimming was not even on the list of events in 1904, because Sullivan felt that nonwhite people could not possibly swim as well as Caucasians. This, too, was an easily disproven misconception. Indigenous African, South American, and Polynesian people had been known as excellent swimmers for centuries. Europeans, in contrast, had a history of being skittish around water. The British poet George Gordon Byron's swimming of the Hellespont in 1810 (and his fondness for open-water swimming in general) was considered almost superhuman by his peers, while regimented swimming in Europe and America was—by the time of Sullivan's "games"—less than a century old. Nevertheless, to Sullivan, the proposition that nonwhite people might excel at swimming wasn't even worth testing.

As a sop to his Hawaiian counterparts—and, doubtless, out of some grudging professional curiosity—Wahle did mention in his rejection letter that if Duke could make it to the national swim championships held in Pittsburgh in February 1912, the AAU would time him again, and would accept the results. Indeed, if Duke was all that he was supposed to be, Wahle intimated that he could be part of the United States swim team for the upcoming 1912 Olympics.

Hui Nalu swung into action and, as the club's meeting minutes show, "after some discussion it was decided to give a dance to raise funds for the Duke" to send him overseas. The club further decided to send Dude Miller and another swimmer, Vincent Genoves, with him. The business community of Honolulu likewise rallied around Duke, calling his potential Olympic run the "best bet" for promoting Hawaiian tourism on the mainland. Local athletes held a benefit baseball game, and Honolulu's best sprinter—"Soldier" King—said that he would take on any challenger in a benefit race for Duke. Even the Outrigger Club, with Ford at the helm, contributed to the fund to send Duke overseas. An item in the early edition of the *Honolulu Star-Bulletin* read in its entirety: "Good morning. Have you helped along the Duke Kahanamoku fund yet?"

Finally, on February 8, 1912, Duke and his fellow swimmers departed for the mainland. The trip would serve as a vindication of Duke's swimming skill as well as a demonstration of some of the very real differences between being a very good swimmer and surfer and being a "natatorial expert." And these differences, too, had much to do with understandings of the place of science, medicine, athleticism, and the human body in the 1920s.

• • •

The first intimation of this difference came at an AAU qualifier at the Pittsburgh Natatorium, known to locals as the "Nat." Immediately prior to the race, the *Pittsburgh Press* put the main question succinctly: "is a swimmer who is accustomed only to saltwater and straightaway courses as accomplished a natator as the man who is used to swimming in fresh water in enclosed tanks with many turns?"

Duke's performance seemed decisively to answer this question with a "no." During the first heat, in the 220-yard event, Duke started off strong, hitting the water smoothly and plowing forward with "terrific speed." Suddenly, after completing two laps, he stopped in the middle of the course and appeared to founder. He began gasping for air and sinking beneath the water, as though caught in a powerful undertow. By the time he was dragged from the pool by a group of fellow swimmers, he could barely move.

What happened? The problem likely had to do with travel fatigue and the chilly temperature of the water. The air in the natatorium was also filled with cigar smoke, making it difficult to breathe, even for spectators. *Pittsburgh Press* sportswriter Ralph Davis, however, summed up the problem as one, essentially, of the beach boy versus the scientific swimmer: "Kahanomoku [*sic*] the Hawaiian," he wrote in a quick one-liner, "has discovered there's all the difference in the world between surf riding and a 75-foot tank." In other words, how could a person like Duke—a man schooled in the wild waves of the Pacific—ever succeed in the rational, regimented structures of American civilization, a context so alien to his own?

Much to the chagrin of critics like Davis, Kahanamoku overcame the problem of the "swim tank" in subsequent matchups and proceeded to dispatch his next opponents with ease. In one of these races, Duke took such a wide lead that he had time to stop in the middle of the race, look back at his competitors, then turn and keep swimming, ultimately to victory. His fellow athletes, thrilled with his performance, draped Duke in an

American flag. This served, on the one hand, as an acknowledgment of Duke's place in America, as an American. It also served, as some scholars have pointed out, as a way of further cementing US rights over Hawaiʻi. After all, if people of Hawaiʻi were competing as part of the US team, who could say Hawaiʻi wasn't American in the eyes of the world?

Nevertheless, even though he could win through sheer strength, it was evident that Duke still had some lasting problems with swimming in enclosed, freshwater pools. His turns, for instance, were inefficient and slowed him down, and his breathing was poorly coordinated with his stroke. To improve would require the intervention of "scientific" swimming.

Duke's difficulty in pools wasn't precisely a problem with Duke. Rather, pools were, by their very design, engineered to force people into a particular, technical way of approaching not only swimming but society more broadly. In the early twentieth century, swimming pools were still a novel technology. In the United States, they had originally achieved popularity at the turn of the century as a way for cities to deal with the question of mass immigration—what was often described as the problem of the "unwashed masses."

Initially, municipal swimming pools were meant as sanitation technologies for people who didn't otherwise have access to water for bathing in their tenements. When they first debuted in East Coast cities, they looked like enormous bathtubs, or pieces of medical equipment—large, white, unmarked basins with railings on all sides. As one pair of early swimming pool designers put it, "The problem [of pool design] is in many ways similar to that of the hospital; fundamentally it must be treated from the standpoint of sanitation, as the mission of the bath is to elevate the standard of cleanliness and public health."

Very quickly, however, pool administrators discovered that their inventions were more attractive for recreation—particularly to young boys—than as hygiene devices, and they gave their inventions over to the project of teaching children how to simultaneously have fun and behave in a proper, American way. Immigrant children, insisted elite reformers, needed to learn to take turns, swim in straight lines, practice particular strokes, move their bodies in a methodical way—and this could be accomplished by teaching them to swim in pools. An article in 1905 described the "ear-splitting" cacophony of a bathhouse during a competition, but also praised the way the swimmers managed to stay in their lanes. Discipline could also be accomplished by brute force. An article in the April 1905 issue of the social reform journal *Charities* noted approvingly that a group of young Italian boys "acting like monkeys" in a public bathhouse had learned a lesson in the ways of proper behavior from a pool attendant wielding a stick.

The difficulty with the unwashed masses, in other words, wasn't simply that they were unwashed, but that they were masses—unruly groups of people whose behavior threatened the civic life of the United States. Teaching children how to swim in pools was part and parcel, in many cases, with "transforming some of these grimy anarchists," as one editorialist put it in the *New York Sun*, into "good Americans."

In this respect, Duke's problems in the pool could be seen as an indication that he wasn't fully suited to life in mainstream American society. Or, to put it a different way, Duke wasn't used to swimming in a pool because, in the early twentieth century, pools were still a novel technology, designed to teach people how to swim in a specific, obedient, modern way.

In Philadelphia, the team enlisted "Professor" George Kistler, the University of Pennsylvania's swimming coach. He was mustachioed and portly, or, as one newspaper put it, a "remarkable specimen of physical manhood . . . as broad as he is long and powerful in every way." He was also one of a new generation of "scientific" coaches who endeavored to understand swimming through what would come to be called biochemistry and biomechanics. As Kistler explained his philosophy in 1906 to a group of fellow coaches, new swimming records were a result not simply of stronger men, but of "knowledge of mechanics and physiology." Duke's new record was a sterling example of this. By understanding the science of the body—in a way not unlike that of Osborn and London and other advocates of the strenuous life—swimmers could increase their gains and their gold medals.

Duke stayed in Philadelphia for several months and worked with Kistler. The "professor" drilled him in proper swimming pool form—how to turn at walls, how to dive, how to maximize his stroke in still water. "I'm getting familiar with fresh water," Duke wrote to his father in 1912, "but I had an awful time with it at first. The turns, of course, bothered me, but I'm getting accustomed to them. Kistler says I have it down pretty well."

In the end, for all of his training in "scientific" swimming, Duke didn't have to deal with an indoor pool during the Olympics. The planning committee in Stockholm had decided on an outdoor course, since there were no pools in the city big enough to meet the hundred-meter length required by

Olympic regulations. They settled on a sheltered part of Stockholm Harbor known as Djurgårdsbrunnsviken. The viewing stands, built to accommodate three thousand people, ran along the water's edge. The other side was enclosed with pontoon bridges floating on the water. The result was, in effect, an outdoor pool with land on one side and a rectangular wooden deck extending on all other sides. The water was colder than was ideal, and murky since the bottom of the bay had recently been dredged to achieve a uniform depth through the course. Nevertheless, the Swedish Olympic Committee felt the pool left "pleasant, happy memories in the hearts of all Swedish friends of the art of swimming."

Duke and his teammates arrived in Stockholm on June 30, and hit the water the next week. On his first day of swimming the 100-meter event, Duke set a new Olympic record of 1:02.6. The next day, he won his heat in the 100-meter quarterfinals. In the semifinals, Duke matched the 100-meter world record of 1:02.4. In the ultimate final event, Duke was set to swim against Kurt Brettling and Walter Ramme of Germany, Cecil Healy of Australia, and his own teammate Ken Huzagh. On the day of the finals, Duke, taking a nap under the bleachers, nearly overslept the event. Even still, he went on to win gold with a time of 1:03.4.

His victory was celebrated around the world. The *Manchester Evening News* in Great Britain wrote that British swimmers were "hopeless outclassed by the Honolulu native, Kahanamoku." The *North China Herald* added, "once again America has demonstrated that she possesses the greatest sprint swimmer in the world, the success of Kahanamoku gaining for her the prize and in addition a record that may possibly stand for decades." And the French *Le Sport Universel Illustré* mused that "the performance of . . . the famous American swimmer Kahanamoku, covering the 100 meters of swimming in a little over a minute, leaves . . . most lay people dreaming."

Praise in the United States was no less effusive. Duke was "one of the heroes of the hour," wrote the *Nashville Banner*, continuing, "the athletic experts believe he is the greatest aquatic star that ever appeared in an Olympic Swimming contest." "Hawaiian Carries US Hope in Swimming" crowed the *Evansville Courier*, noting that "Duke is one of the best swimmers that ever happened in Hawaii." The planners of the Hawai'i pavilion at the San Francisco World's Fair proposed to erect a statue of Duke, and in Hawai'i his photograph and medals were put on display at the popular photo studio of Alfred Gurrey.

But in the eyes of many, the victory was not entirely his own.

In the first place, the simple fact that he was of the Hawaiian "race" seemed to tilt the field in his favor. "Back of Kahanamoku," wrote the Wilbur, Nebraska, *Republican*, "is a long ancestry of semi-amphibious humans." Another commentator wrote, "His feet are big, broad, and shaped like paddles, an inheritance from many centuries of sea-swimming ancestors." Indeed, this author went on to say—in a turn of phrase that would have pleased Osborn—"One could almost imagine that a few more generations of swimming champions in the Kahanamoku line of descent would develop web feet." It was élan vital rather than skill, practice, or persistence that made Kahanamoku an excellent swimmer.

Taking this line of thinking to an extreme, tales of Kahanamoku's swimming prowess gave rise to mythic caricatures and absurd fantasies of Hawaiian prowess. A "True Story in

Pictures," for instance, by cartoonist Stookie Allen relayed that "when a mere tot, Duke was on a Sunday school excursion party wrecked by a squall. The ship overturned, tossing all into the sea two miles off shore, yet no one drowned for men, women, boys, girls and babies paddled to the shore in safety!" The accompanying illustration showed a surprised beachgoer observing a line of happily swimming Hawaiian people stretching all the way to a nose-up sailboat on the horizon. But by all accounts, this "true story" never actually happened.

An even more fantastic tale had Duke doing battle with a giant eel in Honolulu Harbor during a practice swim. Press accounts varied over the precise details of the event, but all emphasized that he had been attacked unprovoked and dragged underwater. Severely bitten on the hand, Kahanamoku gave submarine battle to the fish as it coiled around him, and the water grew cloudy with his blood. Some accounts had him eventually stabbing the eel with a pocketknife; others had him "choking the reptile to death." The illustrated Parisian weekly, *Le Petit Journal*, chose to emphasize both—featuring a full page color print in which an improbably mustachioed Kahanamoku simultaneously choked and stabbed the eel. Most miraculously of all, several accounts emphasized that—although he'd had a finger bitten off in the fight with the eel—Duke was still able to swim in the Olympics. This, too, did not happen. Duke had a full complement of fingers when he went to Stockholm.

And in another tale—this one only marginally more plausible—Duke took a job as a diver shortly after he dropped out of high school with a crew building piers in Honolulu Harbor. Such was his comfort in the water that, while waiting for his colleagues to finish a task topside, he grew bored and sleepy and decided to take a nap on the ocean floor. He was sound asleep when his panicked coworkers sent another diver down to retrieve what they assumed would be Duke's drowned body. It's true that Duke's draft card lists his occupation as "diver," but even with his well-known penchant for sleep, it seems unlikely that he could've fallen into a deep slumber on the ocean floor with the diving technology of the time.

At the same time, many commentators insisted that it was not simply Duke's Hawaiian ancestry that made him a natatorial sensation—it was also American science and know-how. Duke, wrote the *New York Times*, "was only a crude, green swimming phenomenon when he first attained prominence . . . by equaling the then existing worlds record." He had come to "this country devoid of knowledge of even the rudimentary principles of speed swimming"—and had to be whipped into shape by American coaches. Never mind that Duke was already legally an American when he came to the mainland, or that he had broken the American speed swimming record before he left Hawai'i. Through a neat trick of cultural amnesia, the *Times* asserted proudly that "Duke was 'made in America' and by Americans" (even if he was not, strictly speaking, an American himself in the eyes of the *Times*).

What it meant to be "made in America" as a swimmer, however, was unclear—and anyway, Duke broke the rules of "scientific" swimming.

Most casual European and American swimmers—those who *Le Sport Universel Illustré* called "lay swimmers"—used a variety of the breaststroke, a fan-like motion of the arms pushing water away from the body, combined with a frog kick. Otherwise, they simply dog-paddled or improvised their own combinations of leg and arm movements. Competitive swimmers, on the other hand, employed more advanced strokes like the "trudgen" and the "Australian crawl." Both combined an overarm reach with straight-leg kicks. The latter is a conventional stroke in the twenty-first century—taught to schoolchildren and ubiquitous in "freestyle" swimming events—but in the early 1900s it was a cutting-edge technique. Indeed, contrary to AAU president James Sullivan's opinion that nonwhite people couldn't swim, both of these "advanced" strokes had been coopted from Indigenous swimmers in South America and the Solomon Islands, respectively, but had subsequently been regularized and incorporated into the repertoire of energy-efficient "scientific" swimming.

Duke, however, didn't practice these new strokes. Instead, he swam in a style that appeared to defy the laws of natation—or better still, to open new horizons to swimming science. For one thing, he snapped his kicks from the knees and ankles, rather than keeping his legs straight or kicking only from the knees.

For another thing, Duke's technique was to swing his arms more slowly and deliberately than other swimmers, while keeping his legs below the water line, rather than breaking the surface as was typical in the trudgen or the crawl. This forced his chest and head higher out of the water than would have been the case with other strokes. It might be expected that such a posture would produce water resistance against his chest, slowing Duke down. However, as an article in the *Illustrated Sporting and Dramatic News* reminded its readers, "the faster an object travels through water, the better it can be made to plane"—that is, lift up in the water—"thus minimizing its immersion and, consequently, its resistance." This was precisely the principle that made a surfboard zip quickly and smoothly through the water. Combined with the immense power provided by Duke's kicking, his posture in the water made Duke's body behave like a surfboard, imparting "unchecked speed" to his stroke.

Duke's swimming style was "a revelation to experts," reported the *Boston Globe*, "who pronounced [Duke] the most perfect swimmer they have ever seen." Others agreed. "Duke is a smooth, well-oiled machine while in action," wrote the *New York Times*. "He has no energy wasting movements."

For Duke's part, he rejected the notion that his style was innovative. He swam in a "Polynesian" manner, he said, having developed his form principally through maneuvering heavy boards through different sorts of surf. As for the idea of scientifically training to swim, he just shrugged. "Training?" he said, "why I never did go into real training for a race but once, and that time I overtrained and went stale." Instead, he said, "my training consists of going out and swimming around."

• • •

After winning the gold, Duke returned to Hawai'i a hero, albeit an impecunious one. The Duke fund allowed people to donate to him to offset some of his travel costs. The grateful businesspeople of Hawai'i arranged to buy him a house—though they did so through a cleverly conceived trust that allowed Duke to retain his amateur status and the businesspeople to retain control over the house in case Duke wanted to sell it for cash. Tapping into another of Duke's talents, his supporters also arranged a job for him as a draftsman at city hall that had radically flexible hours. This, too, allowed him to make money while retaining plenty of time for swimming and surfing—which he continued to do with his typical, intense focus.

Between 1912 and 1920, from ages twenty-two to thirty, Duke took part in hundreds of swim competitions and natatory exhibitions around the world. Even before he left Europe after the Olympics, he showed off his swimming technique in Paris and London and accepted a rematch in Berlin with his German competitor, Kurt Brettling. He once again trounced Brettling at the 100, setting a new world record of 1:01.6. On his return trip to Hawai'i, he stopped in Atlantic City, New Jersey, where he took part in a few exhibition races and did a demonstration of various strokes—the breast stroke, the trudgen, the back stroke, "the famous Australian crawl," and his own "Kahanamoku kick." After almost eight months away touring US cities, he returned to Hawai'i in October 1912. For the next year and a half, he stayed there, competing in local promotional events like the 1914 Mid-Pacific Carnival, where he set a new world record for the 100 with a time of 54.8. (Until then, most authorities thought it was scientifically impossible to swim 100 meters in under a minute.)

When not swimming, Duke also gave surf exhibitions whenever he was near the ocean. Before he left Philadelphia for the Olympics in Stockholm, he'd asked his brother, David, to send two of his surfboards to Atlantic City, in preparation for his return. When he arrived in New Jersey for the swim exhibitions, the boards were waiting, and he took his favorite to the city's famed "Steel Pier," the center of Atlantic City's carnivalesque boardwalk. There he flung his board off the pier, then dove in after it, paddling out to where the Atlantic Ocean was breaking about a quarter mile away. He then rode back to shore on his first East Coast wave to the riotous applause of onlookers.

Duke even made it as far as Australia, where he was credited (wrongly) with being the first person to surf the subcontinent's waves, and (rightly) with kicking off an Australian passion for surfing that continues to this day. In December 1914, Duke and two other residents of Hawaiʻi—the swimmer George Kunha and their manager, Francis Evans—disembarked in Sydney to begin a series of swimming exhibitions.

Australians were fascinated with swimming, and even more fascinated with the dark-skinned American Olympian who came to visit their profoundly segregated shores. They were also fascinated with the idea of surfing. On Christmas Eve 1914, using a rough-hewn board that he'd quickly fashioned for himself using redwood from a local lumberyard, Duke gave an exhibition before members of the New South Wales Amateur Swimming Association and a handful of reporters at Freshwater Beach, near Sydney. The crowd thrilled as Duke struck statuesque poses on his board, did handstands, and shrugged off bystanders' warnings of the many sharks in the water. In subsequent exhibitions, he took audience members on rides with him, lifting women out of the waves and plunking children onto his shoulders. Some of these impromptu surfing companions—Isabel Letham, Claude West, and Charles "Snow" McAlister, among others—became champion surfers in their own right.

These surfing and swimming exhibitions were not exclusively for the joy of sport. They were also—and sometimes explicitly—promotions for Hawaiʻi. After his Olympic victory, Duke's image became synonymous with Hawaiian surfing and swimming. A poster for the 1914 Mid-Pacific Carnival—designed by Duke's fellow beach boy, Lew Henderson—depicted Duke: smiling, bare chested and with biceps flexed, surfing toward the viewer on a rooster tail of white spray, while the ridge of the extinct Diamond Head volcano loomed behind him. A similar image graced the cover of a publicity pamphlet for Hawai'i with the caption "Duke Kahanamoku—World's Champion Swimmer 'On The Beach at Waikiki.'"

For his part, Alexander Hume Ford used a crisp, black-and-white photograph of Duke for the cover of the premier issue of his *Mid-Pacific Magazine*—a glossy journal highlighting all of the best things about Hawai'i. Inset into a colorful green, yellow, and blue Hawai'i seascape of palm trees and waves, the photo shows Duke balancing on a surfboard, the muscles of his bare torso glistening, his face an easygoing mix of concentration and joy. Inside the magazine, an article—ostensibly by Duke, but more likely written by Ford—detailed the joys of surfing for mainland audiences, accompanied by more photographs of Duke—shooting waves, riding with a woman on his shoulders, ecstatic.

This last bit of promotion was doubly ironic since, before Duke left for the Olympics, Ford had barred him from competing in one of the Outrigger Club's amateur surfing contests on the grounds that teaching Moana guests to surf had made him a "professional"—a move that even the morally flexible Thurston found reprehensible. Kahanamoku was "beyond any question the best swimmer, surfer, and canoeist in Hawaii," fumed Thurston in one of his strongly worded editorials. "I think it is a pity that Duke cannot have a chance to try for the trophy, the possession of which is supposed to carry the title of champion surfer, because he employs his talents to make his living."

Ford wrote back somewhat heatedly with a new explanation, arguing that Duke had only been barred from the competition because he was a member of Hui Nalu, rather than the Outrigger Club—conveniently forgetting that Hui Nalu had been formed in response to the Outrigger's whites-only policy. Anyway, Ford continued, why would Duke want to compete with a bunch of amateurs? As far as the Outrigger was concerned, Ford concluded lamely, Duke was a champion already: "he does not belong to the Outrigger Club, nor does he belong exclusively to the Hui Nalu; Duke Kahanamoku belongs to Hawaii, and all Hawaii is proud of him."

In any event, the Outrigger Club would eventually extend a membership invitation to Duke in 1917—mainly for the prestige of having the world's most famous swimmer on its rolls. Duke would graciously accept, not least of all because his old friend and swim competitor, "Dad" Center, was, by then, also a member.

Duke's promotional efforts extended well beyond Hawai'i. In 1912, he appeared on a series of trading cards issued by Pan Handle Scrap tobacco. These cards—similar to baseball cards—featured popular athletes of the time, mainly in swimming and track-and-field events. Duke appeared on his card in a white bathing suit with a caption on the back stating (in part), "Duke Kahanamoku . . . is a Hawaiian. . . . Caucasians have little chance against Hawaiians."

Even minor mishaps could be good publicity. On one of his transpacific journeys, the Matson liner he was on paused in the middle of the ocean to transfer a stowaway to another ship heading the opposite direction. During the pause, Kahanamoku decided to jump overboard for a swim. The boat started up unexpectedly and began to leave without him, resulting in a moment of alarm onboard. In the end, the captain of the ship didn't reprove Duke's shortsighted enthusiasm, since rescuing Kahanamoku would be "good publicity" for the Matson steamship company as well as burnishing Duke's reputation.

The outbreak of war in Europe in 1914 put a stop to Duke's plans to win gold again in the 1916 Olympics, slated to be held in Berlin. Initially, many commentators expected the war to be over quickly. As the Olympic general secretary (and reserve corporal in the German army) Carl Diem remarked, "we can be reasonably sure that modern war will not last so long, so that long before the dates when we will celebrate the Olympic Games, peace will again reign and peoples will unite in sporting competition." As fighting ground to a stalemate, however, the question of Olympic brotherhood became moot in the face of ongoing mechanized slaughter. The International Olympic Committee wouldn't cancel the games, and Germany wouldn't concede that the games could be held elsewhere. In the end, the question of peaceful international competition simply faded without much additional comment. There were no international Olympic games, but Germany held its own internal games with athletes furloughed from their time in the trenches. In addition to staple track-and-field events, these "war championships" featured sports like hand grenade throwing and an obstacle course in which participants had to fire machine guns and rifles.

After three years, the United States entered the war in 1917, and Duke's promotional efforts took on new importance. His father had died unexpectedly earlier that year, so Duke—as the primary provider for his family—was not in imminent danger of being drafted. He served the war effort instead by joining the American Red Cross. There he put to use some of the skills he'd learned at the Kamehameha School, knitting hats and sweaters and scarves. He also undertook a fundraising tour of the mainland, along with swimmers Harold "Stubby" Kruger and Clarence Lane, and a Major Harold M. Clark of the US Army Air Corps. On this tour he and his fellow swimmers gave demonstrations of lifesaving techniques, staged swimming races, and showed off their diving skills.

After the Red Cross tour ended on the East Coast, Duke stayed on in Washington, DC, to enlist in the Army Air Corps with the intention of becoming a pilot. The decision made a certain amount of sense to press commentators. "As an expert surfboat [*sic*] rider and the most scientific men of swimmers," wrote the *San Francisco Bulletin*, "Kahanamoku can see no reason why he should not make a capable aviator." Indeed, many papers referred to him in the water as "flying Hawaiian," making the connection between scientific swimming and the new technology of human flight explicit.

Duke said that his interest in flying came from his fellow American swimmer, Norman Ross, who was an Air Corps pilot, but Major Clark doubtless had also influenced him. Before they left on the Red Cross tour, Clark had been a suitor of Duke's sister, Bernice, in Honolulu. As part of his friendship with the Kahanamoku family, he had taken Bernice and David for rides in his airplane. David had, by all accounts, loved the trips. It's not clear whether Duke also flew with Clark, but he could not have helped but know about the joys of flying from his brother. Nor, for that matter, could he have failed to know the reason that Clark had joined the Red Cross tour rather than flying for the Air Corps. While showing off over

Waikiki, Clark had crashed his plane rather spectacularly. As one Waikiki resident recalled, he swooped low at first, "bzzz, and . . . back up again. Bzzz, like that. And then, bzzz, he got down too low. And when he went up . . . the tail hit and down he went. Everybody saw it," the resident laughed, and "they sent him away." The accident does not seem to have dampened Duke's enthusiasm for flying.

In any case, even if Duke was the "most scientific men of swimmers," his plans to join the Air Corps were foiled by a force against which science had no response—an influenza pandemic that swept the globe from 1918 to 1920.

The origins of the pandemic are still a matter of debate among medical historians. Historian John Barry presents compelling evidence that the influenza first began in Haskell County, Kansas, in the United States. In January 1918, the local newspaper began reporting unusually strong outbreaks of pneumonia and "la grippe"—seasonal influenza. From there, the strangely aggressive influenza began showing up at Camp Funston, about 250 miles northeast of Haskell. Camp Funston was a training ground for some 40,000 American soldiers destined for the Western Front—the line of battle extending north to south across France. As a precaution against the sorts of epidemics that could run wild through army camps, the incoming men received inoculations against diseases like smallpox, but there was no influenza inoculation.

On March 4, a cook reported to the infirmary with influenza. By the end of the day, thirty more recruits had reported sick. By the middle of the month, more than 1,000 men at Camp Funston had fallen ill. Thirty-eight died. From Camp Funston, the disease spread rapidly as recruits fanned out toward the East Coast and deployed for Europe. By April the disease had reached epidemic proportions across the United States. By May it was running rampant across Europe, severely hampering the abilities of German, French, and British armies to mobilize troops. By the end of the war, in November 1918, a second, more severe influenza wave had spread around the world.

Duke seems to have been caught in this second wave. While he was lobbying the Air Corps in Washington, DC, he returned one day to his room in the local YMCA with what seemed like a slight cold. Overnight, he developed a raging fever, accompanied by muscle soreness, a throbbing headache, and uncontrollable shaking and sweating. One of the characteristics of the 1918 pandemic was that it hit young, strong, healthy people hardest, and Duke fit the bill. Over the course of two days, his fever inched higher, and he developed double pneumonia, making breathing difficult. He began hemorrhaging from the mouth. He was alone—the tour manager had abandoned the group—and began to fear the worst. "It had me scared for a while," he admitted. According to a later account by Joseph Brennan, a friend and biographer of Duke's, he was saved when a former girlfriend, Bernyce Smith, discovered him in his YMCA room. Brennan doesn't say how Smith—who was in Washington on business unrelated to the Red Cross tour—knew that Duke was at the YMCA and in trouble. But, as Brennan writes, Smith stayed with Duke, arranged for a doctor to see him, and managed to patch Duke up enough that he made the trip from Washington, DC, to California, and then onto a steamer for Honolulu.

When he arrived home, he was twenty pounds lighter and "looked like a ghost," but he was lucky to be alive. In California, George Freeth had died of the influenza. Duke settled into an exercise routine to recover muscle and train for the 1920 games.

• • •

By the end of 1919, Duke found his identity split in many parts. He was an outwardly easygoing and inwardly hard-working beach boy. He was a naturally talented Native swimmer, and a rigorously scientific "natatory expert." He was a representative of American modernity and of Indigenous Hawaiian authenticity. He was a pioneer of living on the fringe and a "model youth" in the eyes of American elites. He was being pulled in many different directions at once, and it was against this backdrop that Duke filed his suit against the *Advertiser*.

The attack on him, claimed Duke's lawyer, C. S. Davis, had caused him "great grief and mental anxiety." He had been "deprived of much sound sleep and . . . lost much valuable time, and [was] otherwise greatly injured and damaged" by the article. As a result of the anguish the *Advertiser* had caused, Duke sought $30,000 in compensatory damages and $20,000 in punitive damages—a sum that amounts to somewhere near $775,000 in 2025.

The specifics of Duke's complaint are lost to the annals of law, but the bulk of the court's consideration involved the use of the word "slacker." As the court noted, the term "slacker" was "too new in 1920 to be defined with any accuracy," having only "come into use during the recent world war." Nevertheless, in spite of its recent origins, the term was "known to every one of ordinary intelligence . . . and was most generally applied to a person who unlawfully evaded, or attempted to evade, his military duty." The same was true, the court noted, of the term "loafer," which could either mean (and here the court reached for the dictionary): "One who loafs; a lazy lounger; one who has the bad habits typical of street loafers"—or it could mean "the evasion of one's ordinary moral or civil duties."

In labeling him a "slacker," the court found that the *Advertiser* had falsely implied that Duke had abdicated his duty, both as a citizen of the United States and as a Hawaiian. It was true, the court admitted, that "the average reader knows that there was no obligation, either moral or legal, resting upon plaintiff to enter" a swim contest—"even though he had received 'world wide adulation, pages of publicity and many honors' as a swimmer." Thus, the court concluded, the portions of the editorial that had accused Duke of wrongdoing on the grounds of a sort of selfishness were not libel, since "the average reader would . . . see from the article itself the ridiculousness of the writer's conclusion. Unquestionably plaintiff had the right to stay out of the swimming [*sic*] whatever his excuse or even without excuse, and the publication is nothing more than a hostile comment upon the manner in which he exercised this right." On the other hand, maligning his willingness to do his civic duty was a serious attack on Duke's reputation. In other words, anyone would understand that Duke's participation in a swim meet was a matter of choice—his participation in civic life, however, was, to the court, a matter of obligation.

Ultimately, the court awarded Duke $1,500 out of the $50,000 he had demanded, but he never saw the money. An appeals court in 1922 decided instead that, while the original decision was correct, Duke had erred in suing the *Advertiser*, since there was no proof that the *Advertiser*'s top brass had any say in Withington's editorial. As such, Duke's complaint was valid, but he had no recourse to collect. He walked away empty-handed.

Or not precisely empty-handed. While the case didn't pay off for Duke, it did outline in miniature some of the titanic forces—science, capitalism, the emergence and importance of mass media—that were shaping both his own life and—in short order—the United States and the world. The *Advertiser* had implied, as the court put it, that Duke was "unworthy to be a person of Hawaiian blood and Hawaiian descent." But what did it mean to have "worth" defined by "blood"? Or, more precisely, what did it mean to have worth defined by genetics?

Louis R. Sullivan.

4

A PASSION FOR MEASURING NAKED MEN

Upon Osborn's return to New York from Hawai'i, he wasted no time in summoning Assistant Curator of Anthropology Louis R. Sullivan to his office. Like Duke, Sullivan was known as a champion sleeper. And like Duke, he had nearly died in the 1918 influenza pandemic. But the similarities ended there.

Sullivan was a shy, slender man of twenty-eight with dark hair and small, pale, wide-set eyes. He had a taste for plain suits and a dry sense of humor. He was a "good laboratory man," remembered one of his professors at Brown University where he earned his master's in zoology. He had "mechanical ability" and "horse sense" and took "more pains than he is asked to take." Another remembered him as a "quiet fellow, sane, clear-eyed, persistent, not afraid of work, with a scholarly mind and a whole lot of native ability." His notebooks from Brown are filled with detailed drawings of human bones—skulls, vertebrae, teeth, phalanges—labeled in a careful, meticulous hand.

After graduating from Brown, he took simultaneous positions as a PhD student in anthropology at Columbia University and as an assistant in physical anthropology at the AMNH.

At Columbia, his principle adviser was Franz Boas—a dynamic and outspoken German with fierce eyes and a face scarred from youthful dueling with sabers. Under Boas, Sullivan began working on the question of whether immigrants' body types changed over time when they came to the United States. This was a question of great political importance, since it addressed the genetic suitability—or unsuitability—of different "races" for life in the United States. If people's bodily "types" changed from one generation to the next, then notional "races" were mutable, and the very idea of race as a stable category for biological analysis was incorrect. This, anyway, was Boas's opinion, and for a time he dispatched Sullivan to analyze pictures of immigrants in the tenements of New York's Lower East Side, and to measure the head sizes of different immigrant groups. Sullivan's work with Boas was uneven, and Boas complained to a colleague that Sullivan "was plodding along, but somehow or other I cannot get anything out of him." It turned out that the quiet anthropology student from Maine was deathly afraid of his swashbuckling professor and refused to talk to him.

Sullivan was more comfortable in his work at the American Museum. The curator of the Department of Anthropology, Clark Wissler, put Sullivan to work researching "the hair of Indian half-bloods." Wissler was a rotund, bespectacled psychologist whose PhD focused on the correlation of physical and mental characteristics in different races. He let Sullivan loose in the museum's growing osteological collections, where Sullivan attempted to sort out the different races of the Philippines according to the measurements and characteristics of their bones and teeth.

In many ways, this was the precise political and methodological inverse of his work with Boas. Whereas Boas thought that race was a mutable and poorly defined way of studying people that should be treated with great caution, Wissler saw race as an immutable and stable quality that could be applied unproblematically to all manner of social and political questions. In either case, Sullivan thrived at the museum.

Unfortunately, World War I interrupted Sullivan's museum work and almost ended his life. When America entered the war in 1918, Sullivan took a leave from the museum to join the Surgeon General's Sanitary Corps, the organization in charge of looking after the health and hygiene of US troops. Sullivan worked in the Anthropology Section of the Sanitary Corps, under section chief Charles Davenport—a friend of Osborn's, an opponent of Boas's, and by then the nation's leading eugenicist.

The mission of the Anthropology Section was to compile statistics on troops. These statistics would be useful for reasons of logistic concern to army brass—for determining uniform sizes, troops' food rations, and rates of tuberculosis and other diseases. But the war also provided eugenicists like Davenport with a chance to compile more general data about the stature, health, and psychological qualities of different "races" of Americans from across the country. These data could be used to "test" eugenic theories (or, more accurately, bolster eugenic biases). For this reason, Davenport felt, their study was of greatest importance to "science, and to the Nation at large." It was too good an opportunity to be missed.

Sullivan worked diligently and was rewarded for his successful administration of these tasks with a transfer to Camp Grant in Illinois, where he set to work on his own "racial survey" of the army, supervised by Harvard anthropologist E. A. Hooton.

At Camp Grant, tragedy struck Sullivan twice. First, his quarters burned down. All of the preliminary data for his racial survey went up in smoke. Then the 1918 influenza pandemic exploded through the camp. Within six days, 4,000 men were sick. Within a month, more than 10,000 soldiers had been afflicted. There was nothing to be done in the way of treatment other than palliative care—baths in cooling alcohol, ice packs, liquid diets for those who could stomach any food at all. More than a thousand men died. Sullivan was hit hard and hovered at the brink of death. He eventually recovered and was discharged from the army, returning to work at the museum as an assistant curator in 1919. His lungs, however, were permanently damaged. He never recovered his health. His formerly meticulous handwriting became shaky and disorganized.

It was after all this that Osborn called Sullivan into his office on April 7, 1920.

Osborn told Sullivan to prepare himself to go to Hawai'i. His mission would be to study the "racial problem in northern Polynesia"—that is, to figure out where Polynesians came from in the past, and what the characteristics of the "race" were in the twentieth century. Sullivan was also to study race mixing—to see if he could detect a correlation between the racial characteristics of "mixed" people in Hawai'i and their level of accomplishment, wealth, education, and acculturation. Finally—thinking of Duke—Osborn was particularly interested in "any data regarding swimming adaptations in the limbs and feet" of Native Hawaiians.

Sullivan's ultimate goal was to bring back data and exhibition material for the upcoming Second International Eugenics Congress to be held at the American Museum. In Osborn's mind, concerted work on Hawaiian genetics and race mixing would cement the museum's place as a leader in eugenics on the world stage. This was primarily because Hawai'i—with its diverse population surrounded on all sides by water—made a "natural" laboratory. But it was also because the rest of the world had its eyes on Hawai'i as a particularly American experiment in colonial governance and race mixing. To conduct high-level anthropometric studies in Hawai'i, therefore, was proof both of the museum's importance to science and of its importance to the American government and its place in the world.

Osborn outlined the different "types" that Sullivan was to "collect" for the museum. First and foremost, he should get measurements, photographs, and casts of the "Chieftain type"—the "type" of person of Hawai'i (like Duke and David) characterized by his tall stature and excellent musculature. A full-body cast of a man of this "type" could be "attired in one of our feather robes," Osborn mused, "with feather helmet, spear, etc." He also instructed Sullivan to get a "Fisherman type" with "perfect muscular development, with native nets, etc." As for female Hawaiian "types," Osborn thought that "the most representative female type appears to be the hula dancer." Finally, it was desirable, thought Osborn, to secure a sculpture of a man surfing—though he did not apparently think of surfers as a "type."

Osborn's instructions to Sullivan raise a critical question: What exactly *was* a type, and how did types "work" as objective, scientific entities? It does not appear to have crossed Osborn's mind that his way of defining genetic "types" really relied on identifying people's jobs or cultural activities. People of any genetic makeup could—and, historically, did—study hula. By 1920 people of Hawaiian, Chinese Hawaiian, European, European Hawaiian descent (and so on) all trained in the ancient storytelling art. In the same way, many people were fishermen, with nets and spears and fine—or not so fine—musculature. Beach boys, for example, were men of many different "races" and "race mixtures"—and they all also fished and swam and fought and played music and football and baseball. Osborn himself would've seen some of this at Waikiki. None of these contrapuntal facts seem to have sunk in for Osborn. For the purposes of eugenic study, "culture"—activities and beliefs practiced by different communities of people—could be equated with genetics, which could be condensed into the concept of "types."

Sullivan, for his part, did not question the premise of his mission. Osborn had chosen him, and Sullivan was the man for the job in more ways than one.

Most prosaically, Osborn felt Sullivan needed to be out of New York for his health. The cold, damp New York air—full of smoke and soot—would kill Sullivan, Osborn felt, overworking the assistant curator's lungs and sending him back into sickness from which he might never return. Osborn thought that the climate of Hawai'i would do Sullivan good.

More to the point, Sullivan had the obsessive qualities that made for the best anthropometrists.

American anthropometry had its origins in the Civil War, when the United States Sanitary Commission—a semipublic organization used to coordinate medical services for the Union Army—commissioned its first "Anthropological Survey." This was an ambitious venture to collect "anthropological statistics" from every soldier in the Union Army in order to establish the physical, mental, and hygienic qualities of the average American male.

To accomplish this goal, the survey had been staffed with men possessed of a maniacal, almost erotic urge to apply rulers and calipers to their fellow humans.

Take, for example, Samuel Botsford Buckley—an entomologist who turned his incredibly precise measurements of ants (calibrated to "within one or two hundredths of an inch!" exclaimed an incredulous reviewer) to the measurement of humans. Buckley, who was based in Manhattan, measured every Union soldier he could get his hands on. When he ran out of soldiers, he haunted the bars and circuses of New York, attempting to measure yet more people. At one point he complained to the head of the Anthropological Survey that P. T. Barnum had refused to let him measure the World's Tallest Man. At another circus he attempted to measure Madame Sherwood—a "giant lady"—pleading with her that he "merely wanted to gather height and width of shoulders and circumference of waist, etc. etc." Madame Sherwood said no. Other anthropologists were even less circumspect. One confessed to peering surreptitiously at bathing soldiers, attempting to analyze their patterns of body hair growth. Still another put the matter in its most elemental form: "I have almost a passion for measuring naked men," he exclaimed.

Sullivan, too, was cut from this cloth. If Boas had found him plodding in his work on immigration, in his measuring work for the American Museum he was tireless, even fanatical. As he later recalled, he had "put in a good many of my good evenings" in his research and had "stayed away from church calculating averages, standard deviations etc." His work for the army had likewise been characterized by a meticulous attention to detail, and an unflagging energy for measuring recruits. And when he went to Hawai'i, he worked seven days a week, ceasing only when he was on a boat traveling from island to island, or for the odd, single day of hunting or sightseeing.

Sullivan, in other words, was a born anthropometrist. When Osborn summoned him, he and his wife, Betsy, hastily packed and departed New York like soldiers mobilizing for battle. Within a week they had made it to San Francisco. While Betsy did some sightseeing, Sullivan measured some of the human skeletons in the collection of the California Academy of Sciences. Then they sailed for Hawai'i on April 27, arriving in Honolulu on May 3 after a "fine voyage" with no seasickness.

He immediately got to work. On May 4, Sullivan met with Herbert E. Gregory, the director of Honolulu's Bishop Museum of Natural History—the regional hub of Polynesian anthropology, where Sullivan would be based during his time in Hawai'i. A gray-haired, parsimonious, and often quarrelsome Midwesterner, Gregory had made his name at Yale as a geologist before assuming directorship of the Bishop Museum in 1919. He greeted the Sullivans politely but perfunctorily, showed Sullivan to the museum's collection of Hawaiian bones, instructed him to begin cleaning and cataloging them, and quickly departed for an excursion to study a recent lava flow on Kīlauea's Southwest Rift Zone.

Sullivan worked for the next month in the skeletal collections of the Bishop Museum, doing as Gregory had instructed him and attempting to come up with a systematic description of Hawaiian bone structure. In June, Gregory returned from his geological expedition and the pair took a steamer to the city of Kona, on the island of Hawaiʻi. There, Gregory introduced Sullivan to David K. Kaupiko, a local politician, who took Sullivan by motorcar to a small village about thirty miles away, where he knew there to be a large population of "full-blooded" people of Hawaiʻi. It was there that Sullivan took his first measurements and photographs, with Kaupiko serving as his inaugural subject—the first of many people that Sullivan would measure.

For the next seventeen months, Sullivan ping-ponged around the islands, following the infrastructures set down by the American territorial government. He roamed the roads up and down the west coast of Hawaiʻi Island, measuring the community members of churches and schools. He then returned to Honolulu for a month, where he measured members of marching bands, residents of retirement homes, schoolchildren, police officers, and military men. He journeyed to Lānaʻi, where he measured more police officers and the inmates of a Girl's Industrial School—a kind of reform school for Native children. He measured people in big cities and in small villages. He measured plantation workers on Kauaʻi and descendants of *aliʻi* on Maui. The youngest person he measured was two years old. The oldest was 102.

"I think it would be criminal not to make the most of this opportunity," he wrote to Wissler, and vowed to "pick the chicken clean."

Sometimes Sullivan took photographs, other times he took hair samples. On rare occasions he took blood samples. Always, though, Sullivan carefully recorded his subjects' notional racial "mix." He was particularly keen to find "pure-blooded" Hawaiians, but his notes show a catholic collecting spirit. He photographed and measured Filipino sugar workers and Scotch Irish tour guides; Japanese merchants and Māori missionaries. He carefully noted the fractions of each race that he encountered. One man was "Hawaiian 1/2, Chinese 1/2"; another was "Hawaiian 3/4, Spanish 1/8, English 1/8," and so forth.

Overall, Sullivan collected measurements of roughly three thousand people. The pace was breakneck. Oftentimes he would measure more than a hundred people in a single day. On one day in July, he measured close to two hundred. The sheer throughput necessitated some assistance. When he first arrived, Gregory introduced him to John F. G. Stokes, an Australian archaeologist, and R. T. Aitken, a young ethnologist, both of whom worked for the Bishop Museum. Sullivan endeavored to instruct these men in the rudiments of anthropometry. The team was later joined by Betsy Sullivan and Mrs. Stokes, a botanist by training.

Measuring people was deceptively hard work. Would-be anthropometrists faced a number of philosophical and practical problems.

First and most basically, there was the question of why they wanted to measure people at all. Of course, there are plenty of practical reasons for wishing to know, for example, the average heights and weights of a given community of people at given ages. But anthropometrists like Sullivan were after more fundamental insights. In their measurements, they wished to discover essential qualities about different "races" of people. They might, therefore, have stopped to ask why they thought that some essential idea of human character could be expressed in simple, linear numbers. They might even have dwelled on the reality of "race" in the first place. But they tended to be untroubled by these questions and rarely lost sleep over high-order problems such as these.

Once one believed that race was real and could be expressed in numbers, the next problem boiled down to which features of the human body were worth measuring, and on what grounds. Height and weight seemed obvious enough. Upon reflection, however, it was not entirely clear to discerning anthropologists that height and weight contain salient information about "race" or "type." The height and weight of individual human beings fluctuates—sometimes subtly, sometimes dramatically—over time. Could these possibly be considered stable features of different "races"? For that matter, more esoteric measurements like arm span, or distance between the eyes, or width of nose, or ratio between the length and width of the head might change less over time, but these qualities, too, presented problems. Why measure the space between eyes, but not between nostrils, or between ears? For that matter, why not measure the space between lip and nose, or between fingers on the left hand, or even between nose and knees?

In the view of anthropologists of the day, qualities such as skin color and hair color or texture further complicated the picture. Although in everyday American life, skin color tended to be the single most important determinant of race, when they were honest with themselves, anthropologists questioned whether skin color was really such a salient feature. After all, people of notionally different "races" often had very similarly colored skin and hair—and, rather like height and weight, skin color and hair color changed over time. What did this mean for the validity of color as a measure of race? For that matter, skin color also varied over the body of an individual. Where was the most representative spot to take measurements of skin color?

And then there were the practical problems: even when one did decide what aspects of the human body were worth measuring, the question became how, precisely, to go about it. When an anthropometrist decided to measure an arm, should the measurement be taken from the tip of the longest finger to the armpit—and if so, where did the armpit end and the torso begin? When measuring the space between eyes, did the anthropometrist proceed from the inside corner of one eye to the other? And if so, what to make of the fact that the corners of different people's eyes are subtly upturned or downturned? Slight morphological differences in people would skew any attempts to normalize measurements.

To overcome these problems, anthropometrists relied on professional consensus, strict discipline, and fine-tuned instruments. A "stature rod," for instance, would measure the height of subjects with precision. "Spreading calipers" could be used for measuring head length and head breadth. And "sliding calipers" came in handy for measuring nasal height and nasal width. As for measuring skin color, Sullivan favored a set of thirty-six small, opaque glass bricks developed by German anthropologist Felix von Luschan. Each brick measured roughly two by three centimeters and ranged in color from an almost chromatically white brick labeled number "1," to an almost chromatically black brick labeled number "36." The shades in between varied from pinkish white ("7"), to lemony yellow ("20"), to deep, cinnamon brown ("30"). By holding a tile from the scale next to a subject's skin, the anthropologist could assign a standardized numerical "grade" to the subject's skin color, and thereby group the skin colors of different notional races.

Gregory—a geologist by training and not well-versed in anthropology—had assigned inexperienced data collectors to Sullivan. "I wonder if Dr. Gregory would pump geology into a man for three days or a week and then send him out to do field work," groused Sullivan. "If these men are going to do the work it seems to me they should devote at least a couple of months to preparation for it." He later wrote to Gregory directly to complain that it seemed "very probable" that Gregory did not "appreciate the amount of detail involved in work of this kind."

Nor did it help that Aleš Hrdlička, a famously antagonistic anthropologist from the rival Smithsonian Institution, passed through Honolulu and openly mocked Sullivan's efforts. "Although he stayed only three days, he left his customary odour behind," Sullivan complained to Wissler, saying that Hrdlička had also critiqued the inexperience of Sullivan's team. Some weeks later, Sullivan came to see Hrdlička's point. "I am getting the reputation of being an out and out crab," he wrote, complaining about his undertrained coworkers.

Measuring, moreover, could be boring. "The work grows very monotonous," he wrote to Wissler. "Of course it is very interesting when I'm actually at it, but there is very little variety from day to day. I shall have earned an opportunity to rest from taking measurements for a while and to indulge in a little mental exercise in working up and digesting the data."

Fortunately for Sullivan, the female members of his anthropometry team worked better than his male assistants. Sullivan thought Mrs. Stokes was "undoubtedly the best student I've had. . . . She has worked and read and has a very intelligent grasp on the subject." Betsy Sullivan, likewise, proved to be a capable anthropometrist.

In addition to difficulties measuring people, dealing with living people could also be challenging. Sullivan found, for instance, that as much as he had to rely on regional sources of authority, his local informants could be unreliable. "Time and time again," he wrote to Wissler, "local authorities have told me if I wished to find the pure and primitive Hawaiians I should go to some out of the way and inaccessible place. In every case I have gone only to find Hawaiian Chinese crosses and Portuguese half-bloods who for the most part were born in Hilo or Honolulu." It's hard not to imagine that these "local authorities" were either pulling Sullivan's leg, or else that they themselves had little concern about or care for the idea of "primitive" people of Hawai'i and were just telling Sullivan what they thought he wanted to hear. As a result, Sullivan found himself undertaking trips by boat, motorcar, and horseback to tiny villages, only to realize that the demography of Hawai'i had changed over two hundred years. "The most and best types of Hawaiians are in Honolulu," he concluded, "strange as that may seem." People in Hawai'i in the 1920s were drawn to Honolulu by economic opportunities—but these very opportunities meant that few people wanted to spend hours getting measured when they could be getting paid.

To overcome these difficulties, Sullivan first relied on local authority figures to collect people into one spot for convenient measuring. At Kona, for instance, he retained the services of Thomas C. White, an agent of the Bishop Estate who knew the local leaders well. "Taking Mr. White with me proved a good investment," wrote Sullivan. "He is expert at pulling strings and everywhere we went the people were gathered at some central point where I was able to work rapidly and without loss of time." Typically, Sullivan would show up to these events with a dynamometer—a device for measuring grip strength—to keep the crowds amused while they waited to be measured. If anthropometry could be boring for Sullivan, that went double for his subjects.

Sullivan also devised a card for self-reporting, to be distributed to residents of Honolulu and beyond. The top of the card read: "Anthropological Census of Hawaii." Underneath, Sullivan provided lines for name, address, height in feet and inches, weight in pounds, reach in feet and inches, and head dimensions in length and width. True, Sullivan could not have expected much accuracy in the returns from the cards. But he could at least track down interested parties later. "Tell your relatives and friends about the anthropological census," the card exhorted in cheery type along its bottom. "Have your whole family measured and photographed. Special hours will be set apart by request for measuring family or social groups." Sullivan gave an address and phone number where people could reach him to make an appointment. On the card's back Sullivan listed comparative weights and measures of different people of the world—a way, as Wissler put it, to "stimulate interest in the subject as a whole." Sullivan did, indeed, find that the cards were effective—"I find that they arouse much interest in the work," he wrote.

Even when they could be assembled and made to cooperate, however, people knew about eugenic research and bore ambivalent feelings. When, in 1912, a group of "Ladies" in Līhu'e, the main port in Kaua'i, started a Eugenics Club, a citizen writing under the nom de plume "Ignoramens" asked the editors of the *Garden Island Newspaper* whether eugenics was a "kind of breakfast food, or some kind of contagious disease, or some kind of wild animal." In response, the ladies of the Eugenics Club replied that the writer was, indeed, an ignoramus, for, as they said, "any school boy could tell him that Eugenics is the science of improving things—especially human beings."

They did not exaggerate about the schoolboys. Eugenics was, indeed, taught in schools, as well as written about in newspapers, preached about in churches, and discussed in public lectures.

The Kamehameha School—where Duke and David had attended high school—was a particular source of eugenic enthusiasm. Uldrich Thompson, the school's principal from 1899 to 1914 and thereafter an influential member of the school community, was an avid eugenicist. In 1913 he penned a short book titled *Eugenics for Young People* that was distributed among Kamehameha School students. The book set out the principles of eugenics in language easy for a child to understand. Human "race mixing" obeyed laws like those of chemistry. Everybody had "good" and "bad" qualities, but it was up to individuals to reproduce with people who had good qualities that would accentuate their own good qualities. The book recommended other eugenic texts to curious students: Charles Davenport's *Eugenics* and David Starr Jordan's *The Blood of the Nation*. And it looked forward to a future in which "people who have . . . bad qualities will not be allowed to become fathers and mothers. In time, only the finest men and women will have children. And the weak, the cowardly, the dishonest, the foolish, the lazy and the diseased will die and disappear."

Thompson made sure to give eugenics a particularly Hawaiian flavor in his text, emphasizing the greatness of past Hawaiian "types." In a section addressed "to a remnant"—that is, the

Hawaiian student who was reading it—Thompson wrote that "the old time Hawaiians possessed many of the finest qualities mankind is heir to. . . . They were gigantic in stature and great in strength. How many men of today," he wondered, "could use their spears or their surfboards?" Unfortunately, most of the Hawaiian race had died off, he continued, and it was up to "young men and women of Hawaiian blood" to preserve those "noble and necessary qualities" that were still "in their blood." Thompson closed on a note of hope and of warning. "It remains for this remnant of a people to learn how best to keep and how best to transmit to their children the qualities that they are proud to say their ancestors possessed. And they must learn these things and act upon this knowledge"—that is, knowledge of eugenics—"before it is everlastingly too late."

Thompson's advocacy of eugenics was well known and even led to a brief but inflammatory push in 1913 for "social hygiene" legislation in the Hawaiian congress. Bill 181, as proposed by Dr. Archer Irwin, allowed for the sterilization of criminals and the mentally ill and required physical examinations of all men before marriage. The bill was widely regarded as a "joke"—albeit one that caused heated debate in the territorial government. For one thing, territorial representative William Coney noted, if a man had "manhood enough" to marry, then he should be "man enough" to make up his own mind about marriage, without a scientist telling him what to do. Irwin shot back that if Coney "thought the average man was man enough, then he had another guess coming." An even more serious objection arose around the examination of women, which seemed indecently intrusive if not outright dishonorable. The bill was tabled after being widely and publicly pilloried.

For this reason, Sullivan's mission was not mysterious to many of his interlocutors. Anthropologists poked and prodded physically, and when they were done with that, they poked and prodded into one's family history. In a subsequent manual for would-be anthropometrists, Sullivan advised his readers that, when taking measurements and family histories, it was necessary to "never embarrass the subject more than is absolutely necessary." "Continued success," he wrote, "will follow only an impersonal, kindly, and considerate attitude toward the subjects examined." The fact that this had to be written in a manual suggests something of the character of anthropometric study in the 1920s.

To top it off, anthropologists also had a deservedly bad reputation for stealing people's bones. This was a serious subject anywhere, but in Hawai'i, people's bones had special importance, as they were traditionally seen as repositories of great mana, strong life force. This was why, when an *ali'i* died, his or her body was cooked in an underground oven to strip away the flesh and preserve the bones. These bones would later be interred, often in a secret location to avoid their being stolen.

Sullivan had cut his teeth, as it were, on osteology and was enthusiastic about getting his hands on Hawaiian bones. (Indeed, when he first went to work at the American Museum he confessed he had "little or no experience on the living.") Shortly after arriving in Hawai'i, he was happy to report to Osborn and Wissler that, on Kaua'i, he and his assistants had absconded with "30 crania and considerable miscellaneous skeletal material." Wissler cautioned him in return that "any news from us as to skeleton materials should not get into the papers. The Hawaiians are ticklish on that point." Wissler reiterated this warning in a subsequent letter to an official at the American Museum, writing that "a controversy has arisen over some skeletons removed from another island by other persons, so no news concerning that phase of the work should be given out. So long as nothing is said about graves, skulls, or skeletons no harm will be done. The papers [in Hawai'i] are rather keen on such subjects."

Sullivan nervously watched the progress of another social scientist from the mainland—a psychologist named Ernest Bryant Hoag—whose work became, as Sullivan put it, the "butt of local politics." After surveying the islands, Hoag had criticized the morality and efficiency of Hawaiian government institutions, drawing attention to child labor in canneries and poor facilities in industrial schools and juvenile detention centers. He had also excoriated the ineffectiveness of public health officials in combating syphilis among the youth of Hawai'i. The result was a picture of eugenic degeneration and moral decay at the hands of feckless officials.

Hoag's report caused a firestorm, not simply because of what Hoag said, but because he was perceived as an outsider and an "expert" poking his nose into matters of which he knew nothing. Of course, nobody could object to honest criticism, fumed an editorial in the *Hawaii Herald*. But "we cannot believe that [scientists] have acquired a power of such influence that [they] can look into a child's brain, or heart, or more difficult still, its mind, and tell what, how, and why the wheels go round." Such "mental experts," continued the *Herald*, "rush into a state or territory and after riding over the country in a railway carriage, or in an automobile for days" make sweeping pronouncements on the nature of the people they had studied. "To what pitiful depths we have fallen," lamented the editorial with bitter sarcasm, "that we must depend [on experts] for knowledge of the character of our community life."

Sullivan—who himself had made a habit of rushing into villages for a day or two to measure people with whom he had almost no experience—viewed Hoag's case with some alarm. Hoag, he wrote to Wissler, had "made some pretty bad breaks here on his first arrival and it will take him a good time to live them down. He took the attitude that this was a God-forsaken hole and that the [people] were a bunch of incompetents. . . . Naturally they resented this attitude." When Sullivan contemplated his own interest in the racial testing of children, he wrote to Wissler that when talking to school officials they had better pretend to be mainly concerned with educational goals. "If the real motive . . . is to discover possible racial differences," he decided, "this motive must be heavily cloaked." That is, if it was possible to pretend that anthropometry—including the measurement of psychological attributes—was strictly for the purposes of figuring out better pedagogical techniques, Sullivan thought that might be the prudent course of action, rather than drawing attention to the fact that theirs was a study of race differences.

For all of his apprehension and (sometimes) outright dissembling, it does seem like Sullivan's repeated contact with Hawaiian people began to change his approach to his subjects. This change is particularly evident in his photographs.

In his research for Boas, Sullivan's photographs were antiseptic—clinical to the point of being unpleasant. In each black-and-white photo, a person—usually male—stands against a gray background. The figures are, for the most part, naked, though some are clothed. One man seems incongruously dandyish. On the whole, the naked figures are cropped just below the waistline, but some stand fully nude. Sometimes the figures scowl, looking directly into the lens. Sometimes they look away, averting their eyes toward the ceiling or off to one side. One man folds his arms protectively over his bare torso, but most keep their arms limply at their sides. In the low-contrast exposure, the skin of the subjects merges with the gray background. Each photograph bears the label of the person's ethnicity. One man is "Austrian-Spanish," another is "Hungarian Jew." The people in these photos are made to seem as much like objects as possible.

Sullivan had been assisted in this work by Soichi Ichikawa, an exhibitions expert in the anthropology department. A polymathic museum worker, Ichikawa was skilled in photography, plaster work, sculpture, and anthropometry. His work on restoring an Aztec Sun Wheel would win him a mention in the *New York Times* in 1925. At the museum, Sullivan relied totally on Ichikawa to take photographs for him. At one point he worked so consistently with Ichikawa that he felt the need to apologize to his peers for "monopolizing" the more experienced museum man.

Now, however, Sullivan was on his own and had to figure out how to make the pictures work, often in remote spots far away from the controlled environment that he was used to. Osborn had written to him in an admonitory tone, saying, "I trust that . . . you will find a way of securing the photographs that you need *au naturel*, for it is extremely important to secure these for your series." It was hard work. Sullivan had purchased a new, top-of-the-line Graflex camera before he left New York, but couldn't get it to work. "I am still hopelessly amateur," he wrote to Wissler. Photography took a lot of time. At first, having to photograph people at their houses—or "au naturel" as Osborn had put it—was challenging to Sullivan. He favored the "old fashioned" method of simply putting a subject in front of a dark cloth and snapping a picture, and some of the early shots show an effort to emulate Ichikawa's pictures with a piece of canvas draped over a line.

Gradually, however, Sullivan's photographs loosened up. It might have helped that all of the people in the photos were clothed, seemingly dressed how they had chosen. In one, a uniformed police officer draws himself up to height and puffs out his chest. In another, a plantation worker peeks out from under a straw hat, squinting slightly in the sun. Sullivan was sure to get a picture of a fisherman for Osborn. The man he chose was middle-aged, slight, and bearded. Bare chested, he holds a net loosely in his hands, and his cutoff work pants expose his bare ankles.

Before Sullivan departed from New York for his study, Osborn had warned him that people of Hawai'i were "said to be sensitive to photography"—that is, they didn't like having their pictures taken. This was incorrect. In fact, people seemed to love being photographed. Among the many photography studios in downtown Honolulu, A. R. Gurrey—best known for taking some of the first photographs of Duke and David surfing—had a sideline in anthropological photography, selling aesthetically pleasing photos of different Hawaiian "types" to tourists. Duke even displayed his medals in the window of Gurrey's studio when he arrived back from the Olympics, so public appreciation of Duke's athleticism went hand in hand with the public appreciation of a kind of anthropological photography.

Sullivan's photographic subjects interacted with the camera, and with Sullivan, making each picture a tiny portrait of a moment, rather than a timeless and clinical document. One man cocks his head quizzically and smiles slightly. A soldier assumes a proud and stern face. A grandmother dandles a laughing child on her knee. A couple stand side by side, the bearded man gazing at his wife's shoulder. In one photo, an elderly man presents a small flower to his wife.

It is not clear, of course, that Sullivan the anthropometrist appreciated these subtleties. For Sullivan, photography was useful mainly because it recorded "descriptive characters" that distinguished notional races. Descriptive characters, as Sullivan later wrote, were "characters that were not readily measurable," like hair texture and distribution, or the shape of people's eyes and lips, or the size of and shape of their teeth or face. Whereas a "stature rod" could capture a subject's height—and, as Sullivan noted, "150 centimeters means the same the world over"—descriptive characters were essentially arbitrary and required careful study to discern. The hundreds of pictures he had taken, Sullivan wrote, were "giving me an opportunity to get a real knowledge of the race characters of the Chinese, Japanese, Koreans, Filipinos, Portuguese and Whites, as well as the various Hawaiian mixtures."

Race scientists examined such photos to correlate physical form and mental tendencies. For instance, before he had even articulated the principles of eugenics, in 1877 Francis Galton had composited a number of photographs of criminals into one (blurry) picture in order to identify the facial features of the "criminal type"—in other words, to establish which kinds of nose shape, eye width, etc., would betray a tendency in people toward crime. The implication was that by preemptively identifying criminals, society could take steps to stop them. The same search for "descriptive characters" could likewise apply to the search for features that indicated mental illness, or genius, or piety, or a host of other mental traits. Once these traits were "discovered," eugenicists fantasized that those who possessed them could be shunted into institutions—schools, occupations, asylums—that would ameliorate their shortcomings or elevate whatever "characteristic" talents they had.

This was a narrow and simplistic way of thinking about humans, but the study of "characters" was not a fringe endeavor, on the outskirts of true science. In 1918, for example, E. B. Titchener—perhaps the most celebrated psychologist in early twentieth-century America—wrote to Sullivan to ask for "full length part nude photos of men and women for some psychological study." That Titchener didn't specify what he hoped to find in the photos—and the fact that Sullivan didn't question the assumption that nude photos might shed light on the psychologies of living people—suggests how little critical thinking many researchers gave to the study of "characters."

What was really at stake to these eugenicists was more than just a general correlation between people's exterior appearances and their inner lives. It was the question of whether particular groups—to say nothing of "mixes" of people—had the mental fortitude to participate in American society.

Sullivan saw Hawai'i as an ideal place to conduct such research. "I can't imagine a better place to compare races mentally," he wrote to Wissler. "The correlation or non-correlation of physical and mental traits has been booted around for a century with the evidence 50-50 either way." Now, with a "natural laboratory" full of people of diverse backgrounds in every combination, Sullivan thought, "we have an opportunity to make comparisons which will be of general interest to psychologists and anthropologists." The question, he concluded, "is an important one."

Of all the mental characteristics that interested eugenicists, intelligence was the most central. But here was where even the best anthropometry fell down. Whereas a measurement like "150 centimeters" is the same at different places and at different times, measurements of "intelligence" are, inevitably, simply tests of a subject's ability to comprehend what's important in a particular context, to a particular group of people—like psychologists. Behavior that is "intelligent" in one setting might be profoundly unintelligent in another. The skill sets that mark a person—or a group—as intelligent are as much a matter of learned behaviors as genetic inheritance.

Early twentieth-century intelligence tests tended to overlook this problem and blithely evaluate test-takers' literacy and cultural knowledge rather than any sort of biologically innate mental powers. For example, one of the most common intelligence tests of the early twentieth century—psychologist Robert Yerkes's "Army Alpha" test, which evaluated recruits during World War I—contained items like:

Circle the correct answer:

- The **Orpington** is a kind of
  fowl   horse   granite   cattle

- The most prominent industry of **Minneapolis** is
  flour   packing   automobiles   brewing

and

- Unscramble the sentence, and say whether it is true or false

  happiness   source   of   always   a   crime   is

  money   marry   always   for   men

Clearly this was a test that could only be successfully completed by those who knew how to read English and were conversant in American cultural knowledge and values. Yerkes subsequently released an "Army Beta" version of the test to address literacy concerns. But "Beta's" cultural assumptions about what constituted "intelligence" were little better than its predecessor's. In one section of the test, for example, examinees were asked to correct the errors in a series of pictures. See if you can spot what's missing in the following pictures (this writer could not):

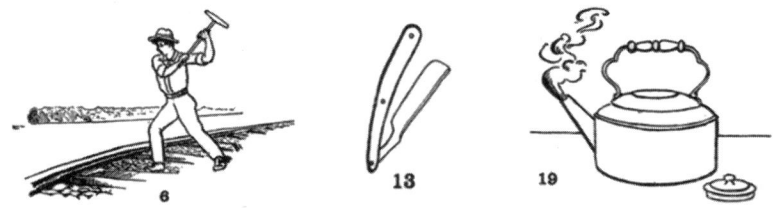

Tests like these appeared to show serious, systematic mental deficiencies in immigrants and nonwhite people throughout the United States. While some commentators called "foul" and pointed out that the tests didn't really indicate *general* "intelligence" as much as *specific* experience at being an American in the 1920s, eugenicists in particular latched onto the results of the tests as grist for their conviction that nonwhite people and immigrants were inherently unsuited for American civic life.

In Hawai'i, Sullivan's subjects recognized the arbitrary nature of intelligence tests and complained about the biases in psychological surveys such as those Hoag administered. "There are many things that are not fair to people whose experience has been confined to Hawaii," Sullivan wrote to Wissler. For example, Sullivan explained, in the tests given to the Hawaiian children, "a picture is given of a boy without a neck-tie and the problem is to find what is wrong. In a school of 1000 children here, there are 3 neckties; so of course there's nothing wrong with him from their point of view. Another set has a boy with a stocking for a necktie and no one saw anything wrong with that. To them, if they noticed it, it was merely a new style. Then there was a Ford Car with Pierce Arrow headlights. That is entirely proper here. Another question was how many brothers have you and name them. If they included themselves the answer was incorrect. As a matter of fact it seems to be a localism here to include oneself. The question seems to be interpreted in the sense of how many boys are there in the family. The principals pointed out ten or a dozen more but I have forgotten them."

As with Osborn's identification of the "fisherman type" and "Chieftain type," intelligence tests conflated cultural qualities with innate, genetic constitutions. This did not necessarily disqualify them, in Sullivan's view, and he wrote to Wissler pleading for extra money to try out a new battery of psychological tests that, he felt, would overcome previous problems. "However imperfect these tests may be," he wrote, "they are admitted by all to be a rough test of mentality, just as my own tests are rough indices of physical development. . . . Since the [new] tests have been devised no one has attempted to correlate the results with physical data." To do so would be "a new stunt," he felt.

Nevertheless, Wissler replied, the "techniques applicable to such a problem" needed to be further refined before the museum could spend money on the effort, and he turned down Sullivan's request. Years later, Sullivan had to admit that "we are not yet in a position to recommend definite tests for primitive people."

• • •

The final and most important part of Sullivan's research was "collecting" plaster casts of people's heads. Wissler had emphasized to him that this was a vital part of his mission. "We need as many casts as possible and at least two figures," Wissler wrote, "maybe more." Wissler later applied significant pressure, reminding Sullivan that "President Osborn is rather anxious to have some casts and photographs of race mixture[s] exhibited" in the Eugenics Congress. To accomplish this, Wissler emphasized, Osborn had set aside $1,000 of the expedition budget—roughly $15,000 in 2025—for facial casts.

From a scientific perspective, casting was important because it captured the very essence of a person in minute detail. As one writer put it, "the value of a plaster cast, as a portrait of the dead or living face[,] cannot for a moment be questioned. It must of a necessity be absolutely true to nature. It cannot flatter; it cannot caricature. It shows the subject as he was, not only as others saw him in the actual flesh, *but as he saw himself.*" Casting, that is, revealed the deepest, most interior truth of a person. In a counterintuitive way, the writer explained, a plaster "mask" created by casting a person's face revealed—as though by magic—the person "with his mask off!"

Done properly, a plaster cast picks up the most minute details. Wrinkles around the eyes and ears, pores on the nose and cheeks, the smallest scars, the development of subcutaneous muscles. For eugenicists, a wide, flat cheekbone, for instance, would indicate that one's family—one's type, one's race—was descended from Cro-Magnons (the Irish were a good example of this). A slightly beetled brow might indicate a descent from Neanderthals. It was even possible to tell—based on casts, measurements, and photographs—precisely what "racial composition" a people possessed. As a news article about Sullivan's research put it, "bodily, facial and cranial characteristics of the Polynesian show that he is eleven parts Mongoloid, five parts European, five parts Mongoloid-European, and two parts Mongoloid-Melanesian." A cast, in other words, served a similar purpose in the 1920s as popular genealogical DNA testing does in the 2020s. Casts were, in many ways, the premier genetic technology of their era. They were a way of understanding the past, present, and future of an individual and a "race" alike.

From the perspective of museum exhibits, casts crucially conveyed the subjects of natural history in a lifelike, compelling way. As the American Museum's director Frederick Lucas remarked, it was easy enough to illustrate scientific ideas with a photograph, or drawing—or, for that matter, a chart or graph. But, he continued, "a museum of pictures would be monotonous and lifeless—most literally flat, stale, and unprofitable; we need three dimensions to give a feeling of reality." Just so, it wouldn't be enough for Sullivan to simply display charts of his measurements or prints of the people he had photographed. From Osborn's perspective, Sullivan needed to secure casts to make his exhibit a success and thereby transform the American Museum into the center of worldwide eugenics—and therefore into an organ for saving the world.

The cranky but conscientious Hrdlička described the basic process of facial casting in his 1904 manual, *Directions for Collecting Information and Specimens for Physical Anthropology*. First, seat the subject in a comfortable chair with adequate back and head support. The anthropologist should then sweep the subject's hair back from their face and fasten it in place with a cloth, leaving a bit of hair exposed just around the hairline. Another piece of light cloth would be positioned around the subject's neck to capture any plaster that might fall. The anthropologist should stuff the subject's ears with cotton, though the nostrils should be left open. "No nasal tubes are required," Hrdlička advised. Lubricate the subject's face—gently spreading a thin layer of oil over their skin "by means of a camel-hair brush"—and rub thick soap (or lard) into the thin band of hair still visible at the hairline, as well as their eyebrows and any other exposed facial hair.

Using a spoon or a spatula, the anthropologist would then spread a layer of fine plaster over the subject's face, starting with the forehead, moving to the area around the eyes, then down to the cheekbones. "The upper part of the face being covered," wrote Hrdlička, "advance rapidly to the ears and lower part of the face. At this stage," Hrdlička continued, "it is of advantage to throw the plaster on, with short, gentle jerks, with the fingers." Depending on how much of a cast the anthropologist desired, they might also cast portions of the subject's neck. Finally, it was time to apply a coat to the entire face, including the eyes and mouth. This had to be done gently, to avoid putting pressure on the eyes and lips and thereby distorting the cast as well as for the comfort of the subject. It was important to leave room around the nostrils for the subject to breathe, and it was especially important not to get any plaster in the subject's eyes, "where it would produce severe burning."

Once they had encased the entire front of the subject's face and neck in a layer of plaster about half an inch thick, the anthropologist had to support the subject's head with their hands while the plaster dried. After about fifteen minutes, when the plaster had set sufficiently, the anthropologist would gently wiggle the subject free, starting from their ears and slowly, carefully, working the plaster mask away from their face, starting with their forehead, and working downward to the chin and neck.

The result would be an exact negative of the subject's face. The mold could simply be kept as it was and filed away for later use, like the thousands of other specimens in a natural history collection. Or it could be lightly oiled and filled with plaster again to make a positive sculpture of the subject's face. Covered with a layer of shellac for preservation purposes, the positive was ready to be used in anthropometric study. If the cast was to be displayed in a museum, it might undergo further modification. The cast might, for example, be altered by a skilled artist, who would sculpt the model so that its eyes appeared open. The artist might also lightly touch up the neck area, or give more definition to features like hair and eyebrows, which would have been matted down by grease. This new face would then be re-cast and a new positive made. For maximally vivid effect, the eyes could be painted and then covered with glossy varnish to make them shine, and exhibitors might apply a coat of flesh-colored paint and "another coat of substance designed to simulate the skin effect."

Hrdlička emphasized that the casting process required a steady and experienced hand. The proper consistency of plaster, for instance, was difficult to describe—it "must be learned from practice." The same went for knowing when the cast was ready to come off: "The proper hardness of the cast is learned through experience; it can be ascertained by tapping on it with a finger or some object."

What Hrdlička did not mention—but Sullivan well understood—was that casting was an arduous process. "It is hard on a living subject," Sullivan wrote. Swallowing, coughing, sneezing, spitting, and twitching of every kind were forbidden while the plaster was being applied. As the mold dried, the experience could be claustrophobic and uncomfortable. Sounds came to the subject through the plaster helmet, weird and muffled. Wet plaster threatened at any moment to work its way into the sitter's nostrils or under their eyelids. Moreover, the chemical reaction that made plaster harden gave off heat. While Hrdlička was of the opinion that the plaster would never get so warm as to injure a subject, other sources cautioned that "it is important that the hardened plaster be removed before it becomes too hot." In all cases, though, "the ordeal through which the subjects had to go," as one report put it, "was somewhat severe." As a result, finding people to sit for a mask was "time consuming and discouraging work," Sullivan told Gregory.

Making matters worse, the man that Gregory had assigned to assist Sullivan, John W. Thompson, was not up to the task of casting humans. Thompson had proved himself a capable "artist and modeler" earlier in the century, producing a celebrated series of plaster casts of fish for the museum. These fish had "received the emphatic approval of the gentlemen of the United States Fish commission," as the Bishop Museum's report from 1901 proudly stated, and the report's author doubted "if so good representations of fish can be found in any museum." Casting dead fish was different from casting live people, however. "Thompson fell down on the bust making proposition," Sullivan complained to Wissler. "He can't model human figures. The busts he turns out look worse than that of a child's." Thompson, Sullivan concluded, was "not an artist. He can just copy and neglects anatomy altogether. His necks look like table legs. I'm much disappointed."

In his despair, Sullivan made some desultory casts at Kona and on Maui, but he didn't know how to turn the negatives into positives. Sullivan had requested that Ichikawa accompany him to Hawaiʻi, but a family crisis had intervened, and Ichikawa returned to Japan before Sullivan left New York. Now, growing anti-Japanese sentiment in the United States as well as an economic crisis in Japan had stalled Ichikawa indefinitely. In a state of slight panic, Sullivan began making plans simply to ship the plaster molds back to New York to be finished at the American Museum. "I miss Ichikawa," he moaned to Wissler.

Fortunately for Sullivan, the infrastructures of American territorial governance once again intervened. In May 1921, Sullivan secured the services of Gordon Usborn, a local sculptor and head of the new design school in Honolulu. Usborn intended the school to teach proper artistic taste to a rising generation of students in Hawaiʻi, and he celebrated a scientific approach to art and education. More importantly to Sullivan, Usborn was a "first class man from a museum point of view." He wrote to Wissler that Usborn could do "a bust in no time at all. He has a great sense of values. . . . If things run smoothly, I shall be able to bring back about forty busts and one or two full figures."

To find subjects for sculpting, Sullivan again leaned on the connections that he had made in conducting measurements and photography. The principal of the Kamehameha School for Boys, Earl G. Bartlett, turned over his more-or-less captive population of teenaged cadets to Sullivan, and one "Miss Nelson," director of the Kamehameha School for Girls, did likewise with her students. Both schools were conveniently located on the Bishop Museum grounds.

Sullivan and Usborn, assisted by Thompson, worked quickly, slathering their subjects in plaster. Within a little under two weeks, they had taken forty casts of students. A reporter examining the proceedings noted that "each subject is represented . . . exactly according to his or her individual facial and cranial lines." Usborn dexterously opened the eyes of the casts and carefully corrected the small eccentricities introduced by bubbles in the plaster. He sculpted missing portions of the necks and accentuated the hair and eyebrows.

The resulting busts are haunting—cold, white faces, lifelike but not alive, evocative of individuals, but representative of "types." Sullivan was very happy. On lined paper, in careful script, he assigned each cast a number, noted the subject's name, and jotted down their racial "type." Cast number 9, for instance, belonged to James Apo: male, "Haw[aiian] 1/4, White 1/4, Chi[nese] 1/2." Number 7 was Elizabeth Kamai, female, simply "Hawaiian." Number 43 in the ledger—a man identified as "Lydgate"—was "American," though the ledger qualified that he was "Haw[aiian] born." Still others were anonymous, unidentified but for a number, and sex, and their notional "type"—and, of course, their image, rendered in plaster.

More remarkable than what they captured, however, was what the casts left out.

Take cast number 11—a boy named Charles Kahaunaele. As with many of his classmates—and, indeed, many beach boys—he was, according to an article in the *Honolulu Star-Bulletin*, a musician and an athlete, performing in the orchestra during the Kamehameha School's musicals, and playing basketball and football. On the gridiron, he was an excellent defenseman, with a "wide but deceptive grin" that "belies the swift, fierce plunging that has come to characterize his play." As a musician, he was considered to be one of the best in the school. Shortly before Sullivan cast his face, Charles had a different encounter with anthropology, after a fashion, when he found a human skeleton while hiking on Mount Tantalus, just outside of Honolulu. He and a few other boys had left the trail to gather maile—a kind of flowering vine used to make lei—and stumbled on the bones. They discovered a small, .25 Colt pistol close by. From fragments of clothes, the boys determined that the skeleton had belonged to a man, and from a book with Japanese writing in it that was next to the body, the boys figured that the skeleton had belonged to a Japanese person. The book, as a newspaper later noted, was determined by Kamehameha School authorities to be a "pessimistic work of philosophy." The man had disappeared some three years previously and had presumably committed suicide.

The lives of other people whose faces were preserved in these castings likewise provide a similar cross section of life on the Islands. James Apo, cast number 9, was friends with Charles. The two played football together at Kamehameha, and James helped build the sets for the musicals that Charles played in. James was a literal Boy Scout and reported on his scout troop's goings-on for the *Honolulu Star-Bulletin*. His earnest dispatches describe hikes and marches and games, after which the Boy Scouts invariably ate ice cream. He was, by all accounts, an excellent marksman, and shortly after having his face cast, he joined the ROTC. Esther Keawekane, Elizabeth Kamai, and Naomi Palama were all about to graduate Kamehameha School for Girls when Sullivan cast them. The three participated in the same plays, did glee club together, and planned to become teachers after they graduated. Elizabeth was a particularly prolific performer, having taken a star turn as a "beautiful and dignified queen" in a play that she wrote about "Indians." Edward Ah Choy was a marksman and baseball player. His great speed earned him fleeting fame when, during a charity "Prosperity Fete," he earned the distinction of catching a greased pig that had eluded other runners.

Such life details had little meaning, however, in eugenics, where the "mix" of one's parentage was of singular concern, and where "race" defined social potential, affinities, and sense of belonging.

Ironically enough, Sullivan's own, much-missed Ichikawa made a similar point from Japan. Writing to inform Sullivan that he couldn't join Sullivan's group in Hawaiʻi, Ichikawa vented his frustrations first with his own home country and then with anthropometry.

His time in America, Ichikawa said, had made him unfit for Japanese life. Regardless of his supposed "race," he wrote, "I am regular black hair yellow skin Yankee and no more suitable to this so called flowery kingdom. The porterhouse steak with mushroom sauce, apple pie and coffee is mine. No chop-suey, no rice dinner for me." He was as "American" as Sullivan, he insisted, even if his anthropometric characteristics said otherwise. His "race" was as much a matter of "taste"—of aesthetics—as any sort of physical characteristics.

At the same time as an erroneous, biological definition of "race" obscured his authentic self, Ichikawa continued, the idea of race also tended to lull largely white anthropologists into a false sense of objective superiority. Ichikawa asked what

Sullivan thought of a new spate of "anti Japanese agitation" in California—referring to anti-Japanese labor demonstrations that were, in the 1920s, sweeping the West Coast. "We are talking about war here," Ichikawa wrote. "Be careful Mr. Sullivan. We may capture you before long, and put you in our Tokio [*sic*] Museum." He then closed with a cheery "I hope you are well and have great success."

Ichikawa meant his remarks as good-natured needling, but it was needling with a strong underlying message. Anthropologists tended to assume that they did their work from a perspective of unimpeachable objectivity. It was they alone (they thought) who had the scientific knowledge and trained objectivity to define others: to tell other people who they were, and what their behaviors, their stories, their traditions meant. On the contrary, however, Ichikawa suggested that the role of anthropologist and anthropological subject might easily be reversed. Seen in this light, Sullivan's casts were not so much a record of an objective, scientific conception of "race" but a snapshot of hierarchies in a volatile system of national and international politics.

By and large, however, people tended to accept the scientific objectivity and significance of Sullivan's casting project. Newspapers of the time praised Sullivan's casts as, in the words of one reporter, "one of the most important contemporary contributions to the science of eugenics and the study of racial characteristics." One of his major conclusions, Sullivan said, was that "the individual of Hawaiian blood mingled with that of one or more of the racial strains that flourish here . . . is an efficient, progressive citizen, morally excellent of body and brain and thoroughly capable of assuming any place in the world for which he is willing to fit himself." Sullivan's conclusions, the reporter emphasized, "may be regarded by anthropologists everywhere as authoritative."

This was a more rosy pronouncement than many of those by eugenicists, but it might have made the reporter wonder what about casting—or photographing, or measuring—could lead to that conclusion. More precisely, what was it about Sullivan's vague statement that made it "scientific" at all?

• • •

With Sullivan's collection of casts complete, there was only one more task to be carried out by the team: securing the most prized "catch" of all—the full-body cast of Duke Kahanamoku. Osborn had been explicit about this part of Sullivan's mission. When Sullivan arrived in Honolulu, Osborn's first letter to him closed with the injunction: "do not fail to make the acquaintance of Duke, the swimmer." Sullivan was to measure him and cast him after "ascertaining if you can, without giving offense, whether he is full blooded."

As with the other aspects of Sullivan's mission, this was harder to do than Osborn's letter suggested.

Sullivan was optimistic about the prospect of casting Duke and envisioned grand plans for the cast's eventual display. "I have talked with Mr. Osborn casually about making a diorama for the Polynesian hall of the museum," he wrote to Wissler, imagining a scene of plaster figures performing "typical" Hawaiian activities for the American Museum's audiences. "The thing that appeals to me is a good group of surf board riders of about four or five figures. Mr. Usborn would make a complete group already to put in a 12 x 12 case including a background for about

$1500. He would submit a wax model for approval. For about $2500 he would make a group suitable for the tower hall of that floor. It seems to me such an exhibit would be attractive and display the physique of Polynesians to good advantage." Given Osborn's fascination with surfing, Sullivan was "sure that President Osborn would take kindly to such a proposition."

Sullivan himself does not seem to have shown much interest in surfing, though others readily made the connection between surfing, physical beauty, and eugenics. In an article titled "Beach Apollos: The Eugenics of Surfing," a journalist postulated that surfing and other beach activities gave men a more developed chest, stronger lungs, and better functioning kidneys—all of which were exemplified by the glowing skin of surfers. "Nearly all swimmers have soft, silky, elastic skins with few blemishes," the author wrote. As a result, this made them a "woman's instinctive choice." Surfing made men excellent, in other words, and excellent men made for excellent genetic "stock," which women readily recognized. Duke and David—variously described as godlike, and perfect specimens of manhood—were ideal eugenic models.

Like many of the Honoluluans that Sullivan met, Duke was a busy man. The life of a beach boy involved constant hustle. Even as a world-renowned athlete, Duke still struggled to make a living. Between his return from Stockholm and his fight with the *Pacific Commercial Advertiser*, he occupied his days teaching surfing and swimming. He made extra money as a clerk in the Hawai'i territorial statehouse. The governor of Hawai'i, Charles James McCarthy, proposed making Duke the "official greeter" for Hawai'i—a salaried government position that involved Duke gladhanding dignitaries when the big ocean liners came in. Duke did this anyway, but an income from this de facto public relations job would ease some of Duke's financial worries. By the summer of 1920, the position seemed like a done deal, but the governor had not yet made it official. To add to Duke's day-to-day stresses, his libel case was slowly wending its way through Hawai'i's courts.

During this time, Duke was also training hard for the 1920 Olympics in Antwerp. The *Pacific Commercial Advertiser*'s wrathful editorial aside, he did swim in countless races and qualifiers, and then—on May 25, 1920, while Sullivan was still cleaning bones in the basement of the Bishop Museum—he hopped on the ocean liner *Wilhelmina* to San Francisco where Olympic qualifiers were being held. He made the Olympic team—a feat in itself for a man of thirty—and beat his own world record at the 100 in the semifinals at Antwerp. He then went from the Olympics to exhibition matches in Paris where he broke another record. By November 7, 1920, he made it back to Honolulu.

Beyond his busy schedule, however—and the fact that he was out of Hawai'i for much of the time that Sullivan might have cast him—it also seems clear that Duke had little interest in anthropometry. Seeking to apprehend Duke, Osborn sent a memo to his museum director in New York, George Sherwood, instructing him to "invite Duke Kahanamoku, the famous Hawaiian swimmer, to visit the Museum on his return from Antwerp. He will make as fine a model as we could secure of the chieftain type, and I would like to arrange, if practicable, to obtain measurements and photographs." In a somewhat defensive mode, Osborn cautioned, "he promised me to make this visit, but unless there is a special invitation sent to him, he may slip through without our seeing him." Duke did, indeed, slip through New York without visiting the museum, though he participated in a parade with other returning Olympic athletes, during which the mayor of New York mispronounced his name.

For months, Sullivan and Usborn worked diligently on their face casts, all the while trying to get Duke into the studio. Ultimately, it took the intervention of Hawaiian Governor McCarthy, who, according to one newspaper report, impressed on both Duke and David "the great assistance which they could render to science through the perpetuation of their physical measurements as type specimens of the Hawaiian race." A sculpture of Duke would "constitute as fine an example of the best type of Hawaiian physical specimen as can be found anywhere, and that it will prove of great value from a scientific as well as an artistic point of view." Given that "the Kahanamoku boys" acceded to the governor's request to pose for Sullivan on the same day that Duke's job as an official greeter went into effect, it seems possible that the governor also reminded Duke that he was owed a favor in return. In any event, as the newspaper put it, "both agreed to submit to the operation."

On July 11, 1921, David showed up at Usborn's studio in the Bishop Museum. He was alone, unaccompanied by his brother. This itself was not unusual. Since Duke had risen to fame as a swimmer, David had assumed a backup role for his brother. When Duke was out of town, it was David who entertained visiting celebrities and showed them how to surf and swim. He was also an accomplished canoeist, and, in 1921, had become head of the Waikiki Lifeguards. Nevertheless, as David's son later explained, by Hawaiian custom, the siblings all threw their support behind the oldest son. David didn't resent this, and so when the time finally came to submit to being cast in plaster, it was natural that David should go first.

Sullivan and Osborn got right to work. They ordered David to strip down to a pair of tiny swim trunks and began posing him like an oversized doll. He was to play the role of the "fisherman type," they decided. The statue of Duke would show Duke as a surfer, with surf behind him. Sullivan and Usborn positioned David with his arm raised as though about to spear a fish. His head tilted slightly forward, as though looking intently into the water, and he tensed his legs.

In his instructions to anthropometrists, Hrdlička explicitly warned that "casts of the body should never be undertaken except by one well practiced in the art, for the operation is not without danger to the subject." When the famous fin de siècle bodybuilder, Eugen Sandow, posed for a full body plaster cast in 1901, he experienced the danger firsthand. "They tell me that only one man in two hundred can stand having his face done," he recalled, "and I'm not a bit surprised. But if that is the case I don't believe that one in a million could be found who could stand to have his chest done." The operation, Sandow said, was simply too painful. "What with the peculiar 'biting' feeling of the plaster as it dried on the skin, and the difficulty in regulating the breathing, I thought I should burst." Having a full-body cast done was the hardest thing Sandow had ever done in a life of strenuous exertion, he thought.

Sullivan and Usborn were not, suffice to say, well practiced in the art of full-body casting. Nevertheless, they gave it a try. First, they marked out the spots on the floor where David's feet were, to aid in repositioning him, should he move during the process. Then, they suspended a pole from the ceiling with some rope so that he could hold on to it with his upraised arm. Then they mixed a batch of plaster and got to work. Moving quickly, Sullivan and Usborn covered his legs and chest and parts of his arms with a layer of plaster. They applied a line of linen thread along his legs where they wanted the cast to break off. When the plaster hardened just slightly, they would draw the thread out and it would cut the plaster for mold making. Then: more plaster, up David's legs, his abdomen, his chest, his neck.

As the plaster hardened, Sullivan and Usborn told David not to move lest he crack the mold. Then they departed for a lunch break.

David was at first surprised. Then he began to get nervous. Just as Sandow had described, the plaster squeezed his chest, making it difficult to breathe. He resolved that this wasn't simply a casting session—it was a fight for his life. Taking short, gasping breaths, he tried to expand his rib cage subtly, giving himself enough room to breathe without disturbing the form of the cast—and necessitating another session. When he accomplished this, he focused on keeping his arm aloft—a difficult task under any circumstance, let alone with plaster hardening around his chest. The strain was awful.

Finally, Sullivan and Usborn returned. They broke David out of the mold, and he was able to relax for a moment before the casting began again: his arms, then his hands, and then, finally, his face and head. David had stuck to his end of the agreement, and after an arduous day, he was free to go. But he vowed that neither he nor any of his family would ever have to experience such a trial again. As Sandow had put it, once someone had been fully cast in plaster, they would "never undergo it again for any amount of money." Duke would not be following in David's wake.

Usborn admitted that making the cast had been a "ticklish

task," but he was happy with the results. As he told a reporter for the *Honolulu Star-Bulletin*, "the cast of David shows to excellent advantage the splendid muscular development of the upper body that results from constant surf-riding. David's development in the shoulders and chest is nothing short of remarkable. He himself is rather light, in my opinion, to make as typical a representative of the Hawaiian race as Duke. Duke is larger and more heavily built, but both are remarkable in their physical develop[ment]." Director Gregory agreed, believing that the cast would be "regarded by all museum experts and anthropologists as a standard and reproductions will be made for museums through the world." Even in faraway Oklahoma City, the *Oklahoma Times* reported that the cast of David Kahanamoku "conform[ed] to the nicest exactitude to the measurements of the subject." A reporter in Hawai'i put the matter in both aesthetic and erotic terms: David Kahanamoku's body made "sculptors' hands itch for clay, and women's eyes turn green with envy."

• • •

In August 1921, the Sullivans packed up their anthropometric equipment and left Hawai'i to return to New York. Notebooks full of measurement data accompanied them on the trip, boxes of skeletal material, crates of facial casts—and "1 life cast of a Hawaiian fisherman," which was David.

Sullivan's work had garnered widespread praise in the American press. One of his peers told a reporter that his measurements, photographs, and casts were "one of the most important contemporary contributions to the science of eugenics and the study of racial characteristics."

The cast of David Kahanamoku displayed at the Bishop Museum in Honolulu.

Osborn was ecstatic over the compelling face casts and the magnificent full-body statue. They would make fine grist for the Eugenics Congress. As Osborn gazed admiringly on the statue of the fisherman, he didn't realize that the statue was not of Duke Kahanamoku. The cast seemed to depict a "Chieftain type," and Duke was a Chieftain type, therefore the cast must be a sculpture of Duke. Sullivan chose not to correct him.

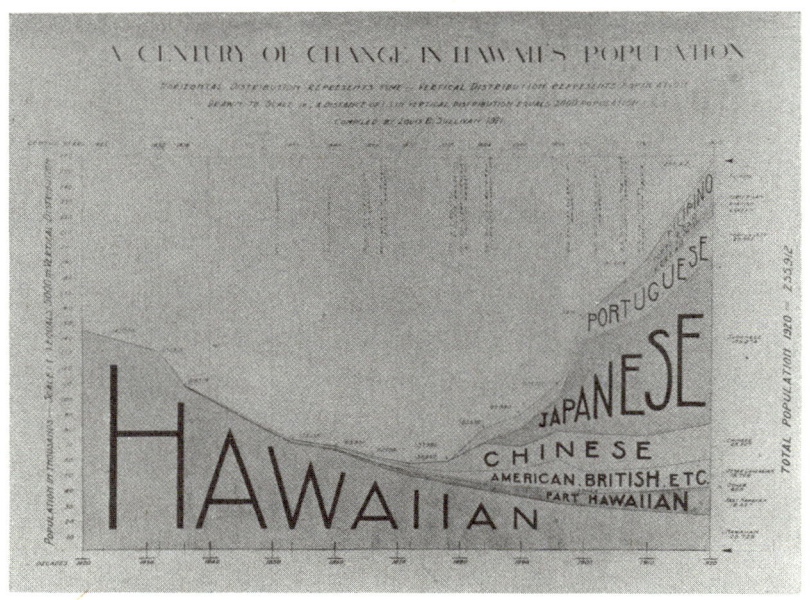

Louis R. Sullivan's graph of demographic changes in Hawaiʻi, presented at the Second International Eugenics Congress in 1921 at the American Museum of Natural History.

5

BARBARIANS AND DEMIGODS

September 22, 1921, was a mild fall day in New York City. Nestled amid the blazing elm trees of Central Park, the Museum of Natural History bustled with activity. In the first floor Forestry Hall, carpenters had blocked the glassed-in cases of taxidermic woodland creatures with gray, fabric-covered boards, and erected a series of cubicles on both sides of the long room. Delegates busily put the finishing touches on their exhibits, tacking photographs and charts to the temporary walls. In the great Hall of the Age of Man on the fourth floor, work crews had moved aside exhibits of stone tools and ancient crafts to set up rows of chairs, a stage, and a lectern. Osborn had ordered a menu of grapefruit, celery, consommé, filet of sole, broiled chicken, peas, potatoes, ice cream, and "fancy cakes" for a grand opening night feast. The museum would sponsor a clam bake on the weekend. The Second International Congress of Eugenics could now commence.

To kick off the proceedings, Osborn took to the lectern and greeted the assembled delegates. "I doubt if there has ever been a moment," he began, "when an international conference on race character has been more important than at the present." World War I, only recently resolved, he reminded his listeners, had depleted some of the best racial stock on both sides of "the fratricidal conflict" of white Europeans against white Europeans. In the United States, he continued, "we are engaged in a serious struggle to maintain our historic republican institutions through barring the entrance of those who are unfit to share the duties and responsibilities of our well-founded government." In Europe, "the worst elements of society have gained the ascendancy and threaten the destruction of the best." In South America, governments were investigating "the relative value of the pure Spanish and Portuguese and of various degrees of racial mixture of Indian and Negroid blood in relation to the preservation of their Republican Institutions." The time was right, he concluded, for men of science to enlighten their governments in the "prevention of the spread and multiplication of the worthless members of society . . . and of all moral and intellectual as well as physical diseases." In his view, the time was right for eugenics.

It was true that some people did not agree with this assessment. *Was America not a nation of immigrants?* they asked. Didn't the very men who called for the restriction of immigration come from the unwanted "stock" of old Europe? And wasn't it this unwanted "stock"—their very ancestors—who had made America great? For that matter, what about individual self-determination—the bedrock of America's system of government and economy? Wasn't it every man's right to choose how they wished to live, to marry whomever they wished, and to pursue their own destiny without the intervention of scientists and doctors? Moreover, while it was fine to think rationally and scientifically about improving society, at their most extreme, eugenicists could sound cold-blooded and positively murderous. Consider, for instance, the popular playwright, committed eugenicist (and future Nobel Prize winner) George Bernard Shaw, who called for mentally ill and physically disabled people to be "put out of existence, simply because it wastes other people's time to look after them." Surely this was not the American way.

Osborn and his fellow eugenicists countered that views like Shaw's were unnecessarily extreme—and, anyway, were not politically viable. By and large, they pointed out, American eugenicists weren't calling for mass killings or mass expulsions of people from America. They proposed what they considered kinder, gentler policies—involuntary sterilization of the "unfit," immigration restrictions based on race, and the occasional (very occasional) postnatal euthanasia of disabled infants. These were, they felt, simply the necessary and "scientific" ways of preserving the greatness of the American population. For those who objected that such proposals violated basic American civic values (in the name of saving America, no less!) eugenicists reserved a particular tone of condescension and injured patience. Eugenics, as Osborn put it in a letter to the (immigrant, Jewish) banker and museum trustee Felix Warburg, simply dealt with "great questions, formerly treated on humanitarian grounds, which must be taken up now on both humanitarian and scientific grounds."

Over the next four days, an audience of some three hundred eugenicists from all over the world mixed and mingled and shared ideas about directed human evolution. The crowd of luminaries included the inventor of the telephone (and ardent eugenicist), Alexander Graham Bell, who told reporters that "the grand spectacle is presented to our eyes of a new people being gradually evolved in the United States by the mingling together of the different races of the world in varying proportions. It is of the greatest consequence to us that the final result should be the evolution of a higher and nobler type of man in America, and not deterioration of the nation." It included Charles Darwin's son, Leonard Darwin, who told the assembled that, by following his father's work and lending a human hand to natural selection, "progress on eugenic lines will make mankind become continually nobler, happier, and healthier." It included Osborn's good friend, Madison Grant, whose book, *The Passing of the Great Race*, had predicted that the "Nordic type" that had made America so powerful would be genetically doomed if strong steps weren't quickly taken to prevent the spread of undesirables.

But it was the French comte George Vacher de Lapouge who gave the clearest voice to the message of the conference. In no uncertain terms, he explained, it fell to American leadership in eugenics to "save civilization" from "barbarism" and "produce a race of demigods."

The problem for eugenics, as Osborn explained, was the problem of racial history. "500,000 years of human evolution," he noted, "have impressed certain distinctive virtues as well as faults on each race." In his opinion "as a biologist" there was "little promise in the 'melting pot' theory. Put three races together, you are as likely to unite the vices of all three as the virtues." However, one shouldn't just trust his opinion. Science looked to "experimental proof or disproof, which will be presented by researches such as those of Doctor Sullivan in the Hawaiian Islands." Through work like Sullivan's, it would be possible to ascertain "what each race is best fitted to accomplish in the world's economy."

• • •

Everything about the Eugenics Congress had been carefully arranged to make eugenics clear and comprehendible to its public audiences and its participants.

The exhibits began in the museum's first floor Forestry Hall and took visitors on a voyage from the rudimentary principles of the eugenics movement to its most advanced work. Audiences first entered the congress's exhibits through a door on the hall's east side, strolling past a booth displaying promotional material for the various eugenical societies of the world. They then encountered, in sequence, exhibits on the basic principles of genetics, on the breeding of domestic animals, on human heredity, and then on "the family," with an attention to "family records," "mate selection," and "differential fecundity." They then learned about "Aristogenetic" families (Osborn's own pet idea)—that is, those whose "pedigrees showed the inheritance of specific talents"—and "Cacogenic families," who showed "the inheritance of specific degenerate qualities." From there spectators could loop around to the other side of the hall to discover booths about the "races of man," "human migration and immigration," and the tools of eugenics: anthropometry, population statistics, and mental testing, each in its own alcove.

To drive home what was at stake in all of this, the exhibitors included two sculptures, each about eighteen inches high, at each end of the Forestry Hall. At the entrance, Robert Tait Mackenzie—a physician and sculptor who had measured Duke while Duke trained in Philadelphia in 1912—had produced a composite sculpture of the "50 strongest men of Harvard." Based on his measurements of Harvard athletes, this sculpture was meant to demonstrate—with scientific, statistical accuracy—the peak of physical, mental, and moral development in white men. Mackenzie's sculpture was cast in bronze and showed a figure flexing his rippling muscles as he delicately, even modestly, fondled a sphere—perhaps just a ball, perhaps the world itself. The figure was polished, poised, and full of kinetic energy waiting to be released.

At the other end of the hall, Jane Davenport Harris—daughter of America's leading eugenicist, Charles Davenport—created a composite sculpture of the Average American Male "based on the proportions of 100,000 white soldiers" that her father had measured during the war. Davenport Harris's sculpture—made of humbler plaster—depicted a slope-shouldered, hangdog figure standing in a pose of incipient defeat. With his soft arms hanging limply to his sides, his sunken chest and ever-so-slightly emerging paunch, the Average American Male seems uncomfortable. His expression is confused, although he manages the slightest, meek smile, as though to apologize for what he's become.

The contrast between the fantasy future of eugenics and the desperate present couldn't be clearer. With the help of eugenics, all humans could be as physically fit—as able, as energetic—as the fifty strongest men at Harvard. Without eugenics, humankind—white humankind, anyway—would become flabby and emasculated.

Once visitors had the basics of eugenics down, they could proceed to the upper level of the museum, to the Hall of Man, where the bulk of the conference papers were presented. Here, in the "general racial exhibit," visitors could travel through time to witness the past, present, and future of humanity. Beginning with paleolithic skulls, congress attendees could take in a "synoptic view" of the "chronology of world cultures"—witnessing the ascendancy of the different races as they moved around the globe. Here early humans trudged out of Asia (where Osborn was sure humans had originated), occupying continents, rising up from "savagery," to "barbarism," until, in the case of white Europeans, they created "civilization." Hung high over the room, two huge murals by painter Charles Knight, whom Osborn had commissioned, depicted paleolithic humans as they struggled for survival and invented culture.

As with the charts on the floor below the murals, this was a just-so story: a quasi-mythical, aestheticized tale about what "culture" ought to look like, and what shape an authentic "civilization" would inevitably take.

Anchoring the whole room was the cast of David Kahanamoku. Usborn had sculpted a modest *malo* for the surfer-and-beach-boy-turned-model-fisherman, and it whipped around his waist. His raised arm now held a spear, and his eyes bulged intently as he concentrated on a fish near his feet. Artists at the American Museum had added color to the cast, and now David's dark hair rippled over his head, and his skin seemed to glow with warmth through layers of red and brown paint. He stood on a piece of black, plaster-sculpted lava rock. If you looked closely, it was possible to read a trace of sadness or anxiety on the face of the figure—perhaps a holdover from his unhappy experience with casting—but the immediate effect was of a figure from the past, brought uncannily to life in the museum.

In a glass case behind David, a selection of Sullivan's face casts looked out impassively. Museum men had colored them, too, and the faces seemed ready to speak—to verbalize the story of race history for their eugenicist audiences. This was the power of David's cast and the importance of Sullivan's work to men like Osborn. Congress attendees would have been interested in his charts of race mixing, and his tables of marriage statistics. But the real message was that—even in a place as racially complex as Hawai'i—it was possible to harness the genetic power of races in the deep past to make the "demigods" of the future.

Sullivan's casts aside, studies in the Eugenics Congress tended to run from the numbingly didactic to the distressingly grisly, with very little room in between.

For the most part, the exhibits had the atmosphere of a PTA meeting or a corporate presentation before the era of PowerPoint. The cubicles and booths created for each exhibit overflowed with charts, maps, and photographs, all tacked neatly if amateurishly to the fabric-covered boards. Viewers could examine, for instance, charts showing the "Theoretical curves of growth of various nations and a colony of fruit flies" (the growth curves all showed the same, gentle, s-shape); and charts depicting the "Approaching Extinction of 'Mayflower' Descendants" (the central diagram coincidentally looked somewhat like a Pilgrim's hat). Sullivan displayed a chart showing the gradual diminution of the proportion of "pure" Hawaiian people in Hawai'i, relative to other "races." Occasionally—as with charts showing the heritability of musical talent—the geometrical figures were inscrutable. Viewers could take in maps of the spread of jimsonweed in the United States (an analogy for the spread of "invasive" races). They could ponder maps of the distribution of different ethnic groups across the United States and take comfort in maps displaying the growth of eugenic research facilities across the United States. One exhibit showed a sequence of photos demonstrating how to properly perform anthropometry. Another, more popular, selection of photographs showed what the white "race" in America would look like in 1950 if eugenics was successful, as determined by composite photographs of different ideal white "types." A high point of visual interest was a display of the heritability of different traits of corn, as exhibited by real pieces of corn hanging from the gray walls of the booth.

The exhibits also lurched frequently and suddenly into the eerie and stomach-churning.

As visitors entered the booth on mental testing, for instance, they saw a series of stark, black-and-white photographs of moist brains, freshly extracted from their skulls, glistening on black backgrounds. Below each brain was a bold, all-caps, sans-serif label reading either "NORMAL" or "CRIMINAL." As though they were themselves the subjects of wanted posters, each of the "criminal" brains had a sort of eugenic rap sheet describing each brain's crime and type. Brain 590, for instance, was a "sex pervert" and a "vagrant" with "unknown parents." It was of a "broad, short, anomalous" type. Brain 576 was an "alcoholic vagrant" whose "mother died insane." It was of a "narrow" and "simple" type. The lists went on, detailing the faults of each "criminal" brain, though the "normal" brains had no such information. Audiences, presumably, would know what "normal" meant.

A similarly lurid exhibit by the Carnegie Institution titled "Comparison of White and Negro Fetuses" included plaster casts. An accompanying chart called attention to the ostensibly salient details of the fetuses, such as the allegedly larger first toe in white fetuses, and the relatively greater length of the second fingers as compared with the fourth fingers in Black fetuses. The exhibitors neglected to say what, exactly, the larger point of these grisly measurements of fingers and toes was, nor did they remark on where they had acquired the subjects for these casts—though surely the question was more pressing to thoughtful viewers than the measurements on display.

When it came time for talks, many lecturers delved deep into the bones of the good and the degenerate. E. A. Hooton of Harvard University, for instance, spent a large portion of his talk on "the effect of race mixture on physical characteristics." He focused on "Negroid skull texture," which he felt was distinctively "bony" (he did not specify what made one skull bone bonier than another). William Goldsmith discussed a skull abnormality found in a particular family in Kansas and came to the conference equipped with an example. Still other lecturers discussed slight variations in arm bones, which seemed to them to indicate a propensity for insanity. As another speaker noted, the growth of finger bones might say something (it was unclear what) about how different "races" developed. Still another speaker discussed how differences in body stature might indicate a disposition toward psychoneuro disease.

And then there was the blood—so much blood. The delegates bathed in discussions of "European blood," "Nordic blood," "Alpine blood," "white blood," "colored blood," "Caucasian blood," "Negro blood," "Jewish blood," and "American blood." Sullivan spoke of "Hawaiian blood" while his peers discussed the "Negrito blood" of some Filipino tribes. Discussants talked about the "richness of blood" of pure racial stocks, the "tainted blood" of impure stocks, and warned against the "gradual dilution of our best blood" by "inferior blood." The more scientifically inclined introduced such pseudoscientific terms as "leptorrhine" blood (the blood of people with long noses) and "orthoganous" blood (the blood of people with long heads). This bloody talk, moreover, had serious policy implications. Britain's Caleb Saleeby argued that environmental poisons were endangering "the young blood of adolescence" and the "blood of young girls and women." Norwegian eugenicist Jon Alfred Mjøen denied the "so called 'purifying effect' of blood mixture when foreign 'fresh' blood" enters a country, and distinguished between "the right to live, and the right of other races to mix their blood with our own." American Maurice Fishberg reassured audiences that "the flow of Jewish blood into the veins of the European and American peoples does not infuse any new racial elements"—though others disagreed. The "purest Germanic blood," noted still another speaker, gave the highest rates of suicide, which could be ameliorated with "an intermixture of Slavic blood."

Even within the American scientific community of the time, the vague conflation of blood and genes, of skulls and behaviors—and, indeed, of objective science and gross prejudice—struck many as preposterous. Abraham Meyerson, a neurologist and speaker at the congress, scolded the assembled delegates, reminding them that science was "very far" from identifying any scientific bases for the heritability of specific traits. "The insane have normal descendants; normal folk have insane descendants in a perfectly bewildering and inexplicable fashion," he chided his peers. There was just no data to support the grand assumptions that eugenicists made.

Thomas Hunt Morgan—whose work on chromosomes would win him a Nobel Prize in 1933—likewise attended the conference, but thought eugenics was bunk. As he wrote to Davenport in 1915, "for some time I have been entirely out of sympathy with this method of procedure [i.e. eugenics]." Morgan pointed to "the reckless statements, and the unreliability of a good deal that is said" as key reasons that he wanted to distance himself from the movement—though not so far that he wouldn't attend its meetings.

All this talk of brains and skulls and blood, however, was simply prelude to a singular preoccupation with "sexual hygiene." At their most optimistic, eugenicists tended to see love and sex as matters easily amenable to eugenic doctrines. As Darwin's son put it, "love is doubtless to a large extent aroused by advantageous moral and mental qualities and as such it . . . forms the finest foundation on which to base a eugenic policy." It was therefore the eugenicist's job, as Darwin thought of it, to help "foster the growth of all that is noble in the ideals of the adolescent"—especially in the case of choosing a eugenically proper partner.

But American eugenicists didn't view "love" so much as a matter of emotion, or happiness, or even personal choice. "Love" meant a dogmatic duty to one's race. Those who chose their life partners out of a sense of connection or desire were at best irresponsible and at worst dangerous to their communities. Any sort of relationship that wasn't sanctioned by science could be perilous, eugenicists thought. As physician (and future founder of the American Lung Association) S. Adolphus Knopf put it, "No license for marriage should be issued except to such as have been found physically and mentally fit to become the fathers and mothers of the future generations." Indeed, such relationships could be seen as a form of societal sabotage. As one delegate put it, drawing on "interracial" marriage as his example, "intermarriages between whites and blacks . . . are essentially anti-social tendencies and therefore opposed to the teachings of sound eugenics in the light of the best knowledge available to both races at the present time." Eugenicists thus argued that it was obviously necessary to forbid marriage—and sex—between notional races. The same went for mental illness, which had to be prevented by "checking [the] procreation of defective stock." Although some delegates murmured objections to the effect that categories such as "fit" and "defective" were unhelpfully ambiguous—difficult to pin down legislatively and impossible to establish with any kind of scientific certainty—challenges of these sorts were largely swept under the rug amid the general eugenic enthusiasm.

And if marriage restriction didn't work, compulsory sterilization would. Harry Laughlin, of the Eugenics Records Office, one of the best-funded, best-known private eugenics organizations in the United States, delivered a laudatory talk on the involuntary "sexual sterilization" of those he saw as "degenerate," saying that "among advanced peoples it must be rated as one of the four or five most practicable measures for purging the human stock of its more degenerate and worthless strains." Laughlin noted approvingly that "Many custodial institutions (for the feebleminded, insane, criminalistic, and the like) are making family history studies of their inmates, and many states are denying parenthood to individuals whose handicaps are based upon hereditary defects, and, as a radical measure, fifteen states have enacted laws providing for sexual sterilization of certain types of defectives." If people couldn't be trusted to police their own sex and family lives, eugenicists would do it for them.

• • •

A fixation on skulls and bones and brains; an obsession with blood; an unseemly interest in sexuality and forced sterilization; an ambient paranoia about the end of the human race: at some point, eugenicists might well have stopped to wonder if they were on the wrong path. Were their fixations not just a bit macabre? Didn't the effort to reduce people to "blood" and "skulls"—to say nothing of transforming them into plaster casts of "types"—dehumanize human beings in the name of saving humanity?

If these paradoxes bothered eugenicists, they rarely mentioned it. The contradictions of eugenics weren't a bug—they were a feature. One of the appeals of eugenics was that it could hold many conflicting impulses at once. It was at the same time conservative and progressive. It was at once scientific and mystical. It cloaked magical thinking about the dark, chthonic forces of genetic history in the guise of rational science. Eugenics was somewhere between surrealism and conspiracy theory.

With American eugenics in particular, conservatism is perhaps its most evident quality. At the core of the American eugenic programs was the desire to quite literally conserve values, customs, morals, and political systems through the preservation of what eugenicists believed were distinct, human "stocks." This meant, first of all, conserving traditional notions of masculinity and femininity, and the social roles of men and women. When they were mentioned at all—which was seldom—forms of family or sexuality that did not conform to the idea of a nuclear family with a male breadwinner at the head were viewed as degenerate. True, the more clear-eyed among eugenicists might note that many groups of people since antiquity had engaged in a cornucopia of sexual and kinship arrangements, but these arrangements were at best viewed as bygone artifacts of more "primitive" and "unscientific" times. In a similar way, American eugenicists seldom deviated from parroting the assumed racial hierarchies that had driven European and American imperialism.

Even for those who would admit that nations like the United States were by their very historical definition composed of a multiracial population, there was still a clear order of racial hierarchy that could not be altered. As one delegate put it, "The negro [sic] is here to stay. He is as much American as any white man. He is of right entitled to his freedom, to his opportunity, and to his pursuit of happiness." However, the delegate continued, "he has no right to claim the exercise of these privileges at the cost of the white man's civilization or the white man's standard of life." In other words, civil rights ended where race science began.

This said, the paranoia about "white civilization" could strike even some devoted eugenicists as a bit overwrought. Sullivan, for instance, confessed during the congress that he was unconvinced by anxieties about the "race suicide" of America's Anglo-Saxons. "Some writers," said Sullivan, referring to Osborn's good friend, Madison Grant, "have been clamoring about the passing of the blond type. Personally I am not impressed with their sparsity." This did not mean he dismissed race mixing as a problem—but the durability of the "north European type" was not as doubtful to Sullivan as it was to some of his peers.

If racial hierarchies were indelible, many eugenicists were willing to argue that differences between the sexes tended to be overstated. "There is good ground for the feminist contention that women should be liberally educated," conceded one manual. Women "should not be regarded by men as inferior creatures, [and] should have the opportunity of self-expression in a richer freer life than they have had in the past. All these gains can be made without sacrificing any racial interests and they must be so made." Indeed, the Kamehameha School's president, Uldrich Thompson, went one step further and wrote that "the higher education of women" would be the "foundation upon which the science of eugenics will be built." It was necessary that (white) women to be on equal footing with (white) men, Thompson thought, for the eugenic project to be successful.

While some eugenicists counted themselves as progressive for their feminism, others embraced left-leaning movements such as socialism, although often on qualified grounds. As one manual noted, "fundamentally eugenics is anti-individualistic, and [is] a socialistic movement since it seeks a social end involving some degree of individual subordination." This did not mean, of course, that all eugenicists embraced the overthrow of capitalism. But more than a few of those voices in American politics and letters that gave full-throated support for reforming the lot of the working man—Jack London was one of them—also subscribed to eugenics.

Moreover, many eugenicists considered themselves "progressive" insofar as their goal was notionally scientific progress. At the congress, Norwegian eugenicist Jon Alfred Mjøen declared "Racebiology [sic] is a new science." It was, that is, still finding its footing. "But," he continued, "I hardly doubt that we will be able someday, perhaps by biological-chemical means (blood-analysis?) to ascertain what races may safely be crossed and the chemical laws will then be fundamental for the moral. The woman of the future will feel antipathy towards a man of strange (disharmonic) blood, just as the woman of the present-day feels antipathy towards one who is not of her standard of life." In Mjøen's vision, eugenics was a positive step toward a new society in which a person's worth was judged by their genes rather than their earning potential. If he had ever paused to consider that his vision of future society was even more oppressive, dystopian, and dehumanizing than the one he proposed to replace, Mjøen didn't mention it.

In any case, if the eugenicists at the congress fancied themselves men of science, their scientific ideas rested on a bedrock of profoundly gothic, mythical, even occult thinking. Vacher de Lapouge's talk of demigods was only the beginning. Saleeby spoke to the assembled delegates about "racial poisons," tracing the idea to "the Roman myth regarding the deformity of Vulcan, supposed to have been conceived when his father, Jupiter, was drunk." Others spoke of "eugenic prophecies" of greatness or doom, or of eugenics as the "seed bed of a new religion." These were not just idle thoughts, or literary allusions. They were fundamental pillars of eugenic thinking, spoken by some of the most influential eugenicists in the world.

For that matter, even when eugenicists groped for scientific concepts, reason and rigor often shaded into imagination and impressions. Take, for instance, the definition of traits. It was the job of the eugenicist to identify which characteristics inhered in particular races. These traits could be obvious and obviously heritable, such as eye color. But they could also be esoteric and weirdly specific to the point of fantasy. For example, Charles Davenport—America's leading eugenicist—compiled obsessive indexes of the qualities of different European "races," with an eye toward the most picayune of details. He thought, for instance, that those of the German "race" were not simply light skinned and of medium build, but were also "lovers of freedom, full of courage and daring." They tended to rise in society if they were poor, and were "as a rule, thrifty, intelligent and honest." Germans, thought Davenport, have an inherent love of art and music, including "the music of song birds." Scandinavians were blond and "independent in thought and action," with a marked sense of chastity and self-control, and a love of agricultural pursuits. About Italians, Davenport wrote that, "aside from his tendency to crimes of personal violence, the average Italian has many excellent characteristics, not one of the least of which is his interest in his work, even as a day laborer." Italians tended to "assimilate well to urban life," felt Davenport. The same was true of the Irish, who were "sympathetic, often chaste" and could be good leaders—though Davenport noted that they were afflicted with "alcoholism, considerable mental defectiveness, and a tendency to tuberculosis." The many traits that Davenport cataloged included thrift, capacity for higher education, musical ability, artistic ability, a love for academic history, the desire to go to sea, skill at woodcarving, and, as he put it, an "interest in weird things."

The world that eugenicists wished to live in, in other words, was one of such paranoiac knowability that it left no room for surprise, for discovery, for individuality. It was one of such conformity—such incuriosity—that even a love of songbirds had to be not merely explained as a cultural idiosyncrasy or a charming individual trait but determined by a person's biology: by their "race." This was a world in which even "genius"—a property, needless to say, that American eugenicists thought could only belong to white people—was down to "superior" genetic factors rather than accidents of life, or insight, or imagination, hard work, curiosity, or perspicacity. Indeed, one of the greatest ironies of eugenics is that, for all of their genuflection to reason and rationality, for all of their stated belief in scientific progress, for all of their conviction that science and technology had elevated white civilization beyond the benighted societies of the primitive past (and their less-evolved, less-white neighbors in the present), eugenicists subscribed to a doctrine that relied deeply on unreasoning fear and a magical wish for control over the uncontrollable.

How else to think about eugenicists' obsession with blood "mixing" other than as unreservedly alchemical? By what processes could one "mix blood" to arrive at a new kind of human? Maine eugenicist Clarence Cook Little reached for the analogy of an old-fashioned drug store to explain. "It is much as though a small boy was given charge of a soda fountain," he wrote, "and he looked at all the various apparatus which squirt out the syrups of different kinds and he saw cherry, pineapple, chocolate, coffee, vanilla, strawberry, raspberry, lemon and orange, and he said, 'aren't we a great and wonderful soda fountain? I am going to have some fun,' whereupon he proceeded to mix together various combinations of these different syrups. Some of them fused and some of them didn't; some made a lovely combination and some gave a most unpleasant feeling." Of these "flavors" of alchemical human, Little—and many of the eugenicists at the congress—felt that pure Yankee "stock" was the most prized, and the most endangered. "I don't want to see that particular element mixed up, or mauled up," wrote Little. "I want to keep it the way a chemist would prize a store of chemically pure substance that he wants to use for testing, that he wants to use for definite purpose when a certain element is needed." It is hard to shake the impression that eugenicists often thought less in terms of genes and more in terms of elemental properties carried in blood, to be mixed and churned, as though human populations were a big, smoking cauldron.

And if blood mixing was alchemical, what was casting faces but a sort of contact magic—a way of absorbing the power and essence of a person or thing through touching it? If eugenicists thought in terms of the new science of genetics, in their practices they nevertheless reverted to those "spirits" and impressions that early modern Europeans believed to be at the source of reproductive power.

In this sense, the cast of David Kahanamoku was not simply a recording of his morphology. A simpler process—a photograph, a sculpture, an outline on the floor—could have done that. The true magic of the cast—even if eugenicists wouldn't have recognized it in this form—was that it could channel the mystical essence of the deep, racial past that had supposedly given David his powerful form, and solidify it—returning David to a time from which he'd been banished by modernity. Scientific humans were no longer meant to believe in totems. That much had supposedly been dissipated by science. And yet here was Sullivan the anthropologist—an emissary of the modern world—himself creating likenesses in dead material that were meant to invigorate the past, to return David Kahanamoku to a "primitive" or "natural" state of which he had never really been a part. It was a strange and self-contradictory view of biology, of culture, and of science.

There was, ultimately, something deeply, unshakably surreal—dreamlike, or rather, nightmarish—about eugenics. It offered a world in which inside was outside and outside was in; in which the beautiful and the disgusting, the moral and amoral, merged to become indistinguishable.

• • •

This strange sense of scientific progressivism and mystical conservatism was confusing even to many advocates of eugenics, both inside the United States and out.

Other countries pursued programs of eugenics that looked similar to the ones propounded in the United States. Japan in particular took the idea of racial purity very seriously and implemented marriage restrictions and sterilization laws. Mexico, too, was unusual among South and Central American countries for aggressively implementing regulations to prevent eugenically undesirable reproduction. A 1917 "Law of Family Relations," for instance, framed marriage as a eugenic act and sought to restrict marriage for people with conditions deemed dangerous to public health, such as habitual drunkenness. After the congress ended, another law in Mexico, passed in 1923, prohibited Mexican-Chinese marriages.

Many places, however, gave far more attention to "positive eugenics"—bolstering the supposed genetic "quality" of a given population—rather than "negative eugenics," which emphasized restricting reproduction. Spain, for instance, sponsored communities in which eugenically pure couples would receive free or heavily discounted housing in return for producing a certain number of offspring. Italy took the opposite tack, imposing a celibacy tax on those genetically desirable individuals who chose *not* to reproduce. Argentinian eugenicists encouraged the immigration of white Europeans as a way of increasing Argentina's desirable "stock" of Nordic types.

For that matter, even the singular desirability of Nordic or Anglo-Saxon types as the taproot of society seemed questionable to many delegates. Japanese eugenicists, for example, took a dim view of the idea that the white race was superior to their own, and they did not accept American eugenicists' blithe assumptions that people of Japanese ancestry were fundamentally of the same racial "stock" as those who populated other Asian nations. In parts of South America, meanwhile, racial mixture rather than racial purity was considered virtuous. Chilean eugenicists celebrated *la raza Chilena*—an amalgam that combined European ancestry with the regal stock of the Mapuche people. In Brazil, with dizzyingly complicated debates about the nature of race mixing, there tended to be fewer policies restricting intermarriage, and, indeed, a positive sense of the potential for intermarriage between notional races.

Outside the walls of the Eugenics Congress, opposition to eugenics could be even more pointed.

"There is nothing to show that all the blond, blue-eyed, tall individuals present excellent strains," wrote Sullivan's adviser, Boas. "There are mediocre and subnormal types among them just as well as among other races; and the proof has never been given that the relative number of excellent hereditary strains in this race is greater than in others. To speak of hereditary characteristics of a human race as a whole has no meaning."

W. E. B. Du Bois, who was Boas's own model for conduct as an antiracist public intellectual, issued an even stronger rebuttal to the program of eugenics in a lecture that he delivered in November 1921, from the stage at the Second Pan African Congress in London. "No one denies great differences of gift, capacity and attainment among individuals of all races," he said, "but the voice of science, religion and practical politics is one in denying the God-appointed existence of super-races, or of races naturally and inevitably and eternally inferior. . . . The insidious and dishonorable propaganda, which, for selfish ends, so distorts and denies facts as to represent the advancement and development of certain races of men as impossible and undesirable, should be met with widespread dissemination of the truth."

Even among the lay public, eugenicists' ideas could be viewed as extreme. Strict eugenic supervision of all marriages, for instance, struck many people as needlessly oppressive, and potentially destabilizing to society itself. "The eugenicist cannot seriously propose that only the fittest shall marry without leaving himself open to the charge of utopianism, or, if he insists, producing a revolution," wrote an incredulous columnist for the *Chattanooga Daily Times*. According to the standards of eugenic studies conducted by men like Sullivan during the world war, "nearly fifty percent of the men examined were found to be unfit. . . . Who would dare deny marriage to the unfit fifty percent?"

Even those who accepted eugenics as a generally positive movement wondered what eugenic ideas would do to values like joy and amorousness. Eugenics was certainly "the means towards a mentally, morally, and physically perfect race," wrote one editorialist. But was it right for advocates of eugenic pairings—who themselves were largely "men and women of mature years," and therefore more phlegmatic about matters of love—to proscribe "romance, the fundamental basis of girlhood happiness"? Certainly not.

For that matter, as far away as Oklahoma, the progressive *New Farmer* newspaper saw marriage restriction as a way for eugenicists to fob off unfair social conditions on working men and women. "Radically irrational is the proposition before the second national eugenics congress in session in New York that only the 'physically fit' be permitted to marry," steamed an editorial. "The selection of the 'physically fit' to monopolize the propagation of the species is visionary and impractical and that ought to settle that part of the equation." The "evil," the editorial went on to say, "is wholly economic. . . . Undernourished, badly-housed, illy clad, overworked fathers and mothers, fathers and mothers incapable of entertaining and holding those ideals and visions which induce the upward climb, an environment which forbids the fullest development of that spirituality, that taste and touch of the artistic and beautiful which is inseparable from human development—these form the basis for that frightful situation which has produced the eugenic radical."

Nor did one have to be a left-leaning social reformer to lampoon eugenics. As an undergraduate at Princeton, author F. Scott Fitzgerald wrote a song titled "Love or Eugenics," in which the chorus poses the question:

> *Ladies, here's a problem none of you can flee,*
> *Men, which would you like to have come and pour your tea?*
> *Kisses that set your heart aflame,*
> *Or love from a prophylactic dame?*
> *Ladies, take your choice of what your style shall be.*

The "prophylactic dame" in this instance is a woman who carries the clinical credentials of a eugenically fit mate—even if she can't set her lover's "heart aflame." Fitzgerald revisited his skepticism of eugenics in *The Great Gatsby* when he had his loathsome antagonist, Tom Buchanan, drunkenly warn that "if we don't look out the white race will be—will be utterly submerged. It's all scientific stuff; it's been proved."

• • •

For all of the public's misgivings about eugenics—to say nothing of the protests of serious scientists—eugenics was popular policy in the United States.

While many people balked at the idea of eugenic screening for *all* marriages, by the 1920s all but nine US states had legislation against "mixed race" marriages, variously defined. Proscriptions in the United States against intermarriage between "white" and "black" people had been common since the beginning of the republic. In the anti-Chinese and anti-Japanese panics of the 1880s, laws against intermarriage were extended to prohibit marriages between white people and people from Asia. Still later, Oklahoma passed a 1908 bill that prohibited marriage "between a person of African descent" and "any person not of African descent"—an attempt to prohibit marriage between Black and Indigenous people. In 1920, Louisiana similarly passed a law proscribing marriage between Black and Indigenous people.

The 1920s saw both an expansion of these laws and a change in their phrasing. Most characteristic was Virginia's 1924 "Racial Integrity Act," a piece of legislation written in consultation with Laughlin and Madison Grant and dedicated to preserving the integrity of "white stock." The law mandated that everyone's race be recorded at birth as "white" or "colored," and that on applying for a marriage license, one had to furnish these as credentials.

Compulsory sterilization, too, was appallingly popular. By the time of the Eugenics Congress, fifteen states had passed legislation allowing forced sterilization of those state authorities deemed to be "unfit" to reproduce. Indiana was first, with a 1907 law that demanded sterilization of "confirmed criminals, idiots, imbeciles and rapists" following inspection by two physicians. By 1909, California followed suit, and shortly thereafter, so did Washington state, New York, Nevada, Michigan, and Wisconsin. By 1921, 3,233 people had been sterilized against their will in the United States, with California performing nearly two-thirds of the operations.

In 1927, the Supreme Court cemented the legality of compulsory sterilization in the case of *Buck v. Bell*. *Buck v. Bell* originated with a pro-eugenic asylum director who contrived to sue his own organization to establish the validity of eugenic sterilization. Writing for the 8–1 majority, Associate Justice Oliver Wendell Holmes—by then widely admired as a protector of civil liberties and defender of progressive reform—reasoned that if the "public welfare" could call on its "best citizens" to sacrifice their lives in its defense, why could the state not call on the notionally worst to sacrifice something less than their lives for the greater good? "It is better for all the world," he wrote, "if instead of waiting to execute degenerate offspring for crime, or to let them starve for their imbecility, society can prevent those who are manifestly unfit from continuing their kind.... Three generations of imbeciles are enough." There was little public protest at Holmes's remarks, and he himself apparently didn't see (or ignored) the obvious contradiction between protecting the civil rights of individuals against government overreach and endorsing the practices of eugenicists.

Meanwhile, if "socially inadequate" Americans posed a genetic threat to the United States from within, immigration seemed to be an equally potent genetic threat from without. Immediately after the Eugenics Congress in 1921, future US president Calvin Coolidge—at the time he was vice president—published an article in *Good Housekeeping* in which he warned against the menace of immigration in eugenic terms. "There are racial considerations too grave to be brushed aside for any sentimental reasons," he wrote. "Biological laws tell us that divergent people will not mix or blend. The Nordic propagate themselves successfully. With other races, the outcome shows deterioration on both sides. Quality of mind and body suggests that observance of ethnic law is as great a necessity to a nation as immigration law."

In 1924, the US Congress took up this call to pass comprehensive immigration restriction along racial and ethnic lines in the form of the Johnson-Reed Act.

Passage of the act relied heavily on input from key figures in the 1921 Eugenics Congress like Laughlin and Osborn's friend, Madison Grant. In Laughlin's testimony before the House's Committee on Immigration and Naturalization, he presented an incendiary mixture of misinformation, xenophobia, and nationalism posing as objective science. "Immigration," he told the congressmen, "is an insidious invasion just as clearly as, and works more certainly in national conquest than, the invading army which may or may not come and go without supplanting national population. If the immigration is of a closely related racial type, and possesses inborn talents higher than those of the native stocks, then the national type is preserved and the character improved. But if, on the other hand, the racial type is not assimilable, and the inborn traits of character are less ideal than those of the foundation stocks, then immigration work toward ultimate disaster." This vision of American apocalypse—substituting speculation for facts, prejudice for reason, "invasion" for immigration—played to the committee's most base, unreasoning fears of the future.

In his testimony, Laughlin pointed specifically toward Sullivan's work in Hawai'i as an example of the worst that might happen if immigration was allowed to continue unchecked. "In the exhibit of the International Congress of Eugenics in New York in 1921," he said, "Dr. Louis R. Sullivan displayed a chart entitled, 'A century of change in Hawaii's population,' which showed how the principles which I have just described worked out as the result of the interaction of immigration and fecundity differential among the several stocks and strains within a country." He showed the chart to the committee. "Hawaii is a veritable laboratory," Laughlin began, leaning on Sullivan and Osborn's old trope. Then he quickly—and misleadingly—took the committee on a tour of Sullivan's data, concluding that they showed how "immigration and differential fecundity determine the rate of extinction of a national race when it is supplanted by other groups."

If anything, of course, the complex history of Hawai'i—as opposed to a single chart, speciously interpreted—told an entirely different story than the one that Laughlin wanted the committee to believe. Regardless of the "race mixing" that Sullivan's charts showed, Hawaiian society functioned more or less harmoniously. People of different "races" held a variety of different jobs, contributed to local politics, played sports with one another, married one another, had children who went to school together—all without any obvious "degeneration" of civic or economic life. For that matter, far from going "extinct," Indigenous Hawaiian people and Hawaiian culture persisted, adapting to American-style industrial capitalism in spite of almost a century of attempts to replace or eradicate it. Although Hawai'i was not without poverty, disease, crime, exploitation, conflicts, or inequality, its people provided a poor example of the perils of race mixing for American civil society.

Only one congressman offered a rebuttal to the torrent of exaggeration and disinformation. Confronting his peers, New York representative Emanuel Celler remarked on how peculiar it was that the Immigration Committee failed to interview any scientist who might contradict their foregone conclusions.

Instead, they only consulted those who would feed them the "buncombe" and "dogmatic piffle" that they wanted to hear. Laughlin's testimony in particular, said Celler, was "redolent with downright and deliberate falsehoods." Laughlin was "predisposed in favor of so-called Nordic Superiority [and] he supports this argument with the most dishonest methods. He has hoodwinked the Immigration committee into believing his conclusions." Seen in this cold, clear light, Celler pointed out, Laughlin's "science" was really just circular reasoning in support of cheap prejudice.

Had the committee called an authoritative scientist like Boas, Celler noted, Boas would have told them that eugenicists' pet measure of superiority—skull shape—changed dramatically from generation to generation in "Nordics" and non-Nordics alike. "How under the sun," asked Celler, "if skulls can so change, can there be any relationship between the form of the skull and the brain inside the skull? . . . In other words, the whole system boils itself down to this: the shape of the skull has nothing whatsoever to do with native intelligence. Nor has complexion or blondness anything to do with intelligence." The same went for "feeblemindedness," criminality, blindness, susceptibility to tuberculosis, and a host of other maladies that eugenic limits on immigration were supposed to solve. In sum, when the bill's sponsor, Johnson, claimed to have found Laughlin's arguments "both biologically and statistically thorough," Celler quipped, "he might well . . . have said that the moon was made of green cheese."

Celler's fellow congressmen greeted his indignant rebuttal with a sort of bemused indifference. They thanked him for his speech, then returned to debating whose ancestry was superior to whose and whether immigrants ought to speak English.

The Johnson-Reed Act passed the House with overwhelming support on April 14, 1924. As historian Lisa Lowe points out, the 1924 Immigration Act was "the nation's first *comprehensive* immigration restriction law." Its provisions held that, among other things, within three years Congress should set racially based quotas for immigrants. It also mandated the absolute exclusion of Asian immigrants. Finally, it included provisions for a border patrol, and it introduced the term "illegal alien" into the American lexicon.

This, along with contemporaneous Supreme Court rulings that affirmed biological race as a valid test for citizenship, cemented the place of eugenics in early twentieth-century American politics and law.

Osborn's program at the American Museum had played a critical role. As Osborn wrote in the museum's annual report, while the public had initially been ambivalent about the mission of the congress, "as the sound and patriotic series of addresses and papers on Heredity, the Family, the Race and the State, succeeded one another, the influence of the Congress grew and found its way into the news and editorial columns of the entire press of the United States."

Within five short years of the Eugenics Congress, the United States had affirmed eugenics with the most sweeping array of pro-eugenics legislation in the world—and this elevated Osborn to the rank of a world leader in eugenic policy and research. Even in Germany—whose delegates had been denied entry to the 1921 congress because of their nation's role in the world war—Osborn's name held the imprimatur of the finest eugenic science.

• • •

Sullivan did not live long enough to see the full extent of the policies that his research had helped to bring about. Two months after the end of the Eugenics Congress, in early in December of 1921, Wissler went to Sullivan's new residence on Ninety-Third Street in New York and found the young anthropologist near death.

The year in Hawai'i had been good for his weakened lungs and had left the young anthropologist feeing stronger than he had in years. But Hawai'i hadn't offered a permanent cure. Upon his return to New York, the hectic schedule of the congress and the cold, damp, soot-laden air of the city had returned Sullivan to his previous state of enervation. Enervation turned into pleurisy. Pleurisy developed into aggressive pneumonia. When Wissler found him, Sullivan gurgled and rasped through each breath, and he could barely move.

Wissler was startled and contacted Osborn immediately. In consultation with a doctor, the two men immediately concocted a plan to send Sullivan far away from New York, to a climate that would save his lungs, and his life. They settled on Tucson, Arizona, as a place that had warm, dry air. It also had a university with a library that Sullivan could use, and plenty of "mixed race" people with whom, Osborn speculated, Sullivan might do some "really fine studies of the Mexican native type, suitable for models in the Mexican hall." (True to form, he also asked a colleague where "the purest descendants of the Aztecs, Mayas [*sic*], and Peruvians are likely to be found," conflating the American Southwest with Central and South America.)

Sullivan and Betsy moved to Tucson in February 1922, where they found life a decidedly mixed bag. The climate "worked wonders" on Sullivan's health, he thought, and after only a few weeks, he began gaining energy and weight and felt "very well indeed." He also managed to direct exhibition work at the museum by mail, write an official guide to anthropometry, and even complete his doctorate.

At the same time, Sullivan worried about his Hawaiian work. He lamented that Roland Dixon, an anthropologist from Harvard, was generating compelling results from his own anthropometric surveys of Hawaiian types, even though to Sullivan's mind Dixon's technique was "weird." Meanwhile, Edward Smith Craighill Handy—an anthropologist with whom Sullivan had occasionally collaborated at the Bishop Museum—had started to get a "stranglehold" on the "Polynesian problem."

Sullivan's letters from this period give the sense of a person trying to get a grip on wildly spiraling moods. In some notes, he seemed hopeful. "I feel very confident that I have staged a comeback," he wrote. "I believe I can stand New York or any other climate with just the least bit of good luck. I believe I have learned how to take care of myself. I am thinking very seriously of coming back to New York." Other times, he gave in to frustration. "On the whole," he complained to Wissler, "you do not seem optimistic about the prospects of raising money for field work here, or for carrying on the work of analyzing my records. The situation is discouraging and hard to understand. I can't understand the psychology of hiring men and then not using them and of spending money on collecting records and then not working them up." And then, he continued, "there are those Bishop Museum face masks. Is the museum passing up the opportunity of duplicating them? If so, I suppose there is little sense in trying to accumulate more. . . . I wish you'd tell me what's the matter."

Finally—placated by Sullivan's assurances of his own improving health—Osborn and Wissler summoned the young anthropologist back to New York to work on a new collection of bones that the museum had recently purchased. Sullivan was thrilled. The collection, he felt, was "pure gold." He'd rather have the skeletal material than a raise in salary, he told Wissler. Since he was "head over heels in the Polynesian Problem," as he put it (his idiom suggested being tumbled by a breaking wave), the materials from New Zealand, Chatham Island, Melanesia, and the New Hebrides were crucial to his work. Wissler, too, seemed happy, telling Sullivan that the collections of bones were "sufficiently rich and varied to keep you busy to the rest of your days."

These words were poorly chosen. Sullivan's health quickly disintegrated, this time for good. Sullivan blamed it on a cold that he'd caught back in Tucson, but Betsy thought it was overwork at the museum. Whatever was the case, within two months, Sullivan was unable to continue his work, and Wissler and Osborn made preparations for him to leave the museum permanently.

The Sullivans returned to Tucson, where the anthropologist's health continued to plummet. He was bedridden in September when Madison Grant stopped by to check up on him. Later that month, X-rays revealed a bad case of tuberculosis. Sullivan was coughing up blood, had an inflamed eye, a raging fever, and was rapidly losing weight. On top of this, he developed appendicitis, and the resulting operation weakened his heart and "sapped his vitality," as his doctor put it.

Sullivan died in Tucson on April 21, 1925.

Sculptor Malvina Hoffman at work.

6

"QUITE A DIFFERENT MAN"

Sullivan's death left a yawning hole in the field of anthropometry. Osborn mourned the loss of Sullivan's "unusual grasp of the problems in his field," and his "logical and critical mind." Director Gregory, at the Bishop Museum, lamented that he saw "no way of carrying on the work unfinished by [Sullivan's] death." And Earnest Hooton, a Harvard anthropologist, eugenicist, and colleague of Osborn's, wrote a lengthy obituary for Sullivan in the journal *American Anthropologist*, lauding Sullivan's "keenly critical mind" and expressing doubt about "the fate of [his] invaluable research."

Just as importantly to Osborn, Sullivan's death also left a gap in the museum's ability to capitalize on its successes during the Eugenics Congress. The goal of the congress, as Osborn saw it, was "to take the whole subject of eugenics out of the hands of faddists and place it on a thorough natural and scientific basis." To do this would require both accomplished scientists and accomplished museum men. The museum's exhibits had to be so compelling, so "self-explanatory and attractive" that they would "draw people to [them] as Nature does."

Unfortunately for them, America of the Roaring Twenties brimmed with attractions every bit as seductive as Nature. The years from 1919 to 1929 produced the biggest bull market in US history, with stocks rising as much as 20 percent per year. The United States became the wealthiest nation in the world, and New York replaced London as the center of global capital. Employment was high, liquidity was high, and everyday people lived high. Mass culture might have been eliminating traditional sources of pleasure like churches and local community; however, it introduced compensatory pleasures: consumer goods like cars and clothing; new kinds of music like jazz; new dances like the Charleston, the Black Bottom, the Shimmy; and new forms of sex and sexuality like "dating"—a term popularized in the 1920s.

All of these new forms of cultural expression drew audiences away from museums. Most challenging of all, however, from an exhibitor's perspective, was the newest form of mass entertainment: moving pictures. As one exhibitor wrote, "in New York City ten thousand people go to see a moving picture for every one that visits the Museum of Natural History. Why? Because the pictures move, they are alive. They have the thrill."

Osborn had, to an extent, come to understand that the museum needed to offer "the thrill" as well. The museum began to show natural-history-themed movies, and crowds packed their theater to see films like *How Life Begins*, *The Why of a Volcano*, and *A New Search for the Oldest Man*. When the museum screened the documentary *Nanook of the North* for eight days in 1922, almost 11,000 people came to see it. That same year, attendance at the museum passed the one million mark, driven largely by people coming to see movies in its theater.

But Osborn hadn't given up on the museum's original mission. Dioramas, displays in glass cases, and casts of Indigenous peoples could provide the thrill of *presence*—the idea that museumgoers were not simply observing natural history but were part of natural history itself, as represented by authentic artifacts, bones, and casts.

The casts that Sullivan had done in Hawai'i were a good example of this. Museumgoers responded viscerally to the eerie, lifelike, seemingly scientifically accurate reproductions of human faces staring out from under glass cases. Indeed, the cast of David Kahanamoku was so compelling that the Peabody Museum at Yale ordered a copy from the American Museum—though their own cast would feature a beard and a sort of mullet haircut made of real, human hair when it went on display.

In the year before his death, Sullivan worked with Osborn—at a distance, from his new home in Tucson—on a grand, new Hall of the Races of Man. This exhibit would, Osborn thought, "demonstrate the slow upward ascent and struggle of man from the lower to the higher stages, physically, morally, intellectually, and spiritually." Sullivan's idea was for a sweeping, panoramic scheme, with busts of the "races of man" arrayed in an arc around a large hall, framing artifacts demonstrating humankind's rise from paleolithic primitivity to masters of nature. Better still, he thought that the plaster casts of Hawaiian faces might be redone in more lifelike wax, "with glass eyes and real hair, eyebrows and eye lashes." By all accounts, Osborn was thrilled.

Now, however, the Hall of the Races of Man—and physical anthropology at the museum more generally—was on uncertain footing. Of course, the museum had tremendous resources, and a first-rate curatorial staff. But it needed eager, young foot soldiers to accomplish its mission.

In September 1925, Osborn instructed the Anthropology Department to contact Earnest Hooton, the Harvard anthropologist who had written Sullivan's obituary, to see if he knew anyone who could fill Sullivan's shoes.

"It just so happens," Hooton replied, "that I have, almost ready for delivery, the best young physical anthropologist who has ever studied under me . . . the most competent man available, now that Sullivan is gone."

Harry Lionel Shapiro—Harvard BA class of 1923, now a PhD student of Hooton's—was, in some ways, a near clone of Sullivan. An anthropometrist who specialized in the study of Polynesian people, he had cut his teeth at the Bishop Museum, arriving on a fellowship in 1922, just after Sullivan left. Like Sullivan's, Shapiro's work concerned the "problem" of race in Polynesia, and race mixing in Hawai'i. And like Sullivan, he was obsessive, even persnickety in his pursuit of people to measure. Indeed, he had even been in contact with Sullivan during the early days of his PhD work, and Sullivan had forwarded him data from the Bishop Museum. Shapiro knew Sullivan's work well and considered his own work as part of a "series" inaugurated by Sullivan.

The similarities between Sullivan and Shapiro ended at their intellectual interests. Where Sullivan was slight, diffident, and sickly, Shapiro was burly, charismatic, and vigorous. He kept his head of dark, curly hair cut in a variation of a high and tight and often clenched a pipe in his chiseled jaw. As Hooton told the American Museum, Shapiro was "a good athlete, having rowed on the Freshman eight" with the Harvard crew team. He was "liked and admired by all of the students who come in contact with him," Hooton wrote, "is extraordinarily well read, and is quite a musician." What's more—and here, Hooton the race scientist couldn't resist reducing his star student to a "type"—Shapiro was a "German Jew." Nevertheless, Hooton continued with disturbing nonchalance, Shapiro possessed "not one of the undesirable qualities sometimes attributed to Jews."

On November 4, 1921, Shapiro was hired as assistant curator of physical anthropology.

It would be years before the Hall of the Races of Man saw fruition—and in the meantime, the American Museum would be scooped in its quest by the rival Field Museum in Chicago.

• • •

Shapiro was not the only person trying out new career prospects.

In April 1925, three days after Sullivan died, *Adventure*, a film by the Hollywood director Victor Fleming, debuted on screens across America. Based on a 1911 novel by Jack London, the movie detailed the trials of a heroic plantation owner in the Solomon Islands who overcomes fever, an insurrection of Indigenous peoples, and rapacious moneylenders with the help of a female mercenary and her crew of Polynesian sailors.

Although the film has since been lost, contemporary reviewers judged it to be, as one column put it, "a smashing action romance that will interest the film fans from eight to eighty." It was "intelligent enough to appeal to the discriminating and fast enough to please those who are content only with red-blooded action," wrote another reviewer.

Some reviewers, however, interpreted the movie as more than just a good story, but a compelling collection of anthropological facts. *Adventure* had a "spirit of realism," thought one columnist, and it captured "present day life in the savage Solomon

Islands in the South Seas." Another reviewer agreed that the movie "shed considerable light on the habits of the native savages." In other words, while the film might have been fictional in its broad outlines (some moviegoers found some of its action sequences "exaggerated" and "unrealistic") many believed it gave an authentic look at the lives of Polynesians.

Among the actors portraying "native" Polynesians was Duke Kahanamoku, making his screen debut as the leader of the sailors.

The years following Duke's victory in the 1920 Olympics had been difficult. He returned to Hawai'i victorious once again, but still struggled to make a living. David had participated in Sullivan's anthropometric casting project at the request of Hawai'i's governor, and in return the governor had granted Duke a position as Hawai'i's official greeter. But the job was more of an honorary title than a viable source of income. At times, Duke worked desk jobs—as a clerk in the Hawaiian governor's office, or in the quartermaster's office at Schofield army base, near Pearl Harbor. He also managed to parlay his celebrity as a swimmer and surfer into a product endorsement for Valspar varnish—supposedly Duke's varnish of choice for his surfboards. Mostly, though, he reverted to his previous means of making money: teaching water sports to the tourists who increasingly flooded Waikiki.

He tried to shrug off his financial struggles, but he couldn't shake the nagging voice in his head. "Out of the water, I'm nothing," he thought.

Hoping to make a change, in 1922, Duke moved to Los Angeles at the prompting of his new "manager," a figure by the name of "Honest Oscar" Henning. Duke had first crossed paths with Henning in Stockholm in 1912, when "Oscar" went by the name of "Thor" and swam the breaststroke for the Swedish Olympic team. Since then, Henning claimed he had been an explorer and adventurer, made and lost a fortune in Russia, and had sailed the Pacific with Jack London before settling down in Honolulu. There, he slipped seamlessly into the role of Hawai'i booster and manager of celebrities like Duke.

In Los Angeles, Henning proposed founding a film company to make Duke a star on the order of Douglas Fairbanks, one of the biggest celebrities of the silent film era. The movies that Henning made would feature Duke performing aquatic feats while surrounded by the finest supporting cast of the day. The first movie was to be a biography of Kamehameha I, shot on location in Hawai'i, and starring Duke as the implacable warrior king. The idea came to nothing, however, and a little more than a year after Duke had settled in Los Angeles, "Honest Oscar" abruptly dropped his client and fled California. He resurfaced a year later in Alabama, having reinvented himself once again as a freelance journalist.

At thirty, Duke felt age nipping at his heels. He was still incredibly fast in the water, but he was well aware that a new generation of swimmers could—literally and figuratively—surpass him. His own brother, Sam, was a lightning freestyle competitor. Sam had "not the powerful physique" of Duke, wrote one sportswriter, but was "seriously figured as a possible heir to his brother's championship estate." More alarmingly, a new swimmer—Johnny Weissmuller, from Chicago—seemed to many as though he had been "grown in a lab" to defeat Duke. Through 1922 and 1923, in qualifying races on the mainland, Weissmuller consistently outswam the older Olympian. Although Duke—along with Weissmuller and Sam—ultimately qualified for the 1924 US Olympic Team headed to Paris, it seemed to many that the writing was on the wall. Even Duke admitted that he didn't think he could beat Weissmuller.

He was right. Paris that summer was blistering hot. In the sweltering barracks where the athletes slept, Duke strummed his ukulele and entertained his fellow Olympians. David had accompanied his brothers across the ocean, and while Sam and Duke practiced, David befriended the other athletes, collecting their signatures on a sweater. A spirit of bonhomie mixed with anxious rivalry pervaded the American swim team. Although one reporter fretted that "foreign nations are developing mermen who will surely tax America's white hopes," the real tension surrounded Duke and Weissmuller's race. While Duke's style of swimming was beautiful, one French newspaper noted, ultimately, "Weissmuller, the speed swimming phenomenon, must triumph."

In the final race for the 100-meter gold medal—Duke's best event—crowds packed the stands despite the blazing heat. Weissmuller stepped up on his starting block, flanked by Duke on one side and Sam on the other. Arne Borg, the "Swedish Sturgeon," and Katsuo Takahashi from Japan took the other blocks.

When the gun went off, Weissmuller dove in and immediately pulled ahead. As one French paper put it, "the Hawaiian with ebony hair, and his younger brother, Sam, fiercely fought throughout the course with the Swede Arne Borg for second place." In the end, Duke took silver, beating his own Olympic record with a time of 1 minute, 0.4 seconds, but losing his shot at the gold medal to Weissmuller's impressive 59 seconds. Sam came in third, with 1 minute, 1.8 seconds. After the Olympics,

Duke raced Weissmuller in a dozen more exhibition matches across Europe, but he was never able to beat the Chicagoan.

With the Olympics over, Duke went back to California instead of Hawai'i, hoping to pick up his movie career where he'd left off.

Stories set among Southern Pacific islands had gained popularity in Hollywood. Films like *McVeagh of the South Seas* (1914), *Aloha Oe* (1915), *The Bottle Imp* (1917), and *Idol Dancer* (1920) presented viewers with encounters between "savagery" and "civilization," often with the daring hint of interracial romance among the palm trees. Sometimes filmed on location, though more often filmed in Los Angeles, the movies typically featured white actors in makeup and wigs depicting the notional Indigenous people of Hawai'i and other Polynesian islands.

In one sense, Hollywood's early fascination with Pacific life tracked with the very history of film, and anthropologists were its earliest users. In 1898, for example, anthropologist A. C. Haddon took a movie camera with him on his expedition to the Torres Strait Islands in the Southern Pacific and came away with roughly five minutes of footage of Strait Islanders making fire, dancing, and hanging around. True, the camera sometimes jammed, the film spoiled easily, and Haddon fretted that the entire expedition would be a failure. In the end, however, Haddon became convinced of the utility of the movie camera for studying humans.

That same year, a team from the Edison Manufacturing Company visited Hawai'i with a movie camera and returned with a short clip of boys in Honolulu Harbor diving for coins. The Edison team returned in 1901 under the direction of photographer Robert Bonine and again shot a reel of boys diving, along with two other films, *Cutting Sugar Cane* and *Loading Sugar Cane*. Finally, in 1906, Bonine returned once more and filmed a variety of scenes, including surfers at Waikiki. It's impossible to tell from the grainy footage if Duke or David were among the surfers and diving boys, though considering their ages at both intervals it's possible.

Further blurring the line between truth and fiction, a new genre of so-called documentary movies offered exciting narratives encapsulating ostensibly nonfiction accounts of people's lives—particularly Indigenous people. The term was first applied to filmmaker Robert Flaherty's 1926 movie, *Moana*, which purported to show the authentic life of a Samoan family living in traditional, prehistoric conditions. In actuality, Flaherty had used hired actors and staged scenarios to recreate what he felt "actual" Samoan life was like.

Flaherty had pioneered this technique four years earlier in his runaway hit *Nanook of the North* (1922), which similarly depicted a week in the life of the titular Inuit man, as he and his family hunted walruses, made igloos, and marveled at modern technologies like phonographs. As with *Moana*, "Nanook" himself was, in essence, a hired actor, and Flaherty designed many of the scenes depicting "actual" Inuit life in order to emphasize the notional "primitivity" of the Inuit's struggle against the elements. This fact did not, however, stop officials at the American Museum from judging *Nanook* a "remarkable film," and from accepting some Samoan artifacts donated by Flaherty into their anthropological collection. Although *Moana* did not make the splash that *Nanook* did, both films nevertheless solidified the idea that movies could be an exciting way of conveying "scientific" ideas.

In their own way, these documentaries were not unlike the casts of Indigenous people in the American Museum. They did not so much "document" Indigenous life as much as they staged a version of it that was compatible with a received notion of slow racial progress, extending from more to less "primitive" races of people. The fact that the real Inuit people that Flaherty filmed no longer hunted walruses with spears, and that they were very familiar with phonographs and other modern technologies, was unimportant for the larger message of the movie. In a similar way, the fact that David Kahanamoku was not often to be found in a malo spearing fish was tangent to the message conveyed by the cast. The point was to provide a glimpse at supposedly disappearing races, rather than the contemporary lives of existing people.

Duke adapted well to Hollywood.

Los Angeles in the 1920s had many similarities to Duke's Honolulu. A port town nestled between mountains and the Pacific Ocean, it possessed a polyglot and often transient population drawn from around the world. Like Honolulu a decade before, LA in the 1920s was in the midst of a rapid transformation from an economy based on resource extraction—oil and oranges—to one based on cultural production. A new film "colony" called "Hollywoodland"—a massive sign for which had just been erected in 1923 in the hills overlooking the city—announced the rapid urban growth.

And while Honolulu's cultural product relied on *importing* tourists to its shores with a promise of sunshine, balmy climate, varied topography, and fantasies of adventure and authenticity, Hollywood reversed that: it *exported* fantasies of adventure and authenticity made by film producers who found the West Coast conducive to moviemaking because of its sunshine, balmy climate, and varied topography.

As a famous athlete, moreover, Duke was comfortable with celebrity, and his easygoing personality endeared him to Hollywood's elites. He hobnobbed with Hollywood stars and directors like Mary Miles Minter and D. W. Griffith, played golf with sports stars like Babe Ruth, and even caroused—in his teetotaling way—with such legendary party animals as John Ford and J. Paul Getty.

He signed a contract with Famous Players–Laskey, one of the biggest studios in Hollywood and the producer of *Nanook*, *Moana*, and *Adventure*. He then followed this turn with a flurry of other small parts in Famous Players–Laskey movies: *Pony Express*, *The Lady of the Hare*, and *Lord Jim* in 1925; *Old Ironsides* in 1926; *Hula* and *The Isle of Sunken Gold* in 1927; *Woman Wise* and *Her Hero* in 1928; and *Where East Is East* in 1929. As a spokesperson for the production company put it, "Duke Kahanamoku, champion amateur swimmer of the world, is one of sportsdom's most valuable contributions to the motion picture world."

In many ways, Duke considered being a movie star similar to being a swimming sensation. It required physical skill, magnetism, and—in the silent era—didn't require much talking. As one item titled "Rules for Gaining Stardom" remarked, to be a film star, one had to be able to fight like Jack Dempsey, dance like Irene Castle, or "swim like Duke Kahanamoku." Certainly, Duke could do that. In a single week during the filming of *Adventure*, Duke reflected, "I took part in three fights, paddled a canoe until my arms ached, and swam a 400-yard course four times under conditions that called for every ounce of strength I possessed."

"There is no better way to keep in trim than to take part in photoplays which contain much action," he told reporters.

Moreover, being a film star required good looks and charisma, and Duke, as one reporter with a knack for understatement put it, "films very well." It was true that, when called on to speak spontaneously in front of reporters, Duke often became tongue-tied. As one of his fellow beach boys explained, Duke's shyness led people to think "that buggah must be dumb!" But in front of a camera, he came alive. His eyes flashed with confidence, and his expressive face would smolder one minute, beam happily the next, and project determination the next. Ever since his days as a beach boy, he enjoyed dressing up in fine clothes and costumes. As one reporter gushed, the reason that Duke was so frequently cast in maritime movies was because his "fine body looks so impressive in the gay, if scanty rags of a pirate." Still another put the matter more succinctly: Duke was "the most magnificent human male God ever put on the earth."

The short silent film *No Father to Guide Him* (1925) provides a standout example of Duke's acting chops. The movie's plot, such as it is, revolves around the efforts of a kindly milkman to wrest his son and estranged wife from the clutches of his overbearing and belligerent mother-in-law. One of the set pieces of the movie takes place on a beach, where the father has taken his son after fleeing the mother-in-law. Gazing at the ocean, the son spots Duke diving flawlessly into the water. "Can you dive in like that, Dad?" the son asks through an intertitle. Wishing to show off, the dad tries, and a series of humiliations follows, culminating in the man losing his swimsuit and foundering naked in the water.

At this point, the camera cuts to Duke in a lifeguard's

swimsuit, sitting under an umbrella and playing ukulele for a gaggle of admiring women. He misinterprets the man's calls for his son to throw him some clothes as cries of distress and rushes to save him. The camera captures some glamour shots of Duke leaping into the water and swimming in his trademark crawl—which does, indeed, seem very fast, particularly in the slightly sped-up register of the film. The man resists Duke. "If you take me out this way, we'll both get pinched!" he cries—presumably worried about the whiff of homosexuality that might accompany his nude emergence from the ocean in Duke's arms. An intertitle then informs the viewer that "when a drowning person starts to struggle," the best idea is to "strike him a firm blow on the point of the chin." Duke does so, but this only enrages the milkman, who punches Duke back and knocks the athlete unconscious. The milkman is then forced to save Duke, while wearing a woman's dress that his son has thrown to him. Duke awakens on the beach, becomes angry, and proceeds to chase the milkman, tripping and somersaulting with some well-rendered slapstick. Eventually, the milkman prevails over his mother-in-law and reunites with his estranged wife, who has collapsed in exhaustion on a pile of sand on the beach. As the two embrace and kiss discreetly, the beach erupts from underneath them—it's Duke buried under the sand! The milkman runs away, this time with his family in tow; Duke gives chase, and the movie comes to a satisfying conclusion.

Duke was a natural at physical comedy. As the *Honolulu Star-Bulletin* remarked, however, more often than not "movie producers were not developing Duke's capabilities before the camera. They were using him in dignified roles, which he plays well enough, but it's in comedy that Duke can really do his stuff." Typically, these "dignified roles" were those of underdeveloped, nonwhite sidekicks. In *Lord Jim* (1925), for instance, Duke played Tam Itam, the title character's manservant. In *Old Ironsides* (1926), Duke shows up briefly as a bearded and turbaned but strangely friendly Barbary pirate who gently manhandles one of the movie's heroes into enslavement before being strangled. In *The Pony Express* (1925) he played an "Indian Chief," appearing on screen decked out in a feathered headdress, ordering a host of generic North American warriors to attack a settlement. And in *The Isle of Sunken Gold* (1927) Duke appeared as a nonspecific Native character, billed third in the film's advertisements, behind "the Devil Ape of Bomo," a man in an ape suit. (The "Devil Ape's" name was "Kong" and his prurient interest in the female lead presaged *King Kong* of 1933.)

The real problem wasn't so much that Duke wasn't able to handle the "dignified" roles. It was that producers and directors—as fond as they were of Duke personally—couldn't quite see him as more than a "Native." Industry magazines emphasized the "natural tan of the Hollywood guest," and expressed consternation over his last name. Duke would "never be popular with film fans," thought one reporter, "unless he adopts a name easier to pronounce." He was "the Duke with the tongue-twisting name" to one reporter; his name "sounded like a muffled alarm clock trying to tell the hour" to another. As late as 1937, child star Shirley Temple spoke fondly of her "friend Duke Kahanamoku," but said, "I call him Duke, because the rest is too long."

Nevertheless, if Duke's on-screen impact was indifferent, his off-screen exploits were larger than life. Duke often worked behind the scenes as a swim instructor, stunt coordinator, and lifeguard. On the set of *Adventure*, Fleming recalled that Duke nearly drowned filming an underwater scene in which he became entangled in seaweed. While filming *Old Ironsides*, he rescued several crewmembers from drowning when the mast of the replica frigate to which they clung collapsed into the ocean near Catalina Island, off Los Angeles. During that same shoot, he caused a panic when he went for a swim offshore in shark infested waters. His costar, Wallace Beery, spied him through binoculars surrounded by fins in deep water, and called out to him, "Wait! The sharks!" Beery and the film's director, James Cruze, leaped into a motorboat and came to Duke's aid. They found him unharmed and laughing. "They're just little sharks!" he said. "I had fun racing with them!"

In his most famous adventure, on June 14, 1925, Duke and two companions woke up on the beach at Corona del Mar, then a secluded cove south of Los Angeles. They had camped overnight, hoping to surf some of the beach's excellent waves. By morning, however, offshore storms had produced angry, roiling surf. "Only a porpoise or a sea lion has the right to be out there," Duke thought. Suddenly, one of his companions spotted a ship nestled in the breakers. The forty-foot yacht *Thelma*, with fifteen passengers and two crew on board, was returning from a night fishing trip when it got caught in the churn. Duke and his companions watched in horror as the ocean swatted the ship back and forth, flooding its engines with seawater. Around its deck railing, fishermen hung on for dear life. The next second, a massive wave reared up and crashed into the *Thelma*, smashing the windows of its pilot house and capsizing the craft. The men on the rails scattered into the sea.

In an instant, Duke grabbed his board and lanced through the waves, paddling until his "arms begged for mercy." When he reached the site of the ship, he began gathering the screaming, frantic fishermen and placing them across his board. With three men on it, the board was at capacity, so Duke turned and paddled toward shore, handing the gasping men over to his companions. In all, he returned to the scene of the wreck three more times, saving a total of eight men. Twelve men survived the wreck. Five drowned.

Afterward, the Newport Beach chief of police described Kahanamoku's performance as "the most superhuman rescue act and the finest display of surfboard riding that has ever been seen in the world." As reporters descended on the scene, Duke melted away. When they finally caught up to him, they peppered him with questions about the rescue, demanding to know how he had saved so many people. He was characteristically shy. "By a few tricks, perhaps," he mused. "It was done. That is the main thing."

The episode cemented Duke's mainland reputation as a legendary waterman, but it also brought surfing to greater public attention. The Santa Monica lifeguard company made surfboards a necessary part of their lifeguarding equipment. Other beach patrols around Los Angeles followed suit.

Duke himself spread the love of surfing among Hollywood's elites. Child star Jackie Coogan, for instance, boasted that after Duke taught him to surf, he rode waves "from Baja California to San Francisco when there were only nine or ten surfers on the entire Pacific Coast." Among those nine or ten were actors Marjorie Daw and Evelyn Brent, whom Duke taught to surf one afternoon in Santa Monica. Clara Bow—Hollywood's "it" girl—tried surfing at least once under Duke's watchful eye.

Thanks to Duke's work, by the middle of the 1920s, the

sport had come to embody, as director Sam Wood put it, "all the mad jazz mania of the twentieth century." It was a sport for people who were "forced to search for new thrills, eager for life and living," Wood thought, and when he went looking for just such a person to star in his films, he approached actress Vera Reynolds, one of Duke's surfing entourage.

"Can you swim?" Wood demanded.

"Can a duck?" she answered. "I was raised right here in Los Angeles, and I know Mr. Pacific's ocean intimately."

"Can you ride a surf board?" Wood continued.

"Bring on any surf board you've got, wild or tame," she replied. "I'll break him."

Based on this discussion, Wood cast Vera Reynolds in his 1923 film, *Prodigal Daughters*, because, wrote a reporter, "she could ride a surf board. Can you imagine making your dearest dreams come true because of a surf board? Of course, there were a few other qualifications—little things like beauty and dramatic ability—but the main thing was the surf board." *Prodigal Daughters* didn't feature any surfing—just lots of other madcap antics. Reynolds did, however, get to show off her skills as a "surf board flapper" in the Cecil B. DeMille film *Feet of Clay* (1924). The film is lost today, but surviving synopses show that it contained a surf race and a shark attack as critical plot points, and it is widely considered to be one of the first fictional depictions of surfing on film.

• • •

In October 1929, the superheated American economy imploded. Wobbling markets in London set off a ripple effect, and within less than a month, Wall Street experienced catastrophic losses. In another month, the world economy went into freefall. In the United States, those who had capital stopped investing, preferring to hoard money. Everyday people pulled their money out of banks and stowed it in mattresses, tree stumps, jars buried in their yards—anywhere but within the US banking system. This caused bank failures and contraction of credit, which further exacerbated economic collapse. People lost their jobs, their farms, their homes, their life savings. Unemployment soared. By 1932, nearly a quarter of Americans had no income.

The winds that blew ill for most Americans, however, blew better for surfers. During the Depression years of 1929 to 1941 the number of surfers in mainland California alone quadrupled. As surf photographer "Doc" Ball pointed out, surfing was essentially immune to economic shocks. It was a sport that could be practiced all day long by unemployed young men (mainly men) who needed only some scrap wood, rudimentary carpentry skills, and a ride to the beach to get started. "Of course, we had a little trouble gettin' gasoline," Ball remembered. "It [the Great Depression] kept us kinda limited in certain ways, but we had surfin' to take care of everything. Long as there's waves, why, you didn't have to pay for those."

Hollywood, too, boomed due to an eager market for escapism. In 1927, a new kind of movie had debuted—the "talkie," in which viewers could hear the actors' voices.

For Duke, though, neither the surge in surfing nor the enduring popularity of movies buoyed his career prospects. As he neared his fortieth birthday, roles dried up. A 1928 article in *Photoplay* magazine listed Duke as one of the many athletes who had "failed" in Hollywood, noting that, in spite of being the "most perfect specimen of his race . . . with a picturesque and splendid face and the carriage of an athlete" his "labors [as an actor] went unrewarded." His film career was over.

Duke faced the end of his time in Hollywood with philosophical resolve. "Lady Luck has gone by," he wrote to David. "I've always heard she was fickle, but at least she was something wonderful I experienced." He moved back to Hawai'i for good in 1929, though he traveled back to Hollywood briefly for a role in the 1930 movie *The Girl of the Port*.

Ironically, one of his last film appearances was in Douglas Fairbanks's vanity project, *Around the World in Eighty Minutes* (1932)—a sort of travelogue in which Fairbanks narrated his adventures around the globe in an upbeat voiceover. The first stop was Hawai'i, where Fairbanks arrived in December 1931. In the film, Duke greets Fairbanks with a handshake and lei, and Fairbanks introduces him to the audience as "the greatest swimmer of all time, the man who made swimming an event."

"Speaking of swimming," says Fairbanks, "how about a little surfboarding?"

"We'll do that," replies Duke.

"I'll bet you . . ." Fairbanks continues, then whispers in Duke's ear, "I'll bet you that, that I can ride a surfboard 100 yards in on my first try and I never tried it before."

"Well," says Duke, shaking Fairbanks's hand, "I'll take you up on that."

The next scene finds Fairbanks awkwardly balanced on a surfboard. "To ride a surfboard requires a little more than confidence," he admits in a voiceover as he wobbles through the waves. "I might look comfortable, but I'm not. . . . It was very much like riding Niagara rapids on a match."

At the end of the sequence, Fairbanks and Duke stand on the beach together, with Fairbanks trying out different supposedly Hawaiian words on Duke: "mai tai" he says.

"That's a drink!" Duke says, good-naturedly.

"I know, I know," says Fairbanks, "come on!" and the two men take off in a trot down the beach, Duke effortlessly toting the heavy, solid redwood board under one arm.

Duke later remarked that, in some ways, this role was the apotheosis of his film career. "First I played a Hindu thief, then an Arab prince, and after that a Sioux chieftain," he told an interviewer. "I was very surprised when at last I received an offer to play what I consider to be my most unusual part—that of a native born Hawaiian."

• • •

Duke wasn't the only one "cast" as a Native Hawaiian in 1931. Just a few months before Duke taught Fairbanks to surf, David and Sargent Kahanamoku took a turn before a movie camera. As the film rolled, the two men showed off their surfing poses—standing straight upright, crouching, kneeling on their boards as they zoomed through the waves of Waikiki at top speed. They demonstrated surfing with clinical precision, showing how the slightest shift of body weight, or a subtle movement of their arms from one side to the other, or a swing of their hips could cause the board to change direction, picking up speed down the face of the wave, cutting across it, gliding to an elegant finish at the shoreline.

This film wasn't a Hollywood production, however, but a hybrid scientific and artistic endeavor. The sculptor Malvina

Hoffman was the director. Her husband, Samuel Grimson, was the cameraman. Jean Marco, Hoffman's studio assistant, served as crew. Hoffman had come to Hawaiʻi as part of a project to sculpt a different vision of the "races of man"—not for Osborn and the American Museum, but for the Field Museum of Natural History in Chicago. Hawaiʻi was her first stop on a transpacific tour, and the Kahanamoku brothers were her ideal subjects.

At forty-six, Malvina Hoffman boasted studios in New York and Paris with a portfolio of clients that included plutocrats and princes on both sides of the Atlantic. She wore her graying hair in a tight bun, and her aquiline nose, high cheekbones, and round face gave her an air of almost querulous confidence. It was her eyes, however, that beamed this self-certainty into the world, focusing tight, bright shafts of curiosity and hauteur on whatever person or thing seized her interest.

She had grown up in New York, in a respectably bohemian family of upper-middle-class musicians. Her father was a composer, her mother a pianist, and her five siblings were accomplished instrumentalists. As a young child, Hoffman became accustomed to the mix of intellectuals, composers, critics, artists, and collectors that filtered through the family home. Mark Twain took her sailing on the Hudson. Gertrude Whitney—founder of the Whitney Museum of American Art—encouraged her sculpting career. Henry Frick, steel magnate and trustee of the American Museum of Natural History, was one of her early patrons.

Unsurprisingly, America's plutocracy and its eugenicists often mingled. Hoffman counted Osborn as a friend, and in 1924 completed a portrait bust of E. H. Harriman—an avid supporter of the arts and eugenics alike. Hoffman herself tended to think in terms of racial types. After a trip through Europe in 1918, for instance, she registered shock at the variation between "Italian types" and "strong jawed and stocky" Yugoslavians. "Not only their appearance but their whole psychology was in sharp contrast to the stolid, slow-speaking Slavic peasants," she wrote of the Italians. In a similar way, she also felt that Croatians were a "primitive race" compared to other Europeans.

It was therefore with little surprise but much excitement that Hoffman received a telegram in February of 1930 from Stanley Field, president of the Field Museum of Natural History in Chicago. "Have a proposition to make," read the slip of paper. "Do you care to consider it? Racial types to be modeled while travelling round the world."

The Field Museum was a relative newcomer among the major American natural history museums. True, it had hired luminaries early on. Franz Boas had originally served as a curator of anthropology at the Field, and the museum gave the most celebrated taxidermist in America, Carl Akeley, his first high-profile job. Nevertheless, the Field was often seen as something of a junior partner to the older institutions.

True progress in public science education could only be made, thought Stanley Field, through "radical changes ... in old museum methods," and one of his keenest desires was to reinvigorate the museum's anthropology halls, which were populated by "dummies of sawdust or painted plaster with staring glass eyes and dusty false hair." He planned a new Hall of Physical Anthropology, featuring an expansive display to be entitled, simply, the *Races of Mankind*. The display would eschew the "old fashioned dry as dust scientific treatment of exhibits"—bones and artifacts in glass cases—in favor of more dynamic sculptures that echoed the excitement of new media such as film.

When Hoffman received Stanley Field's telegram, she packed her bags and traveled to Chicago. The next day, braving bitter winds and biting ice, she strode into Field's "awe inspiring" office—a room of "huge dimensions, with a carpet so soft" that Hoffman felt she was "crossing the ninth green of a golf course"—and squared off against Stanley, Henry, and Berthold Laufman, the museum's director of anthropology. She could not, she declared, be part of a project that cobbled together the work of multiple artists. Such an effort would be a disaster—a hodgepodge that could only end in disgrace. Instead she would do the entire series of the *Races of Mankind* herself. In return, she would dedicate herself "entirely and wholeheartedly to the enterprise and bear responsibility for its success or failure."

After some back and forth, Stanley acceded to her demands, giving her a contract for $250,000 and instructing her to start immediately. Hoffman would produce 120 plaster sculptures depicting the many recognized gradations of racial "types." The exhibit would open in 1933. Stanley later reduced the number of sculptures to 104—and gave Hoffman more money—when she pressed him to have the sculptures instead cast in bronze. As a reward for his acquiescence, she gave him a small, bronze sculpture that she'd produced of a dancing girl from Benin. "Hoffman does get away with it," Stanley remarked, admiring Hoffman's persistence.

Hoffman undertook a crash course in physical anthropology. She went to the Smithsonian to meet with Hrdlička and found him just as grumpy in Washington, DC, as Sullivan had in Hawai'i. "I'd rather know less and enjoy life more than Prof. H.,"

Hoffman wrote in her diary. "Of all 'joy killers' and enthusiasm quenchers he is first prize." She also visited the American Museum and talked to Osborn and Wissler, observing their beloved osteological collections. In London, she met with famed British anthropologist Sir Arthur Keith and impressed him with her supposed ability to discern an individual's race by mere sight. And she read extensively in racial literature, including Sullivan's studies of Polynesian somatology. She marveled, "I had hardly heard of the word anthropology, and now—well, I rarely hear about anything else; perhaps I am becoming an anthropologist in spite of myself."

Intriguingly, one of the scientists that Hoffman met was Marcel Mauss, a French scholar more known for his studies of culture and behavior than of anthropometry. In the 1920s and 1930s he had become increasingly aware, as he said, "that walking or swimming, for example, and all sorts of things of the same type, are specific to determinate societies." For example, he wrote, possibly thinking of Duke, "the Polynesians do not swim as we do, [just as] my generation did not swim as the present generation does." Indeed, all cultures, thought Mauss, had particular bodily movements. Mauss called these styles of movement "habitus" and thought that even if anthropologists since the 1890s had mainly concentrated on the inert body—the body as it could be measured, photographed, and cast—the body in motion truly sparked anthropological interest.

Whether Mauss and Hoffman discussed his theory of habitus is unclear, but its outlines resonated with Hoffman's view of her own task. She firmly rejected the staid anthropology of her predecessors. When, for instance, Henry Field came to visit her to discuss the *Races of Mankind*, she noted with relief that he brought books and photographs—"no skulls, no measurements, no charts." At other times, she disparaged casting as a poor way of representing people, since it did nothing to capture the dynamic motion of the muscles under their skin. She was, for instance, "very disgusted" with the life casts that she found in the American Museum and thought the casts in the Natural History Museum in London were "badly shown and badly painted."

Actions imprinted themselves on the body, Hoffman felt, and thus, as she put it, "certain people represented *race*, while others were mere individuals." A "mere" individual was simply a person, with a particular, finite biography, particular likes and dislikes, particular skills and peccadillos. To represent "race," on the other hand, was to represent an entire branch of the tree of humankind. Ironically, of course, to her it was only the unique skills of a select few individuals—artists and scientists with the vision to see "types" where others saw individual people—that could give form to "race."

Hoffman cared about science—she had studied embryology as a teenager, for example. But she tempered her scientific eye with a belief in the same sorts of mystical, vital forces that fired the imaginations of men like Osborn. She felt that the development of the embryo, for instance, was subject to mysterious organic forces, and that artists, like scientists, were aware of these forces. The artist, Hoffman wrote, was a "superman who has torn away the veils of life, seen behind the walls of reality and tragedy, and penetrated into the wilderness where dwells the primitive savage, the instinct of wild beasts; a man who has listened to the silences of the night, and hears the whispers of the dark forest and the song of the secret bird."

At times, Hoffman didn't stray far from home to "penetrate

into the wilderness." As Hoffman remarked, she "often discovered splendid racial subjects far removed from their original homeland, and more strikingly typical of their own race than those we had actually seen in their native habitat." In Paris, for instance, she counted herself fortunate that 1931 marked the beginning of the Exposition coloniale internationale—a grand fair displaying the products and people of France's far-flung colonies. It was "perhaps the most varied collection of African and Asiatic subjects ever assembled in one place," she thought, and with the assistance of friends among the exposition's directors, Hoffman brought some of these people to her Paris studio for sculpture sessions.

Likewise, in New York, she was delighted to find a bodybuilder to pose for her. This man styled himself "God's Gift to Women" and was a perfect example of the "Nordic type," she thought, even though his self-description caused her to raise an eyebrow. As for the "Anglo-Saxon type," she didn't have to look far. She convinced the British anthropologist Sir Arthur Keith of her keen scientific eye by using him as the model for the best of British racial stock.

But to fully capture humankind in all of its racial typicality, she felt, it was necessary to go, as she put it, on a "head hunting" expedition. This was how she found herself, on October 9, 1931, on the ocean liner *President Garfield*, pulling into Honolulu Harbor. She had packed everything she'd need for her trip—barrels of clay and plaster, rolls of wire for building armatures, snakebite kits and medicine bags. From Honolulu, her party would continue on to Japan, China, India, and then onward across the Eurasian landmass back to her studio in Paris. They would photograph, film, and sculpt racial types of all sorts along the way. But first, she would use her sojourn in Hawai'i to research and sculpt the "Polynesian type."

Her first stop was the Bishop Museum, where she examined Sullivan's casts. She didn't think much of these. She was likewise unimpressed by Sullivan's photographs, which she thought formal and unappealing.

She was more interested in the new curator of anthropology, Te Rangi Hīroa—or, as he was known to his white colleagues, Dr. Peter Buck. The son of a Māori mother and an Irish father, Te Rangi Hīroa had been a rugby player, a medical doctor, and a parliamentarian in New Zealand before turning to anthropology.

He was a complicated figure. On the one hand, he accepted the utility of anthropometry along lines that Sullivan and Osborn would more or less have recognized. "No statement as to the manner of men," he wrote, "can be accepted by intelligent people unless it is based upon a sufficiently large number of measurements of the physical characters of the human body and careful observations as to the form of hair, eyes, nose, skin colour, and other general features." Moreover, he felt, the distinction between savagery and civilization was, in broad strokes, useful, as was the idea that "savage" people had a different constitution than the "civilized." He claimed that he "understood and sympathized with" European doctors, who grew impatient with the "prejudices and superstitions which retard or prevent the recovery of Māori patients."

On the other hand, Te Rangi Hīroa didn't attach an innate, moral value to distinctions between people and doubted both the methods of physical anthropology and the absolute value of modern medicine. He recalled the disgust that he and a fellow Māori classmate had experienced when, on their first day of medical school, they saw posted an advertisement offering money in exchange for the skulls and skeletons of Māori people. "We read it with horror," he later remembered, "and almost abandoned our quest for medical knowledge." Similarly, he noted that it was impossible not to see that under the governance of the "progressive but somewhat forgetful Anglo-Saxon," the "ancient laws and observances necessary to the public health of the Māori have vanished; the conditions of life and living have altered; and the racial physique, vitality, and powers of resistance have deteriorated."

In other words, while Te Rangi Hīroa believed in the concept of "race," he nevertheless felt that culture mattered as much as "type" to understand the health and vitality of a people. Humans were complicated and could hold multitudes. Indeed, multitudes would resurface when one least expected it. "We inherit our fears in our blood," he wrote, "we imbibe them at our mother's breast. The schools and teaching of a father appeal to us as we grow older. We subject customs and faiths to the light of comparative criticism and we ridicule the ideas of more primitive races as absurd. But in times of stress, despondency and lowered vitality, there is a tendency to revert to the mother's fears which slumber within beneath the veneer of civilization." As a result, he was more fascinated with material culture than anthropometry and devoted his career to studying not so much the bodies of Polynesian people but how different people expressed beliefs—about what was good, what was beautiful, and how they should move through the world.

When he met Hoffman, the two evidently got along well. Te Rangi Hīroa indulged both his own fascination with Māori material culture and Hoffman's desire for more dynamic photographs, donning a grass skirt and cape and allowing Hoffman to photograph him practicing a *wero*—a Māori challenge dance. In some of the photographs, he brandishes a spear, demonstrating how it could be used to intimidate an opponent, his eyes blazing and his tongue projecting from his mouth. In other photographs, he is more staid, sitting in a chair, eyeing the camera imperiously, holding in his lap a *mere*—a flat, teardrop-shaped, jade weapon. Hoffman was delighted, describing him as an "eminent member of the Māori race" in her memoirs.

That same visit, Hoffman also met Harry Shapiro, recently arrived from New York to direct his own Hawaiian research.

Like Te Rangi Hīroa, Shapiro believed in the utility of anthropometry for understanding race. At this point in his career, however, he was coming to doubt that "race" had much to do with intelligence or culture. It was more significant what people did than how they looked in a chart when measured.

Hoffman left the Bishop Museum feeling inspired and the next day set up her own studio in Waikīkī and got to work. Through a friend in Honolulu—the wealthy painter, writer, and outdoorsman James A. "Kimo" Wilder—she met David Kahanamoku. The two men knew each other from a pageant that Wilder had written and directed for the sesquicentennial anniversary celebration of Captain Cook's arrival on Maui titled "Hawaii One Hundred and Fifty Years Ago." David's job had been to round up beach boys to play the parts of the Hawaiian villagers who greeted Cook, and to serve as their marshal, directing them around the stage in the costume of an ancient Hawaiian *aliʻi*.

David spent hours with the sculptor, taking her to the house he'd grown up in, and showing her family picture albums. But when it came to modeling, he explained the story of Sullivan's casting process and the sour taste it left. He wouldn't volunteer himself or his family for it. Hoffman recalled, "Every effort to lure any member of his family to my studio failed."

David's reticence called for more direct measures. Donning a swimsuit under her dress, the next day she strode down the beach to the Moana Hotel "to be nearer to the surf-board riders." The scene belonged in an erotically charged Hollywood movie, she thought. Sam Kahanamoku had recently pioneered the idea of swim trunks—that is, men wearing only shorts in the water, rather than the strappy, chest-covering one-piece suit of the 1920s—and all around Hoffman were "beach boys quietly basking in the tropical sunlight," "toast[ing] their splendidly developed bodies on both sides" under the sun, until they became a "rich brown." These "bronzed Apollos," she wrote, "enjoy their unemployment immensely"—"plung[ing] in and out of the azure sea," riding their boards with "an amazing sense of balance and acrobatic agility" and posing both a "menace and lure to the pale-faced visiting ladies" such as herself.

On the beach, she met David and Sargent, who she buttonholed into giving her surfing lessons. Hoffman is uncharacteristically mum on the subject of how the lessons went, except to note that she studied intently "the technique of swimming and surfboard riding" and to remark that "the strength of the waves and the charms of the beach boys" were among the pleasures and "perils" of Waikiki beach. In such a state, she noted, "Words become quite unnecessary as a means of communication—a look of the eye, a smile, or a quick gesture can establish a relationship in which confidence and humor can flow easily from one individual to any other."

The "confidence and humor" that she established in the water won the trust of Sargent and David. The men agreed to surf and pose for her, and, while her husband manned his movie camera, Sargent did "all his best aquatic stunts" on the surfboard. Then they took still pictures around Waikiki: Sargent posed casually at the edge of a swimming pool or standing with his body tensed, as though he was about to dive in; David standing in contrapposto in front of a wall; Sargent demonstrating his surfing stances on land; David posed in white swim trunks, holding a large spear over his shoulder as though he were about to throw it high into the air.

Finally, she was ready to sculpt. She chose Sargent as her model: "21 years old, 5′10½″ tall," and a "surf rider and swimmer de luxe," she wrote in her diary. She instructed him to crouch as though barreling through a curl, and then commenced making a maquette—a small mock-up of the final sculpture—out of clay and wire. It was "the usual mental battle," she wrote in freeform prose, "proportions, construction, wobbly stand, strange new surroundings. Streamers of perspiration exhausted ahead of each hour. Wonder how I can keep up such a fight for months of heat!"

As she worked, she felt the mystical energy of racial history come alive within her. "The world of the spirit has taken hold of me and I am its instrument," she exulted. "Ghosts of long ago revisit me." She sketched a vision in her notebook—racial history spiraling before her. It unfurled like a waterspout from an infinitely small point, expanding into a roiling, conical cloud that spread over the whole universe. "Time, creation . . . race??" she scrawled excitedly. All were collected in this miasma. From singular nothingness she envisioned the emergence of clouds and rhythm; then atoms coalescing from the clouds; then embryos, recapitulating the evolution of life on earth; then human

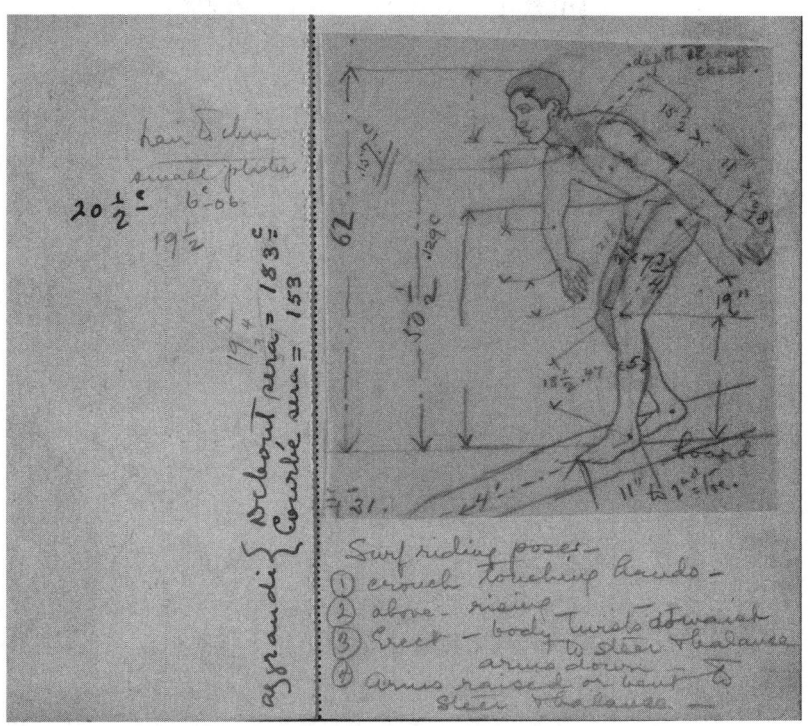

An anthropometric sketch from Malvina Hoffman's notebook depicting Sargent Kahanamoku in a surf-riding pose.

babies; then children; then young men and girls; old men and girls; and finally, those forms evaporated to reveal skulls and bones, like those studied by anthropologists. "And then what?" she wondered. "Immortality?"

If it was indeed immortality, it was realized in bronze.

Three days later, she showed her sculpture of a "Polynesian Male" to David and Sargent, who gave it their approval. She also called on Te Rangi Hīroa and Shapiro who likewise admired her work. She spent several more days in Honolulu, sketching people and searching for other Polynesian "types." At one point, she completed a bust of a "Hawaiian man." At another time, she did drawings and took photographs of Gershon Tupua, a Samoan teenager. She sketched him with a flower over one ear and a necklace of boar's tusks around his neck, extolling him as "one of the typical beach boys quietly basking in the tropical sunlight, with a scarlet hibiscus over his ear, seated in front of the traveler's palm." His head became the bust of a "Samoan man" in the *Races of Mankind* exhibit.

Within two weeks, she finished her work in Hawai'i. Grimson and Jean Marco carefully packed the maquette of Sargent Kahanamoku and shipped it back to her Paris studio. Later, she and her assistants would enlarge the model to full size and cast it in bronze.

The final sculpture was quite unlike Sullivan's cast of David. A life-sized, bronze Sargent, his face taut with a mixture of concentration and pleasure, crouches on a bronze board, riding a bronze wave. Every muscle ripples—his calves tense, his eyebrows pull inward. In Hoffman's sculpture, his body and the wave he rides seem to be almost the same, essential stuff. He appears to be recognizably of the world—Hoffman sculpted him in a pair of well-realized, bronze swim trunks—but also somehow ethereal and out of time. Indeed, as the Field Museum wrote in its description of the sculpture, Sargent's image was intended to be a representative of "physical and mental youth, retarded in sun baked rhythm, smooth, glittering bodies plunging in and out of azure seas. Moonlight, palm groves of tropical splendor and heavy scented blossoms. Athletes of great skill and daring, these boys ride their surfboards over the crests of the breakers."

The *Races of Mankind* opened to much fanfare on June 3, 1933. Its debut purposefully coincided with the "Century of

Progress"—a Chicago fair not unlike the 1893 Columbian Exposition, which showcased the very latest in American science, medicine, and technology.

Hoffman's sculptures were a terrific success. "Impressive as works of beauty," rhapsodized one reviewer, "the statues are modeled with strict regard for scientific accuracy." Another agreed, writing, "the Hawaiian surf-board rider and the Solomon Island tree climber are the most interesting to the majority of people," but all of the sculptures were splendid—and, indeed, provided "scientific displays" that could compete with more vulgar entertainments (like "peepshows") found outside the museum.

Perhaps Osborn was the most stunned by her discoveries. On June 1, 1932, almost exactly a year before the *Races of Mankind* was to open, Hoffman wrote to him to say that she had met David Kahanamoku, "who posed for the plaster cast" at the American Museum, and had told her "all about his sensations inside the mould!" She had been delighted with the meeting and suggested that Osborn might wish to get in touch with his erstwhile subject.

Osborn was taken aback. He immediately sent a memo to the museum's director. "I have just learned that our Hawaiian life cast is not of 'Duke' but of his brother David," Osborn wrote in astonishment. David was "quite a different man," he huffed—though it's not clear that he could have said why or how.

Jane Davenport Harris's statuette depicting the average American male at the Second International Eugenics Congress, 1921.

7

THE DISCOVERY OF NOTHING

By 1934, Shapiro had grown comfortable in his role as Sullivan's replacement. He administrated the Hall of the Races of Man; he did studies of skeletons; he squabbled about money with the American Museum's administrators.

He had also expanded on the role, making it his own. He was an accomplished public speaker, giving radio addresses and public lectures.

In 1929 he embarked on a study of the men of the Honolulu sheriff's office. From 1930 through 1931—when he met Malvina Hoffman—he was in Hawaiʻi to inaugurate a new study on the physical characteristics of Hawaiian Chinese children.

But along the way, Shapiro took a turn. His work at the American Museum showed him the way not to greater understanding of "pure" races or racial hierarchies, but to the conviction that the very notion of racial purity was a myth. More than that, he realized the very idea of heritable racial "factors" was erroneous. Human beings did not, he came to see, fall into easily characterized groups that could be cast in plaster or sculpted in bronze. The entire program of eugenics that animated men like Osborn, Wissler, Hooton, and their protégés like Sullivan relied on bad science.

Or rather, it was worse than bad science. The simple, pleasing, just-so story about racial purity and ideal society that eugenicists peddled was positively dangerous. Shapiro realized that in a society like his own—fast-moving, protean, and possessed of powerful technologies like radio, movies, and airplanes—scientists had to be humble with their pronouncements about matters as serious as race and identity. Without a better sense of what they were doing, Shapiro came to think that his fellow anthropologists were "toying with dynamite."

• • •

By 1933, that "dynamite" had exploded in a series of chain reactions that rocked the globe.

Eugenics, on the rise through the 1920s, received a new stimulus from the global economic Depression. As Roger Babson—an economist who predicted the stock market collapse of 1929—put it in 1935, "vital statistics show that democracy will ultimately collapse unless nations give genetics and eugenics primary consideration"—"our birth standard is far more important than our wage standard, our gold standard, or our living standard!" More to Babson's point, "birth standard" and "living standard"—eugenic policy and economic policy— were inextricably entwined in the American political imagination.

By the middle of the 1930s, America led the world in promulgating eugenic doctrines. Other countries had eugenics programs: Japan, Hungary, Britain, Brazil, Argentina, Mexico, among others. But the United States stood out in both the study of race science and the implementation of eugenic policies.

Germans, especially, esteemed American racial science. This was the case even before 1933, when Adolf Hitler seized power and established the hegemony of his Nazi Party over German politics. German eugenicists throughout the 1920s watched American anti-immigration and pro-sterilization laws with approval. In 1925, Walter Schultze, a physician who would become one of Hitler's closest lieutenants, commented with no small sense of envy that "in the United States racial policy and thinking has become much more popular than in other countries." Indeed, another German physician lamented, in the United States—a country whose people prided themselves on their staunch defense of personal freedoms—compulsory, government-sponsored sterilization of those deemed unfit had experienced widespread legal and social success, while his own countryfolk held too strong a sense of individual "self-determination" to allow such overreach.

Hitler's rise to power tested both this sense of "self-determination" and America's leading status in worldwide eugenics. After 1933, Schultze, for instance, became the head of German universities and orchestrated a purge of Jewish professors. He later served as an architect for the Nazi's program of mass killing. The political program of eugenics was never far from politics. Rudolf Hess, Hitler's deputy, summed up the close philosophical association between Nazism and eugenics by cribbing an aphorism from the eugenicist Fritz Lenz: "National Socialism is just applied biology."

On January 1, 1934, the first of Germany's eugenic laws—the "Law for the Prevention of Progeny with Heritable Diseases"— took effect, allowing the sterilization of anyone doctors deemed likely to bear a heritable illness. Diseases of this sort included "Feeblemindedness," "Schizophrenia," "blindness," "deafness," and alcoholism. The following year, the "Law for the Protection of the German Blood and German Honor" and the "Reich Citizenship Law" went into effect. The first forbade marriage between Jewish people and those of "German blood"; the second limited German citizenship to people of full German heritage.

Nazi academics credited their American forebears. In 1934, officials at Johann Wolfgang Goethe University in Berlin gave Osborn an honorary doctorate, and Osborn personally traveled to Europe to accept it. As he later told Laughlin, "my recent visit to Germany, Austria and Italy and my continuous observation in the United States convince me that of all modern social movements eugenics is far the most important."

• • •

Eugenics in America had always had its dissenters—those who felt it was grim, or illiberal, or bad science, or just creepy. But it took the rise of Nazism for Americans to begin taking a harder look at eugenic doctrines.

Among leading American scientists, it began to become unmistakable that eugenics was really politics masquerading as science, rather than any real science worthy of the name. During a 1936 "Congress on Population," for instance, a delegation from Germany used their presentations to expound "racist propaganda" that alarmed even staunch eugenicists like Hooton. Nazi purges of academia similarly seemed a bridge too far for many of their American peers. In 1939, for instance, Shapiro turned, ironically, to Charles Davenport—founder of the Eugenics Record Office and one of the leading promoters of eugenics in the United States—to try to secure a safe haven for a colleague in Vienna who was run out of his job at the University of Vienna because his wife was Jewish. Davenport promised to help his fellow scientist. Shortly thereafter, Davenport started backpedaling on his strident Anglo supremacy, and prominent supporters of the eugenics movement began to recoil from what they had started.

Outside of academic circles, eugenics increasingly seemed to be marked by bizarre excesses. Newspapers reported on a proposal by Nobel Prize winner and eugenicist Alexis Carrel that children of "high potentialities" should be isolated at birth for up to twenty-five years, to create an order of "engineers": men who lived a monk-like existence studying biology to "understand the mechanisms of the body and soul of the individual and of his relations with the cosmic and social world." These men would act as advisers to governments to "direct the construction of the human being . . . and a civilization based on his true nature." Another article reprinted findings by American Museum researchers stating that unemployed workers became fathers at a higher rate than those employed. The article, entitled "Revolution Would Follow," hinted darkly that the museum's eugenicists wished to sterilize those who used their unemployment time for the pursuit of sensual pleasure. Eugenicists might take away many things, but reprisals for leisure-time sex was too much.

Commentators began to point out with greater force the strong association between Nazism, racism, and eugenics. One commentator compared Nazi racial programs with America's dark history of racial terrorism, noting, for instance, that Nazis were "doing their best to copy the methods of the first Ku Klux Klan." Even Malvina Hoffman weighed in, writing that when it came to defining races, "I will leave the much-disputed subject of what is meant by the word 'Aryan' to be fought out between expert anthropologists and Mr. Hitler." In other words, Hoffman wasn't willing to relinquish the idea of racial "types" altogether but thought that Nazi preoccupations with "Aryan" racial purity went too far.

Rock-ribbed American eugenicists tried desperately to distinguish their own aims from those of Nazism. The Eugenic Record Office's Laughlin, for instance, wrote somewhat defensively that "One may condemn Nazi policy generally, but specifically it remained for Germany in 1933 to lead the great nations of the world in recognition of the biological foundations of national character. It is probable that the sterilization statutes of the several American states and the national sterilization statute of Germany will, in legal history, constitute a milestone which marks the control by the most advanced nations of the world of a major aspect of controlling human reproduction." One might disagree with the Nazi appetite for totalitarianism and violence, Laughlin seemed to argue, but one had to admire their commitment to racist biology.

Nevertheless, even some card-carrying eugenicists had to admit that the field had gone too far. As one wrote in 1935, "it may be admitted that 'eugenics' in the sense in which most of us are now accustomed to thinking of it, has become a hopelessly perverted movement. . . . [I]t does incalculable harm by lending a false appearance of scientific basis to advocates of race prejudice, defenders of vested interests of church and state, Fascists, Hitlerites and reactionaries generally." This author concluded that those who wanted real change—even biological change—should nevertheless devote themselves to promoting social and economic improvements before focusing on genetics.

That same year, a committee consisting of Hooton and three other anthropologists visited Laughlin at the Eugenics Records Office headquarters in Cold Spring Harbor, New York. They had been dispatched by the Carnegie Institution, one of the ERO's main financial backers, to evaluate whether further funding was warranted.

Their final report was damning. The basic character of the science practiced by the Eugenics Records Office was unsound, the committee decided. It failed firstly on purely practical grounds—the ERO had collected more anthropometric and psychometric measurements from American subjects than they could possibly process, and thus their research program looked more like data hoarding than productive science. Secondly, and more damningly, the "data" that they *had* stockpiled were often specious measurements of unmeasurable traits like "self-respect," "holding a grudge," "loyalty," and "sense of humor." Who could possibly develop a scientifically objective way of measuring a person's tendency to hold a grudge? Finally, the committee recognized that the research conducted by the ERO was in the service of "propaganda" rather than "pure research," compromising the office's entire scientific program.

In light of these findings, the committee recommended that the ERO cease research operations until Laughlin and Davenport could get their science on firmer footing and iron out their political biases. The committee also advised that "Eugenics" be struck from the name of the Office, suggesting names like the "Laboratory of Human Genetics" or "Laboratory of Human Biology" instead. This was a telling recommendation: the very word "eugenics" had, by 1935, come to symbolize poisonous bias, rather than good science, even to people who once proudly called themselves eugenicists.

In spite of this scathing report, the ERO bumbled along for another four years, gradually losing steam. By 1939, Carnegie had pulled the plug, and the office closed its doors.

Osborn, for his part, never got to see the full disrepute into which eugenics would fall. He died peacefully in his house in Garrison, New York, on November 6, 1935, sitting at his desk in his study overlooking the Hudson River. He was working on a monograph about the evolution of elephants.

To the very end he was unrepentant about his stance on eugenics. He continued to praise German race science programs and expressed happiness that his nephew, Fredrick Osborn, was taking up "this great world movement." It was his fondest hope that Fredrick would take his place on the International Committee, planning more Eugenics Congresses and shepherding the movement into future decades.

Newspapers eulogized him as "an evolutionist and a scientist," a "successor to Darwin," a "Roosevelt in the field of science." But it was the Eugenics Record Office's house journal, the *Eugenical News*, that gave him the send-off that he might have appreciated most. "Eugenics has lost a good friend in the death of Dr. Osborn," the *News* wrote. He was a man "of fine physique, of a family distinguished in finance . . . administrator of a great municipal museum of Natural History." Most essentially, "as a lover of his country and his race his ideals will long influence the applications of eugenics here and abroad."

To be a man of distinguished "type," with a distinguished family tree, to be lauded for one's contributions to the advancement of the "race"—what more could a eugenicist want? And indeed, Osborn's ideas did have influence both in the United States and abroad, and in a few short years would bring death and misery to millions of people.

• • •

It was in this period that Shapiro's work took a decisive turn.

On December 22, 1935, as an employee of the American Museum, he had arrived on the rumpled coastline of Pitcairn, an island known to be the landing place for the mutineers from the HMS *Bounty*, who killed Captain William Bligh in 1789. Since university, Shapiro had been excited to examine the population—primarily descendants of those criminal Anglo-Saxons and a number of Tahitian women they had taken as wives. Shapiro was, he had to confess, initially disappointed. "I had expected to see definite indications of the Tahitian contribution to their mixed Anglo-Polynesian origin," he wrote. "Instead, the men, *en masse*, were more like a group of Englishmen—dock workers—with ugly, knobby hands and feet, roughened and calloused by labor." They tended to have beaked noses, heavy brows, and dark hair, and reminded him of people from his own, native New England. Others, however, he found more "distinctly Polynesian," like Parkins Christian, the island's chief magistrate.

Shapiro's anthropological work went smoothly, in spite of some initial trepidation on his part. The evening after Shapiro arrived, Christian called everyone together for a meeting, so that Shapiro could tell them about his work. Shapiro remembered the community gathering in a room lit by a "single kerosene lamp" that revealed only the faces of the people sitting in front of him—and behind them, just the alert, "unblinking" eyes of the rest of the crowd, watching him out of the darkness. All at once he was gripped with the realization that "the success of my work depended on the cooperation of these people, and immediately a horrible fear seized me that they might not understand, might even be hostile and resent strangers, however scientific in aim, prying into their intimate lives." To his momentarily "disturbed mind these eyes had taken a hostile look." He briefly wished that he had chosen to study insects or animals—subjects that did not need to be propitiated or negotiated with. "I cursed the personal equation which always confronted me in my study of the human animal," Shapiro recalled. "The suspicious eye of the human subject becomes wearing."

Shapiro needn't have worried. The people of Pitcairn were

eager to discuss their heritage and willingly submitted to Shapiro's agenda. While he went to work with his calipers and measuring tape, a photographer from the American Museum took photographs of each person from the front and in profile, and a physician who had accompanied Shapiro took blood samples. The older members of the island community told Shapiro anecdotes of the past families of the island, which allowed him to compile genealogical charts. The community members lined up to take turns looking into the doctor's microscope, eager for a peek at their own blood.

Within a little more than a week, Shapiro was finished.

In New York, he ran his numbers. He collated his statistics. He compiled tables. And he discovered . . . nothing.

Nothing at all.

Or rather, in that "nothing," he discovered everything. As he put it in his later report of his anthropometric analysis, "the Pitcairn Islanders reveal in their sum total a mosaic of characters, some borrowing their colors from Tahiti, others from England, with an occasional patch where the colors have run to produce a blend." That is to say, no particular "type" or "stock" predominated on Pitcairn.

The same went for the intelligence of the people. The islanders, Shapiro wrote, "seemed to fit into the average range of intelligence." Some seemed "smart," others less smart, but taken as a whole, anthropologists seemed to be incorrect about the degeneration of "hybrid types." Indeed, Shapiro wrote, "as I think back to the individuals I knew on Pitcairn, I am impressed by the relatively large number of men such as

Parkins Christian, Fred Christian, Edgar Christian, Norris Young, and Arthur Herbert Young and of women such as Mary Anny McCoy, Ada Christian, Margaret Lucy Christian, and Harriet Warren, who possessed qualities of leadership or traits of personality that raised them above the level of their neighbors."

The best summary of Shapiro's findings was offered by one of his informants, Edith Young—a shy but ultimately voluble islander who was very conscious of being regarded as an anthropological oddity. When she encountered passengers from the occasional passing steamer, she told Shapiro, "they look on her as a strange kind of creature" and "asked the most intimate questions"—questions about the sexual mores of the island—"which they, themselves, would deeply resent from another."

Edith's response to these questions, Shapiro wrote, was always just to say that "the Pitcairn people are merely human like other folks."

Merely human—like other folks. Shapiro had traveled, round trip, ten thousand miles to a tiny dot in the Pacific Ocean. He had endured bruised feet, deadly cliffs, and swarms of flies only to discover . . . other humans, who were just like other folks. That is to say, the Pitcairn Islanders were like him in some ways, unlike him in other ways. They found some things funny that he did, and some things funny that he didn't. Some things made them mad, some things didn't. They were good at some things, and less good at others. They liked doing things their own way, but also were interested in the way that other folks did things. They had codes of decency and dignity, codes for love and kinship, ways of completing economic transactions—and mostly they held to these codes, but sometimes they broke them. They were human like other folks—as were the people that Cook had encountered, as were the people that Sullivan had studied, as were the mythical people in the past that Osborn summoned up to support his ideas of racial hierarchy.

• • •

Shapiro published his results in 1936 as *The Heritage of the Bounty*. Initially, most members of the scientific community and the general public read Shapiro's monograph as something of a scientifically inflected travelogue, not unlike a documentary movie. It was, as one reviewer put it, "of interest both as a scientific study of inheritance and a vivid account of a friendly visitor's sojourn among the hospitable islanders of today." Shapiro's colleague at the Bishop Museum, E. S. Craighill Handy, wrote that "The Pitcairners have had the good fortune to be registered in the annals of science and history by a scientist whose sympathetic nature responded to theirs so genuinely that the reader feels the book to be as true in subtle human intangibles as it is accurate in fact."

In the next few years, Shapiro continued Sullivan's race-mixing studies in Hawai'i. And again, he came up with a similar result to the one he found on Pitcairn Island. "While innate psychological drives no doubt exist," he concluded, "it is extremely doubtful that they are genetically linked with special physical variations within a mixed population." There was no such thing as the "criminal type" or the "genius type"—just like the natural "racial type" was so physically variable as to be meaningless.

For Shapiro, the problem wasn't simply that people like Nazis had misinterpreted genetic science. The problem was a more general approach by scientists—and people in the modern world more broadly—to matters of identity and belonging. Group identity in the modern world, he wrote, was as much a factor of technology and history as anything "natural." "The radio, the movie, the airplane," he wrote, "have, or should have, taught us that technology may be beneficent, but it may also serve evil purposes." This was as true in America as it was around the world—for "when we look to the world beyond our borders we see there, too, the same forces of intolerance at work poisoning mutual understanding and respect, at a time when the technology of the future is likely to increase rather than to diminish the needs for international and interracial harmony."

With ever more powerful technologies, he continued, "group identities become quickly established and resist the solvents of time and association." Shapiro had discovered that biology was subordinate to society—to culture—when it came to understanding human beings. To think otherwise was not simply foolish. It was dangerous.

Modern humans tended to think that they had mastered nature—compressed time and space through technologies like radio and airplanes; reproduced reality through mediums like books and movies; surmounted nature at an ever-smaller level with physiology, biology, and now the rapidly advancing molecular techniques of genetics.

Far from standing astride the globe, however, modern, industrial societies had—without even knowing it—trapped themselves on a tiny raft, adrift in the ocean of history. "All of us are born into a special group of circumstances and are molded and conditioned by them," wrote Shapiro. "Our views and our behavior are regulated by them. We take ready-made our judgments and tend to react emotionally to any divergence from or interference with them. In a sense we are imprisoned in our own culture."

Surfers crowd a Waikiki beach, 1920s.

8

THIS WAS YOUR LIFE!

Duke stepped out of the glaring California sun and onto a darkened television sound stage. On the back wall of the cavernous room, scene painters had rendered an admirable if anachronistic tropical beach scene, complete with waving palm trees and a little village of grass huts. Set designers had strewn the floor with heaps of sand interspersed with plaster lava rocks. Fake palm trees shook slightly as Duke walked across the stage, and a full-sized replica of one of the painted grass houses stood in the set's corner, with a surfboard leaning against it. Half of a catamaran jutted from the painted wall adjacent to the hut, completing the vision of a vacation paradise.

It was February 20, 1957. Duke was sixty-seven years old. The jet-black hair that sports journalists the world over had fawned over was now silvery and thinning. The chiseled face that once bewitched camera lenses had filled out a bit. But Duke still walked with the leonine stride of an athlete, and his eyes glittered with easy, captivating charisma. Today he was decked out in a style that he'd helped to popularize over the past decade: dark pants and a pale blazer over a flowered "Duke Kahanamoku" brand "aloha" shirt.

Duke was in town to do a television commercial promoting

Hawaiian tourism. Since the end of World War II, visitors to Hawai'i from the mainland United States had increased tenfold, from around 25,000 visitors per year in the mid-1930s to 250,000 people by the end of the 1950s. The arrival of the Pan Am Clipper flying boat in Honolulu Harbor—an event that Duke, his love of flying undiminished, witnessed enthusiastically—had officially opened the islands to air travel. Before the war, tickets from major West Coast airports like Los Angeles and San Francisco were an expensive $500—somewhere around $11,500 in 2025 dollars. This price dropped to around $225 after the war—still expensive (about $2,500 in 2025) but within range for upper-middle-class tourists who could afford relatively expensive airfare, but not monthslong vacations.

By that time, Duke had largely drawn away from the tumult of international fame. In 1932, he'd taken a job running two Union Oil gas stations in Honolulu and Waikiki. He'd also campaigned for sheriff of Hawai'i in 1934, winning the position handily. The life of an island sheriff suited Duke's straitlaced but laid-back personality. He would rise early, check on the prisoners in the Honolulu jail, then eat some waffles for breakfast with friends. He might have a quick surf session, serve some summonses, then surf more before going back to the office to finish work. It was a quiet, pleasant, routine life.

Even as sheriff, Duke served as the unofficial ambassador for the islands, greeting celebrities. He placed leis over the heads of Peter Lawford and Richard Boone, shared a pineapple with Amelia Earhart, hoisted Groucho Marx onto his big shoulders, and taught the sons of presidents Herbert Hoover and Franklin Delano Roosevelt how to surf.

He also spent time fielding questions about Hawai'i from curious mainland folks. One man penned a letter to Duke asking, "inasmuch as you are the ambassador of good will, would you please advise me if it would be possible to secure an authentic Hawaiian hula skirt and what the cost would be?" Duke graciously wrote back with the name and address of the "Aloha Curio Store" in Honolulu and gave the man a short history of the hula skirt. Another man wrote to ask Duke about the feasibility of purchasing a home in Hawai'i. Duke assured him that real estate was "one of the liveliest questions Honolulu is experiencing today," and gave the man some advice about financing. A doll collector wrote to ask if Duke would help her obtain a Honolulu doll. She was writing to Duke, she said, because "no one answers my letters." Duke replied to her as well.

In the midst of all of this, Duke managed to keep a desultory toe in the entertainment industry. In 1952, a TV producer wrote to propose a show titled "Back and Beyond, with Duke Kahanamoku." Duke would appear as "the Epitome of Adventure and masculine Prowess," the man wrote, and he would narrate his own life as a surfer and swimmer in a series of weekly vignettes. In 1958, the chief of police of Los Angeles approached Duke about filming a police procedural not unlike the popular cop show *Dragnet*, but based in Hawai'i. Duke would introduce each episode, ending with the phrase "based on the official files of the Honolulu Sherriff's Office." These ideas went nowhere, but Duke did take a small role as a "native chief" in the satirical 1954 drama *Mister Roberts*, directed by his old friend, John Ford.

Now, as Duke brushed the sand from his shoes and chatted with a studio handler, he spotted someone from the corner of his eye. The television presenter, Ralph Edwards, had emerged from the wings of the stage and was striding toward him. Duke knew Edwards from a transpacific cruise the two men had been on a few years earlier. They shook hands warmly, and Edwards said, "Good to see you, Duke! Last time I saw you was in Hawaii! What are you doing here?"

"Well," Duke said, "we're here for the Hawaiian travelogue."

"You're going to do it here?" Edwards asked. "On this stage, here?"

"Yes," said Duke.

"No, no!" said Edwards. "I'm doing a show tonight."

Duke pushed his hands into his pockets and mumbled a few good-natured protests.

"As a matter of fact," continued Edwards, "I'm doing it right now, and you're an important part of it!"

"OK, you go right along," Duke said, not quite registering the strange shift in conversation.

"Because," Edwards cried, "Duke Kahanamoku, world-famous champion Olympic swimmer and sheriff of Honolulu, Hawaii, This Is Your Life!"

Suddenly, the studio lights blazed on and a heavy curtain at the front of the sound stage swung open, revealing a wildly applauding audience. Duke looked around, startled, and then smiled and shook his head at the realization of a trick well-played. "I never believed I'd be on this program," he said.

This Is Your Life, which Edwards had started in 1948 as a radio show before migrating it to television in 1952, had a simple premise. A guest—often a celebrity, though sometimes an everyday citizen—would be invited to the studio on a pretense, and then surprised by a series of guests who recounted significant episodes in the guest's life. Past guests had included the boxer Jack Dempsey; the singer Tennessee Ernie Ford; and Colonel Dean Hess, a minister who had organized an airlift of orphans during the Korean War.

Edwards told Duke they would be hearing the "story of a little Hawaiian boy who became the most famous swimmer in the world" and who "used his great speed and power in a most heroic way." Then, one by one, a parade of guests filed out of the simulated grass shack. His brothers and sisters recounted Duke's early life against the backdrop of the first territorial government. Former competitors and teammates—including Johnny Weissmuller—spoke of Duke's speed and sportsmanship. His wife, Nadine, who he had married in 1940, talked about how his run for sheriff had been supported by both Democrats and Republicans in Hawai'i. And in a particularly moving moment, some of the surviving fishermen that Duke and his companions had saved from the *Thelma* emerged from the grass shack to thank him in person—for the first time—for saving their lives.

Even at the time, critics of the show called it treacly and lowbrow, but *This Is Your Life* was unquestionably compelling. It presented portraits of people's lives, told in broad strokes, and was reflective of commonly held—indeed, seldom-questioned—American values. Duke's life had certainly seemed like a Horatio Alger story: a young boy who had grown up on a political and economic frontier, who had made good through a combination of athletic skill, moral character, and personal heroism. It was the story not just of one man, but of a way of life—an unchanging story of American grit that someone like Osborn might have appreciated.

But this was not the only way of framing Duke's life.

When a producer approached Duke in 1952 about a TV series based on Duke's biography, he suggested that Duke's story was that of "a man whose feats and exciting past are the foundations for Myths and Legends in the future"—a story not just of "a man of great stature, both physical and moral," but also of a man who was "acquainted with Mainland biases." Duke had experienced prejudice, and had triumphed—and this would be a revelation to others. "It would be most gratifying," wrote the producer, to see the show "serve as an inspiration to youths of all Races and Colors." Indeed, he went on with unexpected candor, "the millions of underprivileged and discriminated against populations . . . present a commercial facet not to be laughed off. These same under privileged [*sic*] for the most part, own TV sets and are potential buyers of a Sponsor's product . . . what an inspiration you could be to them. What a boost to their morale."

Here was a different version of the story of Duke's life: one that acknowledged an America of limits and prejudices, but one that saw a way of turning prejudice into profit.

Then there was still another version of Duke's life. Increasing numbers of "surf-riders" along California's coasts considered him the "spiritual leader" of surfing. They sought to emulate what they interpreted as Duke's style of being in the world: his athleticism, his perceived indifference to money, his cool attitude. In this version, Duke's story was less one of the success of the American system, or triumph over the inbuilt inequalities of the American system, as much as it was a kind of transcendent apotheosis—a means of bucking the system altogether.

Finally, there was the story of Duke—and his brothers, and his neighbors, and, indeed, the people of Hawaiʻi—told through pseudoscientific sculptures in natural history museums. For men like Osborn, it didn't matter much that the casts in the Bishop Museum and the American Museum were not of a particular man named Duke. What these sculptures depicted, in the bleary, myopic, magical thinking of eugenic science, was the natural history of one people's decline and the ascendancy of another.

What, then, was Duke Kahanamoku's life? Or David's, or Sargent's, or any of the men who had so helped to shape not only American sports, but also American science, and even American culture?

The beginnings of an answer could be found not thirty miles from the Burbank studio where Duke sang songs with his family, shook hands with survivors of the *Thelma* wreck, and blinked back tears under the gaze of television cameras.

On the beaches of California, some 100,000 people daily took to surfboards and tried their luck on the waves. Beaches in Oʻahu had become similarly crowded. And Duke had, of course, done more than perhaps anyone else to promote this behavior around the world.

With greater numbers of board riders crowding beaches in Southern California and Oʻahu, commentators increasingly spoke not simply of "surf riders" or "surfers" or even "beach boys" but of "surf culture." Newspaper reporters became amateur anthropologists as they attempted to explain this new "culture" to their readers. Surfers' names were unconventional, as one reporter wrote—they called themselves "Keyhole, Hammerhead, Fritz Magitz, Tarzan, [and] Opie." Their dress code, too, was unconventional: "shoes are unheard of, day or night." Fast-paced jazz-rock hybrid music came to be called "surf music," and new magazines—like *Surfer* of 1960—kept insiders up to date on new developments and opinions about the sport. Surfers even spoke in their own peculiar dialect, and reporters endeavored to translate exotic terms like "wipeout" and "hang five" and "the surf is up!" to their readers.

"Surf culture" was new, because this idea of "culture" itself was new—shaped in part by the work of anthropologists like Shapiro. In a 1956 book written for popular audiences, Shapiro informed his readers that "culture" was, at its most simple, "learned behavior." It included "all the patterned, habitual actions and ideas and values we perform, hold, or cherish as members of an organized society, community, or family." Of course, Shapiro went on, such a sweeping definition could reasonably make a person wonder what culture was *not*. The answer to this was relatively simple. Biological aspects of humankind—tallness, shortness, head size, skin color, metabolism, blood type—were important for many reasons, but they did not explain how different groups organized their societies and family groups; what they found "intelligent" and "unintelligent"; what kinds of art they found beautiful or ugly; indeed, what they classed as "art" at all. Biology, in other words, was not "culture." As Shapiro noted, freeing the concept of "culture" from the idea of "race" allowed science to comprehend individual life stories in greater detail, and with greater scientific fidelity. "In our tendency to generalize people into groups, populations, or race," Shapiro wrote, "we run the risk of losing the individual in the statistical mean or average." To be judged as an individual was an "elementary right," Shapiro thought, whereas judging individuals in terms of their race led to "much prejudice but little understanding."

This idea of culture provided an explanation both for individual life stories and for the ways that these life stories fit into the larger societies around them. Moreover, it explained how people could change society, and how societies could change people. In one final irony, Shapiro noted that the flexible concept of "culture" that had emerged out of the static study of "race" in Polynesia looked a lot like the Hawaiian term "mana." As Shapiro understood it, "mana" carried with it the "notion of a kind of power and virtue residing in certain individuals, animals, or things, that is a sort of essence almost beyond control. It may be precious or sacred and require special care to preserve it from contamination." Upon reflection, Shapiro wrote, "the word culture as I have been using it is somewhat parallel to all this." "Mana" was a kind of life history, in Shapiro's understanding. In this way, Shapiro thought, "history" was the backbone of culture. And history was made through the collective effort of individuals.

This, in essence, was the outline of Duke Kahanamoku's life.

He and his brothers had not only changed sports in the United States, they had changed the meaning of culture itself. And that culture continued to change. The generation of surfers that had followed Duke were aging, just like he was, and for many of the newest members of "surf culture," the term "beach boys" referred to a somewhat corny musical quintet from California, rather than a bunch of hardscrabble guys in Hawai'i earning a living teaching tourists how to surf. David Kahanamoku died on August 10, 1967, just two weeks before Duke's seventy-sixth birthday. As one historian wrote, when Duke died almost six months later, on January 22, 1968, "beach boy culture itself was laid to rest."

• • •

Almost four years after I first saw the plaster masks of Sullivan's subjects in the American Museum's tower, I finally found myself face to face with the cast of David Kahanamoku.

The American Museum told me that they had taken their copy of the cast off display in the 1960s; curators assumed it had been destroyed. The Peabody Museum at Yale had covered theirs in the 1980s, then had taken it down for good in 1993 and it was lost. An early correspondence with the Bishop Museum suggested that they, too, had gotten rid of their cast, probably around 2004. I was disappointed, but such is the way of objects.

Then, in the midst of a different discussion about Sullivan's work and the history of Hawaiian anthropology, another curator at the Bishop Museum offhandedly remarked that she did, indeed, know where the cast of David Kahanamoku was. Would I like to see it?

Would I? I certainly would.

That August, I accompanied a curator across the lawn of the Bishop Museum toward a long, low, metal storage shed. It was eight in the morning, but the sun was already blazing. Inside, the shed was dark and cool. And then: there he was.

Even as I felt my pulse race a bit, the figure was, at first pass, underwhelming. It was just a sculpture of a man wearing a white malo, painted in feathery shades of brown. His pose seemed a bit stilted when viewed from up close. His eyes were sad. The modeling work looked hasty in places, like where the paint on his hair bled onto his temples. Time or careless brushwork had rendered his face blotched, and one of his wrists—the one that once held a spear, but now just gestured into empty space—had cracked and gone unrepaired.

But as I peered in the dim light into the implacably cool face of David Kahanamoku, it was impossible not to think about the man struggling inside the mold; the improbable, immoral obsession that had driven the pursuit of his brother; the titanic shifts in the history of the world and the history of anthropology that had followed in the wake of this statue and others like it.

In the opening narration of Chris Marker's 1953 film, *Les Statues Meurent Aussi* (*Statues also Die*), the French filmmaker observed that "when men die, they enter history. When statues die, they enter art. This natural history of death is what we call culture."

Marker's film is about African artifacts—objects once invested with deep meaning and magic by their creators but subsequently scooped up by the French colonial project and kept behind glass in museums, where their original, spiritual force atrophied and they became mere aesthetic objects.

As much as it is about a different time and place, however, Marker's argument extends to David Kahanamoku's statue as well. The cast was a creation of immense totemic importance to the eugenicists who had made it. And indeed, their notional "science" was, in fact, a sort of "natural history of death." In their dark enthusiasm they had taken the literal impression of a living person in plaster, then reinvested it with an aestheticized scientific mysticism in order to justify preserving some people at the expense of others. A century ago, the cast of David Kahanamoku had not been merely an image of a surfer—it was a powerful, magical, medical technology capable, in the addled minds of the men who made it, of reversing time itself.

Nevertheless, the eugenicists' "natural history of death" was not, in the end, the last word on "culture." Indeed, the recognition of the unreasoning myopia of race science prompted newer, less brittle, more dynamic ideas of culture—including the idea that science itself was an aspect of culture: an exceptionally powerful creation of human beings, but not one beyond human moral concerns. In a new era of reassessing the relationship between science and politics, the cast of David Kahanamoku had lost its original, twisted, occult aura. It's telling that David never brought his son to see the statue, and rarely visited it himself. However, in being removed from public view the cast of David Kahanamoku hadn't died so much as it regained a bit of its original ambivalence, its sense of possibility, its sense of individuality.

Nor was the cast alone. In February 2021, the Bishop Museum opened *(Re)Generations: Challenging Scientific Racism in Hawai'i*, a show about Sullivan's work. As part of the project, the show's curators noted that in the years since the decline of eugenics (though not of racialist thinking), descendants of Sullivan's subjects had come to see his photographs as a resource—a way of connecting with their family members, of discovering genealogical connections, of repurposing a history of racism, small-mindedness, and misinformation into something more powerful and meaningful.

The cast of David Kahanamoku was a reminder that questions of nature versus nurture; the hope of bettering ourselves as individuals and a species; and the desire to harness human potential—for industry, for social and political movements, for communication, for entertainment—have not receded into the background during a hundred years of tumult. If anything, the concept of "culture" hashed out by anthropologists during the 1920s and 1930s provides one powerful tool for contemporary understandings of society. The concept of genetics as developed through molecular biology provides another.

One of the lessons of the story of Duke and David and Sullivan and Osborn—of the rise of surfing and the fall of eugenics, of the creation of new forms of cultural life from the wreckage of the old—is that the future is unpredictable, as are people themselves. There is no particular priority of politics over science, or biology over culture, or reason over feeling. The priority is simply to negotiate rough waves of social and technological change, keep our heads above water, and—through care, open eyes, and lots of practice—not wipe out.

ACKNOWLEDGMENTS

Much like surfing and science, books are collective efforts. I'm thankful for all the help I received during the writing of this book, and for all the people who helped make it possible.

I'm grateful first and foremost for the keen vision and limitless energy of my editor, Elizabeth Mitchell. She leaped aboard an unruly project and—with clarity, balance, and assistance from the indefatigable Anna Calame—steered it safely through perilous reefs and gnashing breakers. At an even earlier stage, my extraordinary agent, Margo Beth Fleming, took this book seriously when it was just a murky fixation kicking around in my head. She nourished it as it went through various permutations, then launched into the world at just the right time. Without their efforts, this book would not exist.

I'm awestruck by the dedication and determination of the librarians and archivists who work tirelessly to protect historical records and make them available for scholars like me. Gregory Raml and Kristen Mable at the central library and anthropological archives of the American Museum of Natural History opened the museum's collections and guided me through their treasures. Sarah Kuaiwa at the Bishop Museum located the original statue of David Kahanamoku in the museum's storage; and her colleagues Jillian Swift, Cheyenne Velez, and Krystal Kakimoto searched out photographs, letters, and journals tied to its creation. Barbara Narendra at the Peabody Museum looked far and wide for records related to Yale's own sculpture of Kahanamoku, and Ramona Kincaid at the Kauaʻi Historical Society showed me gems in this small but formidable library. Archivists at the Smithsonian Institution, the Field Museum, the Getty Research Institute, the New York Historical Society, the Hawaii State Archives, and the California Academy of Sciences supplied me with scans and folders of historical wonders, while the librarians and archivists at Brown University, Truman State University, the University of Wisconsin, the University of Hawaiʻi, the University of Pennsylvania, Ball State University, the University of Southern California, and Utah State University generously made their collections available.

The web of people who supported me and this project includes old colleagues and new friends. I'd like particularly to thank Ivory Lloyd for her deep knowledge and profound generosity in helping me to work through matters of Hawaiian orthography and pronunciation. Tom Pōhaku Stone was openhanded with his encyclopedic knowledge of surfing and Hawaiian cultural history (and he also happens to be a cool guy and great storyteller). Jeremy Lloyd showed up on the beach at dawn to show this poor student how to surf on a wooden board (difficult! fun!). David Kahanamoku II received a message out of the blue one day from a historian who wanted to talk about his dad; he unselfishly gave hours to interviews and follow-ups. The extraordinary historian of surfing, Matt Warshaw, was quick to respond to the strange and arbitrary questions that I lobbed his way, and his answers illuminated this text. Lida Zeitlin Wu and Carolyn Kane provided an early venue for exploring some of the ideas in this text. Bob Richards, Adrian Johns, Hussein Ali Agrama, Huan Saussy, Shadi Barsch Zimmer, Joel Isaacs, Alexander Hofmann, Joe Yalowitz, Zi Yun Huang, and Topher Kindell all offered encouragement, advice, and criticism at various points through the writing of this book. Finally, at the University of Chicago, the Fishbein Center, History Department, Social Sciences Division, Institute for the Formation of Knowledge, and MacLean Center are peopled by devoted, conscientious, energetic, and fascinating folks who provided me with invaluable financial and administrative backing, and—most important—time and space to write. I'm grateful to them.

My friends made the writing of this book not only possible, but pleasurable. Thank you to Will and Rose for venturing west in search of rainbows; Nick, Mathieu, Alexander, Louisa, Brian, and Candice for supporting last-minute drafts, even in a bumping jeep, even on the side of a mountain; Sophia, Alma, Lev, and Sasha for unleashing frenetic fun at every opportunity; Singerman for his sharp wit with a hint of sugar; Jake for countless afternoons spent climbing and cooking. Christine kept me mindful and even-keeled; Ian brought cool breezes to the deepest doldrums; Nikki talked me out of more than a few flat spins. Dan, Rebekah, Willa, and Hazel sustained mind and body with laughter and the best pizza in HP; Karl and Holly kept me energized with oysters and corpse revivers; Jim and Sonia opened their home and tortoise sanctuary to me.

And then there's family. My youngest kid sometimes says our family is "weird," by which (I think) she means it's energetic, extended, creative, unpredictable, argumentative, amorphous, and hard to pin down—in other words, ideal in every way. Within this wild and woolly family, Joanie sustained this writing with research support, but more importantly with fizzy water, Scrabble, and long afternoon conversations. Jennefer made the lights at the end of the tunnel seem attainable, even when they were far away. My brothers—Matt, Joey, and Jason—are relentlessly funny, and also pretty insightful and upright fellows, for younger brothers. Mom and Joe, Dad and Loretta gave unsparingly of comfort, support, good advice, and love; I can't thank them enough. Lynn: I'm grateful for the calming counsel and steadfast resolve intermixed with fits of hilarity. Also, especially, there was the holy water. I think it worked. How did you know?

Dean and Apollonia have the amazing ability to catch the world like a prism and throw it back at me in a way that never fails to astonish, delight, and humble me. I used to worry about not being able to teach them enough before they grew up; now I'm happy to learn from them. As Duke might say, "Now that's a switch!"

Throughout the writing of this book, Zoë dealt gently but firmly with the rotating cast of 1920s characters and obsessive demons who showed up in our lives, overstayed their welcome, and tromped rudely on our domestic tranquility. She also showed me how to plunge courageously through rough storms and crashing waves; how to blaze paths along steep slopes and slippery rocks; how to race the sun to the horizon through salty afternoons. There are too few waves in the ocean, too few words, to express my love and luck and gratitude. So I'll just say: thank you.

NOTES

1 | THE CAST OF DAVID KAHANAMOKU

1 *"charismatic personality"*: Mike Jay, "Champion Saver of Lives on the Beach at Waikiki," June 30, 1923.

3 *"fight for survival"*: Malvina Hoffman, *Heads and Tales* (Scribner's and Sons, 1936), 183–84.

4 *"museum artists"*: Hoffman, *Heads and Tales*, 183.

9 *"while they are yet to be had"*: "Report of the President," *AMNH Annual Report for 1911*, 32.

11 *factors that could be inherited:* For a concise view of the debate over whether genes were even "real," see T. H. Morgan, "The Theory of the Gene," *American Naturalist* 51, no. 609 (September 1917), 513–44. Morgan, for his part, believed that genes were real, that they were carried on chromosomes, and that chromosomes were made of reproductive material—an insight for which he won the Nobel Prize in 1933.

12 *seven hundred fifty:* Daniel Kevles, *In the Name of Eugenics* (University of California Press, 1985), 63.

15 *"history always has the upper hand"*: Michel Foucault, *Society Must Be Defended!* (Picador, 2003), 143.

2 | THE GOSPEL OF THE BODY

17 *"extremely hard to preserve"*: "Hawaiian Race Vanishing, Says U.S. Naturalist," *San Francisco Chronicle*, April 8, 1920, 4.

22 *ride waves after fishing:* Filipe Pomar, "Surfing in 1000 B.C.," *Surfer* 29, no. 4 (April 1988).

22 *a very young age:* Kevin Dawson, *Undercurrents of Power: Aquatic Culture in the African Diaspora* (University of Pennsylvania Press, 2018).

23 *relatively short-lived, however:* See, e.g., Daniel Esparza, "Reconsiderando las fuentes para el estudio del surf arcaico: Polinesia, China, Perú y África occidental," *Materiales para la Historia del Deporte*, no. 15 (July 7, 2017): 193–213.

24 *aesthetic expression:* There are many excellent histories of surfing, both in the twentieth century and before. Some of the more helpful are, e.g., Ben R. Finney and James D. Houston, *Surfing: A History of the Ancient Hawaiian Sport* (Pomegranate, 1996); Kristin Lawler, *The American Surfer: Radical Culture and Capitalism* (Routledge, 2010); Matt Warshaw, *The History of Surfing* (Chronicle Books, 2010); Isaiah Helekunihi Walker, *Waves of Resistance: Surfing and History in Twentieth-Century Hawai'i* (University of Hawai'i Press, 2011); Peter Westwick and Peter Neushul, *The World in the Curl: An Unconventional History of Surfing* (Crown, 2013); Scott Laderman, *Empire in Waves: A Political History of Surfing* (University of California Press, 2014).

24 *"affluent society":* Marshall Sahlins, *Stone Age Economics* (Routledge, 1972), 1.

24 *human-made ponds called* loko i'a: Patrick Vinton Kirch, *A Shark Going Inland Is My Chief: The Island Civilization of Ancient Hawai'i* (University of California Press, 2012), 99.

24 *population:* Estimates of pre-contact Hawaiian populations are controversial and range from 100,000 to 1,000,000. See, e.g., Robert C. Schmitt, "New Estimates of the Pre-Censal Population of Hawaii," *The Journal of the Polynesian Society* 80, no. 2 (1971): 237–43; David E. Stannard, *Before the Horror: The Population of Hawai'i on the Eve of Western Contact* (University of Hawai'i Press, 1989); David Swanson, "A New Estimate of the Hawaiian Population for 1778, the Year of First European Contact," *Hūlili* (July 3, 2019).

NOTES

25 *and cliff jumping*: H. Carrington Bolton, "Some Hawaiian Pastimes," *Journal of American Folklore* 4, no. 12 (1891): 21–26. See also *Ka Nupepa Kuokoa*, December 23, 1865, as recorded in John R. K. Clark, *Hawaiian Surfing: Traditions from the Past* (University of Hawai'i Press, 2011), 10.

25 *"favorite activity of chiefs"*: S. M. Kamakau, *Ruling Chiefs of Hawai'i* (Kamehameha Schools Press, 1961), 106.

25 *"the livelong day"*: David Malo, *Hawaiian Antiquities: (Moolelo Hawaii)* (Hawaiian Gazette Company, 1903), 294.

26 *"surfing, canoe racing, swimming"*: Curtis Pi'ehu 'Iaukea and Lorna Kahilipuaokalani Iaukea Watson, *By Royal Command: The Official Life and Personal Reminiscences of Colonel Curtis Pi'ehu 'Iaukea at the Court of Hawaii's Rulers* (Hui Hanai, 1988), 29.

27 *"the best looking"*: Kamakau, *Ruling Chiefs*, 53.

27 *Kōleamoku seduced him*: Kamakau, *Ruling Chiefs*, 25.

27 *"according to your wish"*: S. N. Haleole, *The Hawaiian Romance of Laieikawai* (US Government Printing Office, 1918), 214.

27 *"noted for his debaucheries"*: This translation comes from Patrick Moser, *Pacific Passages: An Anthology of Surf Writing* (University of Hawai'i Press, 2008), 24.

28 *Hawaiian surfing in 1778:* It is possible that Cook was not the first non-Polynesian to visit Hawai'i. On his visit, Cook noted that the Hawaiians he encountered had a few metal blades—and metallurgy was not technology known to the Islands. This and sporadic other accounts suggest that Japanese and Spanish sailors might also have found their ways to Hawai'i, e.g., through shipwrecks, and might have been assimilated into Hawaiian society.

29 *"sharkboards"*: Moser, *Pacific Passages*, 67.

29 *"their perfect element"*: Moser, *Pacific Passages*, 67.

30 *why it happened is contentious:* For one of the more fiery examples of this debate, see, e.g., Gananath Obeyesekere, *The Apotheosis of Captain Cook* (1992), and Marshall Sahlins, *How "Natives" Think: About Captain Cook, for Example* (1995).

NOTES

31 *"a distinct recollection":* Melville, *Moby-Dick*, Norton Critical 2nd ed., 191.

32 *untouched island paradise:* Mackinnon Simpson and John Brizdle, *Streetcar Days in Honolulu: Breezing through Paradise* (J. L. B. Press, 2000), 113.

32 *Filipino plantation workers:* A good description of early twentieth-century Honolulu can be found in Edward D. Beechert, *Working in Hawaii: A Labor History* (University of Hawai'i Press, 1985), esp. 149–56.

35 *the two went to war:* Ralph S. Kuykendall, *The Hawaiian Kingdom* (University of Hawai'i Press, 1938); Noenoe K. Silva, *Aloha Betrayed: Native Hawaiian Resistance to American Colonialism* (Duke University Press, 2004); James L. Haley, *Captive Paradise: A History of Hawaii* (St. Martin's Publishing Group, 2014).

37 *"gobbled up":* David Malo, 1837, quoted (among many other places) in Kuykendall, *The Hawaiian Kingdom*, 1:153.

40 *cane fields:* The Honolulu Iron Works, founded in 1853, became the largest producer of sugar refining equipment in the world—an irony, as historian David Singerman points out, insofar as Hawai'i has barely any iron ore.

43 *"Henry Cabot Lodge?":* Recounted in Marion Mills Miller, *Great Debates in American History: Foreign Relations, Part 2* (Current Literature Publishing, 1913), 197.

43 *"the operation of the Constitution":* Harlan dissent, *Downes v. Bidwell*, 1901.

44 *"the finest peoples in the Pacific Ocean":* Vaughan Mac-Caughey, "The Physique of the Ancient Hawaiians," *Scientific Monthly* 5, no. 2 (1917): 166–74.

45 *"status," and "belonging":* Quoted in Ty P. Kāwika Tengan, "The Mana of Kū: Indigenous Nationhood, Masculinity, and Authority in Hawai'i," in *New Mana*, ed. Ty P. Kāwika Tengan and Matt Tomlinson (Australian National University Press, 2016), 55–76.

45 *bird or fish or human:* Noenoe K. Silva, "Mana Hawai'i: An Examination of Political Uses of the Word Mana in Hawaiian," in

New Mana, ed. Matt Tomlinson and Ty P. Kāwika Tengan (Australian National University Press, 2016), 37–54.

45 *the power of the natural world:* Author interview with Tom Pōhaku Stone, November 3, 2023.

46 *"to great advantage":* Isaak Iselin, *Journal of a Trading Voyage around the World, 1805–1808* (McIlroy and Emmet, n.d.), 71.

46 *"a way of preserving health":* Henry Theodore Cheever, *Life in the Sandwich Islands; or, The Heart of the Pacific, as It Was and Is* (A. S. Barnes, 1851), 68.

47 *adjusting to hot climates:* In the late nineteenth century, it would be discovered that yellow fever, like malaria, is transmitted by mosquitos, which explains the surge in these diseases during hot weather in swampy, riparian, and coastal regions of the United States. However, it is easy to see why—without a clear idea of the cycle of these diseases—hot weather itself might be to blame.

48 *self-reinforcing feedback loop:* This viewpoint wasn't limited to people beyond America's borders. American reformers likewise blamed the notional backwardness of society in the American South on its hot climate. See, e.g., Fidel Tavárez, "'The Moral Miasma of the Tropics': American Imperialism and the Failed Annexation of the Dominican Republic, 1869–1871," *New World New Worlds*, July 13, 2011.

48 *the cause of disease:* See Oliver Pomeroy Emerson, *Pioneer Days in Hawaii* (Doubleday, Doran, 1928).

49 *"a love affair":* In Clark, *Hawaiian Surfing*, 47.

49 *"pahʻe i ka nalu haʻi o Makaīwa":* From Pukui, Hawaiian Proverbs, #504, #2433, respectively (note: this is the proverb number, not the page number).

49 *"intercourse with the sexes without discrimination":* In Clark, *Hawaiian Surfing*, 49.

49 *"related to sex":* "No na hana lealea" (on fun activities), *Ka Hae Hawaii*, May 26, 1858, 29.

50 *thousands of people:* Beechert, *Working in Hawaii: A Labor History*.

50 *"the result of this [indolence]"*: Emerson, in Richard Armstrong, Levi Chamberlain, and Samuel Northrup Castle, *Answers to Questions Proposed by His Excellency, R.C. Wyllie, His Hawaiian Majesty's Minister of Foreign Relations, and Addressed to All the Missionaries in the Hawaiian Islands* (Hawaiian Foreign Office, 1848), 7.

50 *"indolence, indifference, and improvidence"*: Parker, in *Answers to Questions*, 6.

50 *"surfing is wrong"*: In Clark, *Hawaiian Surfing*, 18.

51 *banning it entirely from the island:* Paaluhi, "No Ka Heenalu, A Me Kona Ino" (About Surfing and Its Evil), *Ka Nonanona*, February 15, 1842, 81–82.

51 *"diving into the ocean"*: Owlahie, "No Ka Molowa," *Ke Kumu Hawaii*, January 31, 1838, 70.

51 *"nothing but surfing"*: Noelani Arista and Mary Kawena Pukui, "Kepelino's Traditions of Hawaii," ed. Martha Warren Beckwith, *Bernice P. Bishop Museum Bulletin* 95, 1932, 94.

51 *"industry can hold out"*: "Hulahulas," *Pacific Commercial Advertiser*, July 2, 1857.

52 *"Is it not possible to quit surfing?"*: In Clark, *Hawaiian Surfing*, 17–18.

52 *"pervaded the land"*: Charles Wilkes, *Narrative of the United States Exploring Expedition during the Years 1838, 1839, 1840, 1841, 1842*, vol. 4 (Lea and Blanchard, 1845), 47.

53 *"oppressive enactments against it"*: Hiram Bingham, *A Residence of Twenty-One Years in the Sandwich Islands* (H. Huntington, 1848), 137.

54 *"nearly forgotten sport"*: Sereno Edwards Bishop, *Reminiscences of Old Hawaii* (Hawaiian Gazette, 1916), 18.

56 *"evils of civilization"*: H. Carrington Bolton, "Some Hawaiian Pastimes," *Journal of American Folklore* 4, no. 12 (1891): 21–26.

57 *"praise for Hawaiian manliness"*: Walter Murray Gibson, *Sanitary Instructions for Hawaiians in the English and Hawaiian Languages* (J. H. Black, 1880), 195–98.

NOTES

58 *"grounded in life itself":* Stefan Helmreich and Sophia Roosth, "Life Forms: A Keyword Entry," *Representations* 112, no. 1 (November 1, 2010): 27–53.

60 *immorality, climate, or bad airs:* It is worth noting that even such medical luminaries as Florence Nightingale specifically resisted germ theory *because* it appeared to strip morality from medical practice. If germs—rather than sloth or indolence or sexual depravity—caused disease, what incentive was there for people to behave well?

61 *financial tycoon:* For excellent biographies of Osborn, see, e.g., Ronald Rainger, *An Agenda for Antiquity: Henry Fairfield Osborn and Vertebrate Paleontology at the American Museum of Natural History, 1890–1935* (University of Alabama Press, 1991); Marianne Sommer, *History Within: The Science, Culture, and Politics of Bones, Organisms, and Molecules* (University of Chicago Press, 2016); Brian Regal, *Henry Fairfield Osborn: Race and the Search for the Origins of Man* (Routledge, 2018).

61 *Victorian Gothic mansion on Park Avenue:* For more on the Osborn house, see Baker, *Richard Morris Hunt* (MIT Press, 1986), 230–31. See also Susan Stein, ed., *The Architecture of Richard Morris Hunt* (University of Chicago Press, 1986).

62 *"poor, weak, delicate":* Quoted in Regal, *Henry Fairfield Osborn*, 31.

64 *"to the utmost advantage":* Francis Galton, "Eugenics: Its Definition, Scope, and Aims," *American Journal of Sociology* 10, no. 1 (July 1904).

64 *"Measure of Fidget":* Francis Galton, "The Weights of British Noblemen during the Last Three Generations," *Nature* 29 (January 17, 1884): 266–88; Francis Galton, "On Head Growth in Students at the University of Cambridge," *Journal of the Anthropological Institute* 18 (1889): 155–56; Francis Galton, "The Measure of Fidget," *Nature* 32 (June 25, 1885): 174–75.

66 *"imagination of the mother":* Quoted in Justin E. H. Smith, "Imagination and the Problem of Heredity in Mechanist Embryology," in Justin E. H. Smith, ed., *The Problem of Animal Generation in Early Modern Philosophy* (Cambridge University Press, 2006), 93.

69 *"reviving past sensations":* Galton, *Inquiries into Human Faculty and Its Development* (Macmillan, 1833), 255.

69 *Galton thanked Osborn warmly for his collaboration:* Galton, *Inquiries*, 24–25.

70 *a brontosaurus:* The skeleton later gained a sort of paleontological infamy when it was discovered that Osborn's team had put the wrong head (that of a camarasaurus) on the brontosaurus's body. To complicate matters further, the designation "brontosaurus" was replaced in the late twentieth century with "apatosaurus" because the species "brontosaurus" was thought to be, in fact, simply a misidentification of an immature apatosaurus. Only in 2011 did some scientists suggest that the AMNH brontosaurus, née apatosaurus, was, in fact, an authentic brontosaurus, which was a distinct subspecies of apatosaurus. Thus did poor brontosaurus, in effect, go extinct twice, only to come back to life once more. Taxonomy is a wild ride.

70 *"Ancient form [sic] of life":* "Brontosaurus Receives a Tea to Celebrate Opening of the Fossil Hall," *New York Tribune*, February 17, 1905, 1.

70 *"epoch making":* "Big Thunder Saurian Viewed and Approved," *New York Times*, February 17, 1905, 9.

70 *"highly strung nervous organization":* Regal, *Henry Fairfield Osborn*, 30.

71 *"may be unbearable and harmful":* George Miller Beard, *American Nervousness, Its Causes and Consequences: A Supplement to Nervous Exhaustion (Neurasthenia)* (Putnam, 1881), 106. Edited for punctuation and spelling.

71 *known as neurasthenia:* On neurasthenia, see George Beard, "Neurasthenia, or Nervous Exhaustion," *Boston Medical and Surgical Journal* 80, no. 13 (April 29, 1869): 217–21.

72 *"a factor in personal history":* Gregory, "Biographical Memoir of Henry Fairfield Osborn," *National Academy of Sciences Biographical Memoirs* 19, no. 3 (1936?): 56–57. It's worth noting that Gregory's use of the term "elan vital" is somewhat anachronistic, but not inexplicable. Bergson first proposed the idea of *elan vital* in 1907—well after Osborn

had established his manner of thinking about life history and human history as guided by an elemental force. Nevertheless, Osborn was a correspondent of Bergson's, and Gregory would have known about Bergson and his philosophy. Bergson was one of the most—if not the most—famous philosophers in the United States in the early twentieth century. In claiming that Osborn was a believer in a kind of *elan vital*, Gregory was drawing on a close-to-hand analogy for the sort of thinking that Osborn pursued his whole life. Also worth mentioning here is the fact that Gregory was an opponent of Osborn's views and found them to be pseudoscientific and galling. Probably not the person Osborn would have picked to author his "biographical memoir."

73 *"repetition of an ancient type"*: Henry Fairfield Osborn, "The Hereditary Mechanism and the Search for the Unknown Factors of Evolution," *American Naturalist* 29, no. 341 (1895): 418–39.

74 *"perhaps hundreds of thousands—of years"*: Henry Fairfield Osborn, *Impressions of Great Naturalists*, 1913, xvii.

74 *"racial soul"*: Osborn, *Impressions*, 1913.

74 *"a continually advancing frontier line"*: Ray Allen Billington gives a thorough account of the first reading of "The Significance of the Frontier" in *Frederick Jackson Turner: Historian, Scholar, Teacher* (Oxford University Press, 1973), 124–29.

75 *"that I have read in several years"*: Quoted in Billington, *Frederick Jackson Turner*, 130.

75 *"floating around rather loosely"*: Quoted in Billington, *Frederick Jackson Turner*, 130.

75 *in newspaper digests*: See Billington, *Frederick Jackson Turner*, 184–208.

79 *"doing battle for his female"*: Jack London, "The Son of the Wolf," in *The Son of the Wolf* (Bernhard Tauchnitz, 1914), 52.

79 *"bloody and red"*: Jack London, "The League of Old Men," in *Children of the Frost* (Macmillan, 1902), 261.

80 *"the grain of sand I crush under my foot"*: Jack London, *The Cruise of the Snark* (Macmillan, 1911), 18–19.

NOTES

80 *"will imagine it is godlike"*: London, *Cruise of the Snark*, 19.

80 *"into the sea and to death"*: London, *Cruise of the Snark*, 19.

82 *"her great black eyes"*: Charmian London, *Our Hawaii* (Macmillan, 1917), 56.

82 *"[her] cold hatred of everything American"*: Charmian London, *Our Hawaii*, 57.

83 *"Now look here, London"*: Charmian London, *Our Hawaii*, 53.

84 *"bull-mouthed monsters"*: London, *Cruise of the Snark*, 82–83.

84 *"the sea's depth from which he rose"*: London, *Cruise of the Snark*, 83.

85 *"the art of surf-bathing thoroughly"*: Mark Twain, *Roughing It* (Hippocrene Books, 1872), 526.

85 *he could do better:* London, *Cruise of the Snark*, 84.

85 *"wrestle with the sea"*: London, *Cruise of the Snark*, 84.

87 *"the bathers on the beach grow distinct"*: London, *Cruise of the Snark*, 89.

89 *London's biographer, Earle Labor:* For this and other biographical details about London, see, e.g., Earle Labor, *Jack London: An American Life* (Farrar, Straus and Giroux). See also C. W. Denko, "Jack London: A Modern Analysis of His Mysterious Disease," *Journal of Rheumatology* 20, no. 10 (October 1993): 1760–63.

89 *"torn to pieces"*: London, *Cruise of the Snark*, 306.

90 *"The New Order of Sainthood"*: Henry Fairfield Osborn, "The New Order of Sainthood" (C. Scribner's Sons, 1913).

92 *"good government and welfare"*: Osborn Diary, March 2, 1920, Henry Fairfield Osborn Papers, Box 28, New York Historical Society.

92 *"spend a large part of it in vacation"*: Osborn Diary, February 28, 1920, Box 28, New York Historical Society.

92 *(and "excellent"):* Osborn Diary, March 19, 1920, Box 28, New York Historical Society.

NOTES

92 *"highly intelligent head"*: Osborn Diary, March 29, 1920, Box 28, New York Historical Society.

94 *the physicality of Hawaiian people:* Osborn Diary, March 5, 1920, Box 28, New York Historical Society.

95 *"model youth"*: Osborn Diary, n.d. 1920, Box 28, New York Historical Society.

3 | THE "MODEL YOUTH"

97 *"Mahape a ale walaʻu"*: quoted in David Davis, *Waterman: The Life and Times of Duke Kahanamoku* (University of Nebraska Press, 2015), 39.

99 *"the athletic honor roll"*: Leonard Withington, "Duke Kahanamoku," *Hawaiian Gazette*, July 12, 1912.

100 *"overhanging crags and masses of rock"*: Hubert Howe Bancroft, *The Book of the Fair* (Bancroft, 1893), 854–55.

100 *"the sights they saw at the fair"*: "Hawaiian Singers," *Pacific Commercial Advertiser*, November 25, 1893, 3.

101 *in "the best of health"*: "They Come Home Happy," *Pacific Commercial Advertiser*, July 14, 1894, 2.

101 *"toadying up to the Royalists and Queen Lili"*: "The Midwinter Fair," *Rochester Democrat and Chronicle*, January 22, 1894, 2.

102 *"in peace and equity"*: A Lover of Justice, "Hawaiian Annexation," *Brooklyn Daily Eagle*, January 22, 1894, 10.

104 *beach houses there:* George S. Kanahele, *Waikiki 100 B.C. to 1900 A.D.: An Untold Story* (Queen Emma Land Company, 1995); regarding Castles break, see Clark, *Hawaiian Surfing*, 470–71. In 1918, Castle's widow sold the mansion to the Elks club: see Michael Keany, "A Long Gone Honolulu Landmark," *Honolulu Magazine*, April 20, 2010.

105 *"practically all* delicious *eating"*: Kathryn Heily, "Scrapbook of Hawaii," 1921, MS 41, Box 1, Folder 5, Kauai Historical Society. Emphasis in original.

105 *born on August 24, 1890:* Davis's *Waterman* offers perhaps the most comprehensive and insightful biography of Duke as of this writing. See also James Dean Nendel's "Duke Kahanamoku—Twentieth Century Hawaiian Monarch: The Values and Contributions to Hawaiian Culture from Hawai'i's Sporting Legend," PhD diss., Pennsylvania State University, 2006; Joseph L. Brennan, *Duke: The Life Story of Hawai'i's Duke Kahanamoku* (Ku Pa'a Publishing, 1994).

106 *"Kaisers," "Fours," and "Threes":* In a series of oral interviews with Waikiki residents between 1985 and 1986, former beach boys identified many of the breaks from the early 1920s using the same names as today and described them as having similar sorts of surf properties (Castles is rough; Canoes is sloping and easy, etc.).

106 *errant duck eggs:* See, e.g., oral history interview with Mary Ellen Kealohapauole (Paoa) Clarke, interviewed by Warren Nishimoto, May 20, 1985, 652; Leslie Fullard-Leo, interviewed by 'Iwalani Hodges, June 12, 1986, 1046; Wilbur Craw, interviewed by Michael Mauricio, April 11, 1985; and Louis Kahanamoku, interviewed by Warren Nishimoto, May 20, 1985, 857. All were interviewed as part of *Waikiki 1900–1985: Oral Histories*, Oral History Project, Social Science Research Institute, University of Hawai'i at Mānoa (hereafter *Waikiki 1900–1985*).

107 *"rice and potatoes and taro":* Doveline "Tootsie" Notley Steer, interviewed by 'Iwalani Hodges, April 1, 1985, *Waikiki 1900–1985*, 1644.

107 *the rocks near shore:* Fred Paoa, interviewed by Warren Nishimoto, March 25, *Waikiki 1900–1985*, 542, 533.

107 *The Ah Leong Store:* Interview with Mary Clarke, 649.

107 *a minor operative in Honolulu politics:* "Democratic Endorsements Announced," *Honolulu Advertiser*, December 15, 1908, 1.

107 *Hawai'i's Fourth Congressional District in 1908:* "Democratic Rally," *Honolulu Advertiser*, October 14, 1908, 5; also, "L. L. McCandless on Land Laws," *Honolulu Advertiser*, October 22, 1908, 2.

108 *kids were constantly running in and out:* Rossi, oral history interview with David Kahanamoku II, November 2, 2023.

108 *jump off into the water at the last minute:* Simpson and Brizdle, *Streetcar Days*, 85

109 *"did not show them our 'Ōkoles":* Oral history interview with Lemon Holt, by Michi Kodama-Nishimoto, March 15, 1985, *Waikiki 1900–1985*, 805.

109 *"we wanted to learn to surf":* Interview with Louis Kahanamoku, 857.

110 *"So I saved myself":* Quoted in Davis, *Waterman*, 4.

110 *"And that was our surfboard":* Interview with Lemon Holt, 806.

111 *"the rest of the week, surfing":* Interview with Lemon Holt, 790.

111 *the school's athletic fields:* Theodore Richards, "From 89–99—A Flare Up of Memories," *The Friend* 98 (December 12, 1928): 307.

111 *The mission of the school:* Frank Metcalf, "Development of Educational Opportunities," *The Friend* 98 (December 12, 1928): 309.

111 *"fonder of ease than of toil":* Quoted in Davis, *Waterman*, 16.

111 *"America's and Hawaii's existence":* Metcalf, "Development of Educational Opportunities," 310.

112 *"machines, blacksmithing, and carpentering":* Duke Kahanamoku, interview, "KGU—7:30, Tuesday," July 19, 1949, folder: "Radio: TV: Biographical," Duke Paoa Kahanamoku Collection, Hawaii State Archives.

112 *"it evinces itself in sportsman-like conduct":* Metcalf, "Development of Educational Opportunities," 310.

112 *"the reason for our success in athletics":* Ethyl M. Damon and Josephine Sullivan, "A Historical View of the Kamehameha Schools," *The Friend* 98 (December 12, 1928): 267–88, on 277.

113 *"the play was heartily applauded":* "School Socker [sic] Has Commenced," *Pacific Commercial Advertiser*, January 25, 1908, 2.

113 *"that was a real switch":* Quoted in Davis, *Waterman*, 28.

113 *"disgusted us quite a bit":* Quoted in Davis, *Waterman*, 30.

115 *"giving them swimming lessons"*: Oral history interview with Ernst Steiner, by Michael Mauricio and Michi Kodama-Nishimoto, March 5, 1985, *Waikiki 1900–1985*, 84.

116 *"that's what they liked very much"*: Interview with Fred Paoa, 558.

116 *"everybody went there"*: Interview with Fred Paoa, 565–66.

117 *"We made money those days"*: Interview with Fred Paoa, 558.

117 *"the Waikiki beach boys of Honolulu"*: Ned Steel, "Spear Fishing in Hawaii," *Outing Magazine: The Outdoor Magazine of Human Interest*, June 1917.

117 *"the amusement they afford others"*: Frances Parkinson Keyes, "Aloha from Hawaii," *Good Housekeeping*, December 1925, 185.

117 *"the big hotels at night"*: Rosita Forbes, *Unconducted Wanderers* (John Lane, 1919), 21.

117 *"the scum of the earth"*: Interview with Louis Kahanamoku, 875.

118 *"in that line [of work]"*: "Ross Says Dave Made a Wise Move," *Honolulu Star-Bulletin*, November 7, 1917, 8.

118 *"And that's all / You need to do"*: Interview with Joe Akana, 52. See also Grady Timmons, *Waikiki Beachboy* (Editions Ltd., 1989), 137.

119 *spoke in a "nasty way"*: "David Kahanamoku Accused of Striking Bather, Gives Version," *Honolulu Star-Bulletin*, August 2, 1922, 18.

119 *"We all surfed on those"*: Interview with Fred Paoa, 539.

120 *Movies and photographs from the era*: See, e.g., Robert Bruce's 1926 silent movie *Sons of the Surf*.

121 *"upon the sandy shore"*: Rosamond Swanzy Morgan and J. P. Morgan, "About Maui and Kauai," *Mid Pacific Magazine* 20, September 3, 1920, 269.

121 *"Two, three times"*: Interview with Fred Paoa, 556.

121 *"good Hawaiian fucking"*: Quoted in Peter Westwick and Peter Neushul, *The World in the Curl: An Unconventional History of Surfing* (Crown, 2013), 329.

NOTES

122 *"Skin to skin. In the water"*: Quoted in Westwick and Neushul, *World in the Curl*, 58.

122 *"your arms in the pits, you know"*: Interview with Louis Kahanamoku, 863.

123 *"the girls look at us . . ."*: Interview with Louis Kahanamoku, 872.

123 *"stranger than fiction"*: The Stranger, "Stranger Than Fiction," *Pacific Commercial Advertiser*, May 13, 1926, 12.

123 *"We go out and think of making money"*: Interview with Louis Kahanamoku, 873.

124 *"swimming instructor to a pupil"*: "Kahanamoku Is Very Indignant," *Los Angeles Times*, October 15, 1913, 30.

124 *"we were all the experienced ones"*: Interview with Joe Akana, 17.

124 *"You ain't coming down this end"*: Interview with Louis Kahanamoku, 869.

124 *"fight, boy"*: Interview with Wilbur Craw.

124 *"pretty rugged buggers"*: Interview with Wilbur Craw, 339.

126 *"the most scientific men of swimmers"*: "Duke Kahanamoku Would Be Aviator," *San Francisco Bulletin*, June 7, 1918, 14.

126 *"I could swim"*: Duke Kahanamoku, Interview, "KGU—7:30, Tuesday," July 19, 1949, folder: "Radio: TV: Biographical," Duke Paoa Kahanamoku Collection, Hawaii State Archives.

127 *"records are forwarded to the mainland"*: "Aquatic Meet Will Attract Big Crowd," *Honolulu Advertiser*, August 9, 1911, 3.

128 *"take our hats off to him"*: "Clarence Lane a Student in Swimming: Paddling as Science Has Forged Ahead: Has Confidence in Kahanamoku," *San Francisco Chronicle*, June 9, 1918.

128 *eighty-seven coins*: "At One Dive Man Picks Up Seventy-Five Coins with His Mouth," *San Francisco Examiner*, February 21, 1897, 29. Note that while the headline emphasizes seventy-five coins, the text specifies that eighty-seven was his record.

129 *"studied by competent men"*: Davis Dalton, *How to Swim: A Practical Treatise upon the Art of Natation* (G. P. Putnam's Sons, 1899).

129 *the "science of swimming"*: C. W. Saleeby, "Science: Swimming," *The Academy and Literature*, July 1903, 44–45.

130 *according to the* Advertiser: "Lively Contests expected in the Aquatic Meet Saturday," *Honolulu Advertiser*, August 9, 1911, 6.

130 *"experts in the territory"*: "Lively Contests Expected in the Aquatic Meet Saturday," *Honolulu Advertiser*, August 9, 1911, 6.

130 *Crowds lined the sides of the pier:* David Davis provides an excellent and detailed narrative of the race in *Waterman*, 37–39.

132 *"is unheard of"*: Davis, *Waterman*, 40.

133 *his "scientific" views on race and athletics:* See Susan Brownell, ed., *The 1904 Anthropology Days and Olympic Games: Sport, Race, and American Imperialism* (University of Nebraska Press, 2008).

133 *considered almost superhuman:* See Charles Sprawson, *Haunts of the Black Masseur: The Swimmer as Hero* (Pantheon Books, 1992).

134 *"funds for the Duke"*: Meeting Minutes, May 8, 1912, Hui Nalu Collection, Hawaii State Archives.

134 *"Have you helped along the Duke Kahanamoku fund yet?"*: "Good morning. Have you helped along the Duke Kahanamoku fund yet?" *Honolulu Star-Bulletin*, July 15, 1912, 4.

135 *"in enclosed tanks with many turns"*: "Hawaiian Stars in Big Race," *Pittsburgh Press*, February 22, 1912, 18.

135 *"a 75-foot tank"*: Ralph Davis, "Ralph Davis' Column," *Pittsburgh Press*, February 26, 1912, 14.

137 *"cleanliness and public health"*: Harold Werner and August P. Windolph, "The Public Bath V," *The Brickbuilder* 17 (June 1906): 115.

137 *"ear-splitting" cacophony:* "Youthful Swimmers Revel in Tanks," *New York Times*, April 26, 1908, S1.

137 *Italian boys "acting like monkeys"*: See Christopher Capozzola and Michael Rossi, "Duesler's Third Law: Social Control and the Politics

of Fun in the Modern American Swimming Pool," *Widener Journal of Law, Economics, and Race* (January 9, 2010).

137 *"good Americans"*: "Public Baths," *New York Sun*, March 31, 1891.

138 *"powerful in every way"*: "Philadelphian to Swim the English Channel," *Rochester Democrat and Chronicle*, August 31, 1903, 13.

138 *generation of "scientific" coaches:* Dave Day and Margaret Roberts, *Swimming Communities in Victorian England* (Springer, 2019), 267.

138 *"knowledge of mechanics and physiology"*: "Trainer Down on Meat," *Monongahela Daily Republican*, August 6, 1906, 2.

138 *"I'm getting familiar with fresh water"*: Quoted in Davis, *Waterman*, 46.

139 *"Swedish friends of the art of swimming"*: Swedish Olympic Committee and Sveriges olympiska kommitté, *The Fifth Olympiad: The Official Report of the Olympic Games of Stockholm, 1912* (Swedish Olympic Committee, 1913), 217.

139 *"the Honolulu native, Kahanamoku"*: "Path, Road, and Track," *Manchester Evening News*, July 20, 1912, 6.

140 *"a record that may possibly stand for decades"*: "The Olympic Games," *North China Herald*, July 20, 1912, 172.

140 *"lay people dreaming"*: "L'Olympiade de Stockholm," *Le Sport Universel Illustré*, July 7, 1912, 473.

140 *"an Olympic Swimming contest"*: "Three American Athletes Who Have Added Winning Points to United States Team at Olympics in Sweden," *Nashville Banner*, July 15, 1912.

140 *"Hawaiian Carries US Hope in Swimming"*: "Hawaiian Carries US Hope in Swimming," *Evansville Courier*, July 11, 1912, 4.

140 *"photo studio of Alfred Gurrey"*: "Would Raise Statue to Duke Kahanamoku," *Hawaiian Gazette*, July 16, 1912, 6.

140 *"semi-amphibious humans"*: "Swimming Feats of Hawaiians," *Republican*, July 5, 1912, 8.

141 *A "True Story in Pictures"*: Stookie Allen, "The Human Fish of Hawaii," *The Argosy* 246, April 14, 1934.

142 *"'made in America' and by Americans"*: "Studies of Present American Champions," *New York Times*, 1916.

144 *"the most perfect swimmer they have ever seen"*: "Honolulu's Champion Swimmer," *Boston Globe*, March 24, 1912, 63.

144 *"Duke is a smooth, well-oiled machine"*: "Studies of Present American Champions," *New York Times*, 1916, S3.

145 *"the famous Australian crawl"*: "Hawaiian Broke Record at Pool," *Press of Atlantic City*, August 17, 1912. Note the phrase "Kahanamoku kick" does not figure in this article.

147 *"make his living"*: Bystander, "The Bystander," *Pacific Commercial Advertiser*, August 13, 1911.

148 *"all Hawaii is proud of him"*: Outrigger (probably Hume Ford), "Letters from the People: Champion Not Barred," *Pacific Commercial Advertiser*, August 14, 1911, 4.

148 *"Caucasians have little chance"*: Davis, *Waterman*, 78.

149 *"good publicity"*: Davis, *Waterman*, 24.

149 *"unite in sporting competition"*: Quoted in Volker Kluge, "Cancelled but Still Counted, and Never Annulled: The Games of 1916," *Journal of Olympic History*, 2014.

149 *machine guns and rifles:* See Kluge, "Cancelled but Still Counted"; also Allen Guttmann, *The Olympics: A History of the Modern Games* (University of Illinois Press, 2002).

150 *"a capable aviator"*: "Duke Kahanamoku Would Be Aviator," *San Francisco Bulletin*, June 7, 1918, 14.

150 *"flying Hawaiian"*: See, e.g., "About Swimming," *Philadelphia Inquirer*, May 5, 1918, 19; "Two Gotham Fair Natators in 'Frisco Free Style Race," *New York Tribune*, May 5, 1918, 20.

150 *rides in his airplane:* "Duke Kahanamoku and Major Clark in New Jersey, Far from Waikiki," *Honolulu Star-Advertiser*, September 29, 1918, 14.

NOTES

151 *"sent him away":* Oral history interview with Earl Vida by Warren Nishimoto, March 18, 1985, *Waikiki 1900–1985*, 604.

152 *"It had me scared for a while":* Bob Shand, "Champion Swimmer Files Application with Flying Corps," *Oakland Enquirer*, October 22, 1918, 9.

154 *the court concluded:* Kahanamoku vs. Advertiser Publishing Company, Hawaii Supreme Court, Docket 1227, 25 Haw. 701, 22 December 1920.

4 | A PASSION FOR MEASURING NAKED MEN

157 *a "good laboratory man":* Pomeroy to Wissler, April 23, 1916, AMNH Anthropology Archives.

157 *"mechanical ability":* H. E. Walter to Wissler, April 5, 1916, AMNH Anthropology Archives.

157 *"native ability":* "Robert Louis Sullivan," *AMNH Annual Report for 1925*, 263.

158 *"I cannot get anything out of him":* Quoted in Rosemary Lévy Zumwalt, *Franz Boas: Shaping Anthropology and Fostering Social Justice* (University of Nebraska Press, 2022), 242.

159 *"the Nation at large":* United States Surgeon-General's Office, Charles Benedict Davenport, and Albert Gallatin Love, *Army Anthropology: Based on Observations Made on Draft Recruits, 1917–1918, and on Veterans at Demobilization, 1919* (Government Printing Office, 1921), 34.

159 *"racial survey":* Sullivan to Greene, September 29, 1919, AMNH Anthropology Archives; on Hooton, see *Army Anthropology*, 56.

160 *"the limbs and feet":* Osborn to Sullivan, April 23, 1920, AMNH Central Archives.

162 *do Sullivan good:* Osborn to Judd, March 16, 1922, AMNH Central Archives.

163 *"within one or two hundredths of an inch!":* William Morton Wheeler, "A Consideration of S. B. Buckley's 'North American Formicidae,'" *Transactions of the Texas Academy of Science* 4, no. 2 (1902).

163 *"circumference of waist, etc."*: Buckley to Gould, December 7, 1864, Box 2, USSC Records, NYPL.

163 *"a passion for measuring naked men"*: Lewis to Gould, February 20, 1865, Box 2, USSC Records, NYPL.

163 *"my good evenings"*: Sullivan to Weitzner, December 23, 1929, AMNH Anthropology Archives.

164 *seven days a week:* Sullivan to Wissler, November 3, 1920, AMNH Anthropology Archives.

164 *a "fine voyage"*: Sullivan to Wissler, May 6, 1920, AMNH Anthropology Archives.

165 *"pick the chicken clean"*: Sullivan to Wissler, December 8, 1920, AMNH Anthropology Archives.

169 *"the best student I've had"*: Sullivan to Wissler, September 28, 1920, AMNH Anthropology Archives. Sullivan also recruited a Miss Madge Yonge from the museum as well as Mrs. Adeline Kinney, and both proved good at anthropometry.

170 *"strange as that may seem"*: Sullivan to Wissler, November 3, 1920, AMNH Anthropology Archives.

170 *"a good investment"*: Sullivan to Wissler, November 3, 1920, AMNH Anthropology Archives.

171 *"they arouse much interest"*: Sullivan to Wissler, September 28, 1920, AMNH Anthropology Archives.

172 *"the science of improving things"*: Ignoramens, "What Is or Are Eugenics," *Garden Island*, December 3, 1912, 1.

173 *"another guess coming"*: "Eugenics Bill," *Honolulu Star-Bulletin*, March 22, 1913, 2.

174 *"never embarrass the subject"*: Louis R. Sullivan and Harry L. Shapiro, *Essentials of Anthropometry* (American Museum of Natural History, 1928), 65.

174 *"no experience on the living"*: Sullivan to Hrdlička, May 22, 1917, Louis R. Sullivan correspondence (1917–1924), Box 62, Hrdlička Papers, National Anthropological Archives, Smithsonian Institution.

NOTES

174 *"skeletal material"*: Report of Louis R. Sullivan, March 25, 1921, AMNH Anthropology Archives.

174 *"ticklish on that point"*: Wissler to Goddard, July 25, 1920, AMNH Central Archives.

175 *"keen on such subjects"*: Wissler to Pindar, July 25, 1920, AMNH Central Archives.

175 *"what pitiful depths"*: "The Hasty Dr. Hoag," *Hawaii Herald*, February 11, 1921, 4.

178 *"sensitive to photography"*: Osborn to Sullivan, April 15, 1920, AMNH Central Archives.

179 *"descriptive characters"*: Sullivan to Wissler, November 3, 1920, AMNH Anthropology Archives.

179 *"various Hawaiian mixtures"*: Sullivan to Wissler, December 8, 1920, AMNH Anthropology Archives.

180 *"for some psychological study"*: Sullivan to Weitzner, n.d., but around October 1918, AMNH Anthropology Archives. See also Anderson, "Estimation of Intelligence by Means of Printed Photographs," *Journal of Applied Psychology* 5 (1921): 152–55.

182 *See if you can spot what's missing:* Some thoughts on possible solutions to the ostensible missing elements of the pictures: Does the error in figure 6 have to do with the croquet mallet that the worker appears to be using to drive spikes into the railroad? Or is the error that there are no spikes in the picture for him to hammer? Or is it that the railroad is already complete, so why is he still hammering it? Or is it the featureless landscape between the worker and the mountains in the distance? It's not clear to this writer what should be added to make the picture more accurate (a different hammering implement? Some spikes? A bit of gravel and cactuses?). Similarly, in figure 19 one can only suppose that the problem with the picture is that there's no steam coming from the open top of the kettle, even though the lid's been removed. Or is the problem that the kettle is still steaming away without a source of heat? But if that's the case, perhaps the kettle was just recently removed from the stove. I tried heating my own kettle to boiling and then taking it off the stove, quickly removing the lid, and

comparing it to the diagram. I didn't see a distinct difference. As for figure 13, this writer has no idea what's wrong, and no idea how to correct it.

182 *"There are many things that are not fair"*: Sullivan to Wissler, December 8, 1920, AMNH Anthropology Archives.

183 *"a new stunt"*: Sullivan to Gregory, April 19, 1921, AMNH Anthropology Archives.

183 *"definite tests for primitive people"*: Sullivan, *Essentials of Anthropometry*, 62.

184 *"President Osborn is rather anxious"*: Wissler to Sullivan, January 7, 1921, AMNH Anthropology Archives.

184 *"with his mask off!"*: Laurence Hutton, *Portraits in Plaster: From the Collection of Laurence Hutton* (Harper and Brothers, 1894).

185 *"characteristics of the Polynesian"*: "Whence Come the Ancient Hawaiians?" *Chanute Daily Tribune*, February 18, 1921, 6.

185 *"a museum of pictures"*: F. A. Lucas, "Wax and Other Casts," *Museum Work*, January 1920, 118.

187 *"simulate the skin effect"*: Arthur C. Parker, "Habitat Groups in Wax and Plaster," *Museum Work* 1, no. 3 (December 1918): 78–85, on 83.

188 *"hard on a living subject"*: Sullivan to Wissler, November 3, 1920, AMNH Anthropology Archives. Note this is about mouth casting in particular, but the same can be said for faces.

188 *"it becomes too hot"*: Parker, "Habitat Groups in Wax and Plaster," 83.

188 *"somewhat severe"*: Sam Putnam, "Eyes of Eugenics Experts Focussed [sic] on Hawaii," *Honolulu Star-Bulletin*, July 23, 1921, 15.

188 *"discouraging work"*: Sullivan to Gregory, March 18, 1921, AMNH Anthropology Archives.

188 *"good representations of fish"*: Margaret Titcom and Mary Kawena Pukui, "Native Use of Fish in Hawaii," *Journal of the Polynesian Society* 60, no. 2/3 (1951): 1–96, at 51.

NOTES

189 *"I'm much disappointed":* Sullivan to Wissler, September 28, 1920.

190 *"cranial lines":* Sam Putnam, "Eyes of Eugenics Experts Focussed [*sic*] on Hawaii," *Honolulu Star-Bulletin*, July 23, 1921, 15.

190 *Sullivan was very happy:* See, e.g., "Traces Origin of Polynesians," in the *Oklahoma Daily Live Stock News*, August 30, 1921, on 2.

191 *"wide but deceptive grin":* "Fighting Micks Figure on Chance Against Kams Squad," *Honolulu Star-Bulletin*, November 7, 1919, 8.

191 *best in the school:* "Kamehameha Pupils Give Play Tonight," April 22, 1921.

191 *committed suicide:* "Skull Pierced by Bullets Found on Tanatalus," *Honolulu Star-Bulletin*, May 10, 1921, 1.

192 *"no rice dinner for me":* Ichikawa to Sullivan, October 14, 1920, AMNH Anthropology Archives.

193 *"study of racial characteristics":* "Traces Origin of Polynesians," 2.

194 *the reporter emphasized:* "Traces Origin of Polynesians," 2.

194 *"make the acquaintance of Duke":* Osborn to Sullivan, July 7, 1920, AMNH Central Archives.

195 *"woman's instinctive choice":* "Beach Apollos," *The Sun*, October 17, 1921, 8.

196 *"invite Duke Kahanamoku":* Osborn to Sherwood, August 4, 1920, AMNH Central Archives.

197 *as David's son later explained:* Rossi, oral history interview with David Kahanamoku II, November 2, 2023.

198 *simply too painful:* "Sandow in Plaster of Paris," *Strand Magazine*, October 1901, 462.

200 *"both are remarkable":* "Racial Exhibit to Be Sent to Eugenics Meet," *Honolulu Star-Bulletin*, July 11, 1921, 1.

200 *Doctor Gregory agreed:* "Bishop Museum Ships Exhibit for Display at Second International Eugenics Conference at New York," *Honolulu Star-Bulletin*, July 29, 1921, 11.

200 *"green with envy"*: Mike Jay, "Champion Saver of Lives on the Beach at Waikiki," *Honolulu Star-Bulletin*, June 30, 1923, 34.

200 *"most important contemporary contributions"*: "Traces Origin of Polynesians," 2.

5 | BARBARIANS AND DEMIGODS

205 *"put out of existence"*: Quoted in Edwin Black, *War against the Weak: Eugenics and America's Campaign to Create a Master Race* (Dialog Press, 2012), 248.

205 *"scientific grounds"*: Osborn to Warburg, April 14, 1923, AMNH Central Archives. Warburg was a powerful figure in New York finance and took a dim view of eugenics. Here, Osborn was speaking specifically about race science and immigration and less about disability—but the observation applies to both.

206 *"the grand spectacle"*: See, e.g., "Eugenics and Immigration Laws," *Times-Tribune*, August 11, 1920, 10.

206 *"nobler, happier, and healthier"*: Leonard Darwin, "Aims and Methods of Eugenical Societies," *Scientific Papers of the Second International Congress of Eugenics, Vol. I* (Williams and Wilkins, 1923), 19.

207 *"the world's economy"*: Osborn, "Address of Welcome," *Scientific Papers of the Second Congress, Vol. I*, 2.

215 *"sexual sterilization"*: Laughlin, "Present State of Eugenical Sterilization in the United States," *Scientific Papers of the Second International Congress of Eugenics*, Vol. II, 286.

217 *"standard of life"*: Hoffman, "The Problem of Negro-White Intermixture and Intermarriage," *Scientific Papers of the Second International Congress of Eugenics, Vol. II*, 187–88.

217 *"I am not impressed with their sparsity"*: Sullivan to Greene, September 29, 1919, AMNH Anthropology Archives.

218 *differences between the sexes*: Harriette M. Dilla, "Control of Parenthood," *Scientific Papers of the Second International Congress of Eugenics, Vol. II*, 270.

218 *"feminist contention"*: Paul Popenoe and Roswell Hill Johnson, *Applied Eugenics* (Macmillan, 1918), 383.

218 *"higher education of women"*: Uldrich Thompson, "Ideals of Marriage," *Honolulu Star-Bulletin*, April 19, 1909, 10.

218 *"a socialistic movement"*: Popenoe and Johnson, *Applied Eugenics*, 367.

219 *"The woman of the future"*: Jon Alfred Mjøen, "Harmonic and Disharmonic Race Crossings," *Scientific Papers of the Second International Congress of Eugenics, Vol. II*, 58.

219 *"seed bed of a new religion"*: Fisher, "Conscience in Relation to Sexual Vices," *Scientific Papers of the Second International Congress of Eugenics, Vol. II*, 317.

221 *"a soda fountain"*: C. C. Little, "Unnatural Selection," *Birth Control Review 10*, 1926, 256.

222 *"certain element is needed"*: Little, "Unnatural Selection," 256.

225 *"has no meaning"*: Franz Boas, "Inventing a Great Race," *New Republic*, January 3, 1917, 305.

225 *rebuttal to the program of eugenics:* For more on Boas's and Du Bois's relationship, see Lee D. Baker, "W. E. B. Du Bois and American Anthropology," in *The Oxford Handbook of W. E. B. Du Bois*, ed. Aldon D. Morris et al. (Oxford University Press, 2024).

225 *"dissemination of the truth"*: Du Bois, "Manifesto of the Second Pan African Congress," *The Crisis* (November 1921): 7.

225 *"the unfit fifty percent?"*: "Make the Unfit Fit to Marry," *Chattanooga Daily Times*, September 27, 1921.

226 *"visionary and impractical"*: "Second National Eugenics Meet," *New Farmer*, October 1, 1921, 4.

227 *"Ladies, take your choice"*: quoted in Daylanne K. English, *Unnatural Selections: Eugenics in American Modernism and the Harlem Renaissance* (University of North Carolina Press, 2004), 76.

227 *"It's all scientific stuff"*: F. Scott Fitzgerald, *The Great Gatsby* (Scribner, 1925), 16.

NOTES

229 *"immigration law"*: Calvin Coolidge, "Whose Country Is This?" *Good Housekeeping*, February 1921, 13–14.

231 *"supplanted by other groups"*: "Statement of Dr. Harry H. Laughlin," *Hearings Before the Committee on Immigration and Naturalization of the House of Representatives*, March 8, 1924, Government Printing Office, 1305.

232 *"made of green cheese"*: Emanuel Celler, 68th Congress, 1st session, Congressional Record 65, April 8, 1924: R 5911–17.

233 *"immigration restriction law"*: Mae M. Ngai, *Impossible Subjects: Illegal Aliens and the Making of Modern America* (Princeton University Press, 2004), 3.

233 *"patriotic series of addresses"*: Osborn, "Report of the President," *AMNH Annual Report for 1921*, 32.

234 *"the Mexican native type"*: Osborn to Hay, December 9, 1921, AMNH Central Archives.

235 *"worked wonders"*: Sullivan to Osborn, May 21, 1922, AMNH Anthropology Archives.

236 *"what's the matter"*: Sullivan to Wissler, October 1, 1922, AMNH Anthropology Archives.

236 *"the rest of your days"*: Wissler to Sullivan, November 7, 1923, AMNH Anthropology Archives.

237 *"sapped his vitality"*: Metzger to Wissler, March 23, 1925, AMNH Anthropology Archives.

6 | "QUITE A DIFFERENT MAN"

239 *"logical and critical mind"*: *AMNH Annual Report for 1925*, 72.

239 *"carrying on the work"*: Gregory to Osborn, May 25, 1925, AMNH Central Archives.

239 *"invaluable research"*: Earnest Hooton, "Louis R. Sullivan," *American Anthropologist* 27, no. 2 (April 1925): 357–58.

239 *"the hands of faddists":* Osborn to Tait McKenzie, November 23, 1921, R. Tait McKenzie Papers, Box 1, Folder 35, University of Pennsylvania Archives.

239 *"as Nature does":* "Report of the President," *AMNH Annual Report for 1922*, 13.

240 *a term invented in the 1920s:* Jonathan Levy, *Ages of Capitalism* (Penguin Random House, 2022), 364.

240 *"They have the thrill":* Ballard, "Museums and Movies," *Museum Work*, 1920, 251.

240 *11,000 people came to see it:* AMNH Annual Report for 1922, 44.

241 *"struggle of man":* Osborn, "The American Museum and Citizenship," *AMNH Annual Report for 1922*, 2.

241 *"glass eyes and real hair":* Sullivan to Lucas, May 8, 1922, AMNH Central Archives.

242 *"Sullivan is gone":* Hooton to Goddard, September 26, 1925, AMNH Central Archives.

242 *a "series" inaugurated by Sullivan:* Shapiro to Wissler, December 11, 1926, AMNH Central Archives.

243 *"attributed to Jews":* Hooton to Goddard, September 26, 1925, AMNH Anthropology Archives.

243 *"a smashing action romance":* "'Adventure' Introduces New Screen Character," *Mansfield (Ohio) News*, July 15, 1925, 11.

244 *"the savage Solomon Islands":* "Jack London Story in a Feature Film," *Helena Daily Independent Record*, June 12, 1925, 3.

244 *"habits of the native savages":* "'Table Duel' Seen in Photoplay 'Adventure,'" *Lansing State Journal*, May 14, 1925, 6.

244 *"Out of the water, I'm nothing":* Quoted in Davis, *Waterman*, 135.

245 *reinvented himself:* Zipp Newman, "Oscar Henning, Internationally Known Swimming Star, Locates in Birmingham," *Birmingham News*,

September 23, 1923, 3. See also, e.g., William Unmack, "Will Kahanamoku Ever Actually Race Again?," *Sacramento Union*, January 14, 1922, 6; Lobby Limerick, "Fan to Fan," *Arizona Daily Star*, December 29, 1921, 11.

245 *"heir to his brother's championship estate"*: "Battle Royale Expected at Title Swim," *Tucson Citizen*, March 9, 1921, 5.

246 *"the speed swimming phenomenon"*: "Une Apotheose," *L'Auto*, July 20, 1924, 1.

247 *the utility of the movie camera*: See Chris Long and Pat Laughren, "Australia's First Films: Facts and Fables," *Cinema Papers* 96 (1993).

248 *"remarkable film"*: AMNH Annual Report for 1922, 49.

250 *"the motion picture world"*: "Duke Has Role of Tripoli Sea Captain in 'Old Ironsides,'" *Honolulu Star-Bulletin*, May 4, 1926, 8.

250 *"swim like Duke Kahanamoku"*: "Rules for Gaining Stardom," *Closeup*, March 5, 1923, 2.

251 *"no better way to keep in trim"*: "Duke Not to Quit Swim Game, Movie Work Simply Training," *Hawaii Tribune-Herald*, July 29, 1925, 4.

251 *"films very well"*: "Pauline Starke Tames Natives of Wild Island," *Los Angeles Evening Express*, May 18, 1925, 10.

251 *"that buggah must be dumb!"*: Quoted in Davis, *Waterman*, 39.

251 *his "fine body"*: "Duke Kahanamoku Another Pirate," *Variety*, June 6, 1926.

252 *"it's in comedy"*: Mike Jay, "Mike Jay's Jabs," *Honolulu Star-Bulletin*, August 17, 1925, 20.

253 *"easier to pronounce"*: Lobby Limerick, "Fan to Fan," *Arizona Daily Star*, December 29, 1921, 11.

253 *"I call him Duke"*: Ida Zeitlin, "A Letter from Shirley," *Modern Screen*, December 1937, 72.

254 *Duke nearly drowned*: "Mike Jay's Jabs," *Honolulu Star-Bulletin*, May 9, 1925, 8.

254 *"They're just little sharks!"*: "Les cinémas: Petites nouvelles," *Le Gaulois*, August 14, 1926.

254 *"Only a porpoise"*: Duke quoted in Bob Sigall, "Kahanamoku, fellow surfers, came to rescue in California," *Honolulu Star-Advertiser*, July 11, 2014, B3.

255 *"That is the main thing"*: "Duke Kahanamoku on Surfboard Saves Eight Shipwreck Victims," *Honolulu Star-Bulletin*, June 24, 1925, 1.

255 *"the entire Pacific Coast"*: Quoted in Davis, *Waterman*, 141.

255 *Duke's watchful eye*: *Exhibitors Trade Review*, October 6, 1923, 857.

256 *"the surf board"*: Ivan St. Johns, "A Surf Board Flapper," *Photoplay*, September 1924, 65, 121.

257 *"Long as there's waves"*: John Ball, *California Surf Riders*, 1946. Quoted in Lawler, *The American Surfer*, and Davis, *Waterman*, among others.

258 *His film career was over:* Charley Paddock, "Why Athletes Fail in Pictures," *Photoplay*, September 1928, 124.

258 *"Lady Luck has gone by"*: Quoted in Davis, *Waterman*, 172.

261 *"Slavic peasants"*: Hoffman, *Heads and Tales*, 127.

261 *"a proposition"*: Hoffman, *Heads and Tales*, 3.

261 *"dummies of sawdust"*: Hoffman, *Heads and Tales*, 3.

262 *Hoffman's persistence:* Quoted in Marianne Kinkel, *Races of Mankind: The Sculptures of Malvina Hoffman* (University of Illinois Press, 2011), 34.

263 *"quenchers he is first prize"*: Hoffman, Datebook, October 16, 1930, Box 37, Folder 3, Malvina Hoffman Papers, Getty Research Collections.

263 *"in spite of myself"*: Hoffman, Colony Club Talk, March 26, 1933, Box 135, Folder 2, Malvina Hoffman Papers, Getty Research Collections.

263 *"specific to determinate societies"*: Marcel Mauss, "Techniques of the Body," *Economy and Society* 2, no. 1 (1973): 70–88. Translated

and republished from the *Journal de Psychologie Normal et Patholigique*, 1935, 271–93.

264 *"badly painted"*: Hoffman, Datebook, November 27, 1930, Box 37, Folder 3, Malvina Hoffman Papers, Getty Research Collections.

264 *"mere individuals"*: Hoffman, *Heads and Tales*, 117, italics in original.

264 *"the secret bird"*: *Sculpture Inside and Out* (George Allen & Unwin, 1939), 76.

265 *"native habitat"*: Hoffman, *Heads and Tales*, 155.

265 *raise an eyebrow:* Hoffman, *Heads and Tales*, 166.

266 *"as to the manner of men"*: Peter Buck, *Vikings of the Sunrise* (Frederick A. Stokes, 1938), 14. He goes on to say, "There is only one way by which we can arrive at an understanding of the physical characters of a people and that is by measurements, measurements, and yet more measurements."

267 *"our quest for medical knowledge"*: Buck, *Vikings*, 15.

267 *"health of the Māori"*: Peter Henry Buck, "Medicine amongst the Māoris in Ancient and Modern Times" (MD thesis, University of Otago, 1910), i.

269 *"pale-faced visiting ladies"*: Colony Club Talk, March 26, 1933, Box 135, Folder 2, Hoffman Papers, Getty Research Collections; also Hoffman, *Heads and Tales*, 184–85.

269 *"Words become quite unnecessary"*: Hoffman, *Heads and Tales*, 14.

271 *"Immortality?"*: Hoffman, Sketchbook "1930–31 World Trip Hawaii, Japan, Bali," Box 178, Folder 9, Hoffman Papers, Getty Research Collections.

272 *"physical and mental youth"*: Field Museum Postcard, Scrapbook, "[Hoffman's] Personal Descriptions and Thoughts Regarding Models for Field Works [Hall of Man]," circa 1930–33, Box 143, Hoffman Papers, Getty Research Collections.

273 *"works of beauty"*: "Human Varieties Shown in Museum," *Nanaimo Daily News*, June 20, 1933, 4.

273 *"peepshows"*: Agnes Selin Schoch, "Back to Yesteryears," *Selinsgrove Times-Tribune*, June 29, 1933, 6.

273 *"inside the mould!"*: Hoffman to Osborn, June 1, 1932, AMNH Central Archives.

273 *"a different man"*: Osborn to Sherwood, June 1, 1932, AMNH Central Archives.

7 | THE DISCOVERY OF NOTHING

276 *"toying with dynamite"*: Harry L. Shapiro, "The Responsibility of the Anthropologist," *Science* 109, no. 2831 (1949): 323.

276 *"our birth standard"*: Roger Babson, "Character Building Most Important Today," *Honolulu Star-Bulletin*, August 10, 1935, 10.

276 *America led the world:* On eugenics in Hungary, see Marius Turda, *Eugenics and Nation in Early 20th Century Hungary* (Palgrave Macmillan, 2014); on eugenics in the Baltic states, see Björn Felder and Paul Weindling, *Baltic Eugenics: Bio-Politics, Race, and Nation in Interwar Estonia, Latvia, and Lithuania, 1918–1940* (Rodopi, 2013).

277 *"racial policy and thinking"*: Walter Schultze, "Der Nordische Gedanke," *Ziel und Weg* 2 (1932): 4.

277 *individual "self-determination"*: Robert Eugen Gaupp, *Die Unfruchtbarmachung geistig und sittlich Kranker und Minderwertiger: Erweitertes Referat, erstattet auf der Jahresversammlung des deutschen Vereins für Psychiatrie am 2. September 1925 in Kassel* (J. Springer, 1925).

278 *"of all modern social movements"*: Osborn to Laughlin, October 3, 1934, Laughlin Papers, Box D-2-4, Folder 11, Truman State University Special Collections.

279 *"racist propaganda"*: Boas to Shapiro, October 26, 1937, Box 1, Folder 23, AMNH Central Archives.

279 *a safe haven:* Shapiro to Davenport, March 1, 1939, AMNH Central Archives.

279 *"construction of the human being"*: Carol Bird, "Science Can Build a Superior Race," *Hawaii Tribune Herald*, February 15, 1936, 9.

279 *sensual pleasure:* "Revolution Would Follow," *Honolulu Advertiser*, June 27, 1936.

280 *Nazism, racism, and eugenics:* "Nazis Would Assure Nordic Dominance," *Honolulu Advertiser*, December 30, 1931, 14.

280 *"Mr. Hitler":* Hoffman, *Heads and Tales*, 159.

280 *"controlling human reproduction":* Laughlin, "Eugenical Sterilization in Germany," *Eugenical News* 18, no. 5 (September–October 1933): 89.

281 *"a hopelessly perverted movement":* H. J. Muller, *Out of the Night: A Biologist's View of the Future* (V. Gollancz, 1936), 10–11.

282 *the name of the Office:* Earnest Hooton et al., "Report of the Advisory Committee on the Eugenics Record Office," 1935, Laughlin Papers, Box C-2-3, Folder 7, Truman State University Special Collections.

282 *"great world movement":* Osborn to Laughlin, October 3, 1934, Laughlin Papers, Box D-2-4, Folder 11, Truman State University Special Collections.

283 *"the death of Dr. Osborn":* "Obituary: Henry Fairfield Osborn," *Eugenical News* 20 (November–December 1935): 98.

284 *"distinctly Polynesian":* Shapiro, *The Heritage of the Bounty* (Simon and Schuster, 1936), 19.

284 *community gathering in a room:* Shapiro, *The Heritage of the Bounty*, 24–25.

285 *"to produce a blend":* Shapiro, *The Heritage of the Bounty*, 200.

286 *"the level of their neighbors":* Shapiro, *The Heritage of the Bounty*, 226.

287 *"hospitable islanders of today":* "Pitcairn Island Life Is Revealed," *North Adams Transcript*, May 21, 1936, 13.

287 *"the annals of science":* G. R. C., "Review of: Heritage of the Bounty," *Geographical Journal* 90, no. 3 (September 1937): 279–80.

287 *"variations within a mixed population":* H. L. Shapiro, *Migration and Environment* (Oxford University Press, 1939).

288 *"interracial harmony":* H. L. Shapiro, "Anthropology's Contribution to Interracial Understanding," *Science* 99, no. 2576 (1944), 374.

8 | THIS WAS YOUR LIFE!

292 *relatively expensive airfare:* See, e.g., "3 Air Lines Make New Requests for Fare Increases," *Honolulu Star-Bulletin*, January 7, 1954, 4. The nonlinear divergence in relative price vis-à-vis 2024 dollars comes from the weakness of 1930s currency versus the 1950s, owing mainly to the Depression.

293 *the hula skirt:* Kahanamoku to Robinson, May 28, 1952, Duke Kahanamoku Papers, Hawaii State Archives.

293 *a home in Hawaiʻi:* Hall to Kahanamoku, February 1, 1954, Duke Kahanamoku Papers, Hawaii State Archives.

293 *"no one answers my letters":* McNeil to Kahanamoku, May, n.d., 1957, Duke Kahanamoku Papers, Hawaii State Archives.

293 *a police procedural:* Walton to Kahanamoku, April 25, 1958, Duke Kahanamoku Papers, Hawaii State Archives.

296 *"boost to their morale":* Walkin to Kahanamoku, November 23, 1952, Duke Kahanamoku Papers, Hawaii State Archives.

297 *"the surf is up!":* See, e.g., Patrick McNulty, "Surf Boarding Gets to Be Real Habit," *San Bernardino County Sun*, May 26, 1958, 7, "'Ironing Boards' Go to Sea," *Long Beach Independent*, September 11, 1960, 12; Eric Opel, "Paddleboard Cove Has No Season," *Long Beach Independent*, March 20, 1960, 26.

298 *"mean or average":* Harry L. Shapiro, *Race Mixture* (UNESCO, 1953), 51.

298 *"little understanding":* Shapiro, *Race Mixture*, 52.

299 *"laid to rest":* Warshaw, *History of Surfing*, 123.

301 *"what we call culture":* Chris Marker et al., "Les Statues Meurent Aussi" (1953). Marker's exact words are: "Quand les hommes

sont morts, ils entrent dans l'histoire. Quand les statues sont morts, elles entrent dans l'art. Cette botanique de la mort c'est que nous appelons la culture." For ease of reading and understanding I've translated Marker's term "botanique" as "natural history" rather than the more accurate "botany." This seems fair to me insofar as "botany," in Marker's usage, refers not to plants specifically, but to Linnean natural historical classification more generally—that is, the process of abstracting living forms into taxonomical tables; preserving the dead forms of living things (like pressing flowers into the page of a book, or making taxidermic animals); and, of course, displaying objects in museums, where they are at once recontextualized from "natural" into "aesthetic" objects.

SELECT BIBLIOGRAPHY

This book brings together several different lines of scholarship, each too extensive for its own, detailed rundown in this space. As a quick reference for some major monographs on themes in the book, readers might consider the following texts. (Information on primary sources can be found in the endnotes.)

For biographical details about Duke Kahanamoku's life, David Davis's *Waterman: The Life and Times of Duke Kahanamoku* (2015) offers the most comprehensive and insightful biography as of this writing. See also Joseph L. Brennan's *Duke: The Life Story of Hawai'i's Duke Kahanamoku* (1994) and James Dean Nendel's "Duke Kahanamoku: The Twentieth Century Hawaiian Monarch: The Values and Contributions to Hawaiian Culture from Hawai'i's Sporting Legend" (PhD dissertation, Pennsylvania State University, 2006).

For histories of Hawai'i, see especially Noenoe K. Silva's *Aloha Betrayed: Native Hawaiian Resistance to American Colonialism* (2004); James L. Haley's *Captive Paradise* (2014); and David A. Chang's *The World and All Things upon It: Native Hawaiian Geographies of Exploration* (2016). See also Hi'ilei Julia Kawehipuaakahaopulani Hobart's *Cooling the Tropics: Ice, Indigeneity, and Hawaiian Refreshment* (2022) for Hawaiian history with a technological focus, and Christopher Kindell's

"The Sanitary Sieve: Public Health, Infectious Diseases, and the Urbanization of Honolulu, c. 1850–1914" (PhD dissertation, University of Chicago, 2019) for a public health history of the Islands. Edward D. Beechert's *Working in Hawaii: A Labor History* (1985) does as its title suggests, and does it well.

Among the most useful histories of physical anthropology and eugenics for readers of this book will be Maile Arvin's *Possessing Polynesians: The Science of Settler Colonial Whiteness in Hawai'i and Oceania* (2019); Christine Leah Manganaro's "Assimilating Hawai'i: Racial Science in a Colonial 'Laboratory,' 1919–1939" (PhD dissertation, University of Minnesota, 2012); Kerry Kamakaoka'ilima Ellen Long's "Unfit for a Queen: Mo'okū'auhau National Consciousness and Eugenics in Territorial Hawai'i" (MA thesis, University of Hawai'i, 2014); and Warwick Anderson's twin articles "Hybridity, Race, and Science: The Voyage of the Zaca, 1934–1935," *Isis* 103, no. 2 (2012): 229–53, and "Racial Hybridity, Physical Anthropology, and Human Biology in the Colonial Laboratories of the United States," *Current Anthropology* 53, no. S5 (April 2012): S95–107. For more general histories of race science and eugenics, see, for example, Stephen Jay Gould, *The Mismeasure of Man* (1981); Daniel J. Kevles, *In the Name of Eugenics: Genetics and the Uses of Human Heredity* (1995); Ann Fabian, *The Skull Collectors: Race, Science, and America's Unburied Dead* (2020); and Adam Rutherford, *Control: The Dark History and Troubling Present of Eugenics* (2022).

Finally, for histories of surfing, start with Matt Warshaw's sweeping *The History of Surfing* (2010) and his *Encyclopedia of Surfing* (2005). For more explicitly political histories, see Kristin Lawler's *The American Surfer: Radical Culture and Capitalism* (2010); Isaiah Helekunihi Walker's *Waves of Resistance: Surfing and*

History in Twentieth-Century Hawai'i (2011); Peter J. Westwick and Peter Neushul's *The World in the Curl: An Unconventional History of Surfing* (2013); and Scott Laderman's *Empire in Waves: A Political History of Surfing*. Finally, it's neither quite history nor quite natural history, but read Melissa McCarthy's *Sharks, Death, Surfers: An Illustrated Companion* (2019). It's good.